# Around The Races
# In Eighty Days

1 Cook
2 Hameed
3 Root
4 Bairstow wk
5 Stokes
6 Ali
7 Rashid
8 Butler wk
9 Broad
10 Anderson
11 Woakes
12 Wood
13 Finn
14 Rayner
15 Batty.
16 Robson

# Around The Races
# In Eighty Days

*A personal journey against the odds*

Neil Andrew

Published by Atried Publishing

A CIP catalogue record for this book is available from the British Library.

ISBN  978-0-9935065-5-0

Printed in the United Kingdom.

*For The Wife and my two boys*

*Thanks to all my friends for being there
and experiencing the absurd odyssey with me.
You know who you are, and I hope you know
how much I cherished your company.*

*In addition I would like to thank the following
kind people who were generous with their time
to help this project succeed:-*

*Lisa Hancock of The Injured Jockeys Fund
John and Jackie Porter at Oaksey House
Graham Oldfield and Sue Collins of
The Racehorse Sanctuary
Nicky Henderson, who needs no introduction
Julian Thick and Andy Clifton of Newbury Racecourse
Richard and Minty Farquhar of Walking The Courses
Francesca Bullock at Aintree Racecourse*

*All of what follows really happened.*
*I still can't quite believe it.*

# Prologue

It is Wednesday 27 May 2015, it is raining hard, and I am sat in a crappy rental car that is parked on the outside lane of a Scottish motorway. We haven't moved an inch in over an hour. That time has been punctuated by various dawning realisations, my travel-weary mind struggling to keep up with the unfolding situation:- police cars and ambulances have been going up the hard shoulder, nothing has been coming down the other carriageway, and I can hear the menacing, machine-gun throb of a helicopter somewhere in the murk.

Windscreen wipers and engines were turned off long ago. I have busied myself as best I can with jotting a few notes and finalising the last bits of planning, but now there is nothing left to do except stare out of a rain-glooped windscreen and face my fate. This is my penultimate racecourse, and if the traffic doesn't start moving soon it shall have gone, the great dream that took twenty years to become reality, washed away under the wet tyres of thousands of stationary vehicles. The last three months of quiet goodbyes and strained phone calls will have all been for nothing.

I have been away from home for six days now on the last big trip of the tour, and I ache to be back with my family, the family I have chosen to desert in one of its formative life-moments. They seem to be forgiving me, but I am not sure forgiveness will come so easily to myself. What once seemed an eccentric frivolity now seems a monumental error of judgement. Guilt is a powerful emotion, but love is a stronger one. Hopefully we can get through this if we can just keep loving each other?

Gradually, to the persistent drumming of rain on a cheap metal roof, I realise it is not all about my guilt. I shall have to process that, and a small price to pay it shall be for as absurd a mid-life crisis as this. And it is certainly not about the racecourses or the horses, the friends or the gambling. I'd worked that out a long time ago. My epiphany comes late in the journey, and quite possibly at the very end of it if this bloody motorway doesn't start flowing soon:- this is a story about love.

# Part 1

*Before Cheltenham*

# Leaving Teaching

I can recall the exact moment when I knew I would leave teaching. It was about three years ago now, but I can remember it like it was yesterday, although since I've turned 40 it is increasingly difficult to remember what I was doing yesterday.

The classroom looked out over one of the college playing fields. A warm May afternoon prompted even more of the students than usual to be fighting their post-lunch siesta, some of them unconvincingly. The muted sounds of early summer drifted through the small crack in the window (the Health and Safety executive dictating that anything more than a slit of an opening would encourage students to throw each other out of a first floor window) and I glanced across at the grounds staff as they changed the sporting seasons from spring football to summer cricket.

"Oh look," I said in genuine surprise, not at the scene itself but the opportunity to deliver my corny one-liner that I had been storing up for years, just waiting for the chance to unleash my ready wit on the adoring audience, "they are literally moving the goalposts!"

Ben barely stirred from his coma. Sajida dropped her pen for the third time in the brief history of the lesson. Megan looked confused, perhaps wondering if this foray into sports ground management was part of the syllabus. I pondered whether I should say it again, observing the traditional teaching rubric that if they don't understand it first time around, just repeat it slower and louder until they do.

But then Dan at the back perked up. Dan would be my saviour. Dan would show me in his knowing glance that I was not talking to myself. A keen sportsman with a youthful glow and a shock of blond hair, and a promising mathematician had he shown even the slightest inclination to do any work, he would confirm that I wasn't wasting my time here, that I could connect with my class, a camaraderie forged in the cauldron of education. He would prove that this would be a unifying and light-hearted moment in the daily battle for hearts and minds. Dan would justify my choice 15 years earlier to desert a budding financial career with the promise of more money and less stress, and pursue the utter privilege and extraordinary challenge that is teaching.

"Oh yes," Dan said simply, rising from his seat to survey the scene outside, "they are."

I had loved teaching for so many years, but was beginning not to any more. It was far from Dan's fault, I must point out. He, or rather that moment, was merely the catalyst (a slow-acting catalyst, as it happened) for me to leave teaching.

Perhaps I should have gone then, that summer, when I knew I didn't love it any more, rather than struggle on for two more years. Teaching is so hard to do properly when you love it; virtually impossible when you don't. I apologise to my last few classes that they got the worst of me, and I pompously credit myself that the worst of me was still enough, just.

And the college, and my colleagues, and the kids, they were just great. It was the best place I had worked in my life. I would walk barefoot over upturned drawing pins fallen from the noticeboards for my department, and they would do the same for me. I knew it wasn't them. It was me. I had become entirely adept at what I was doing, and utterly bored. This was as good as teaching could get, and it is still of enormous regret to me that it was not enough.

The early adrenaline of being a teacher had seeped away as I stared at yet another year of monotony. I knew that I could do it, that I could perpetuate the suspended reality for one more repeat performance, but I really didn't want to. Same subject, same routines, same old jokes. In a way, I find it absurd that I have just described teaching as monotonous, a profession where the landscape is constantly shifting and there are a million possible interactions every lesson. But when you've done it for as long as I had, everything seemed a subtle rehash of earlier situations.

Even the students seemed to be the same, hiding their insecurities behind a wall of casual indifference and wearing their false bravado like a hoodie. Perhaps a different haircut from last year, a new brand of mobile phone, but kids don't change that much, you know. What had changed over the years, and I use this phrase in the emotional rather than the Criminal Records Bureau sense, was my ability to touch them, and for them to touch me. The connection was lost.  I had become just another teacher.

The college, well run and Ofsted-outstanding, was in financial trouble for the first time in its history. Changes to the government's funding structure, favouring academies and schools over sixth forms, meant that the management had to act swiftly to beat the shortfall. So they grew student numbers, suddenly opening the doors to young people that weren't really suited to further education. From an institution that five years earlier was oversubscribed in a matter of minutes after its online application process went live, the message had suddenly changed and it became a game of bums on seats.

The management also cut its major expense – staff. Senior teachers at the top of the pay scale were incentivised to leave by the lure of tax-free lump sums, a practice virtually unheard of in the profession, to be replaced by cheaper and inexperienced newly-qualified teachers, if they were replaced at all. I was one of quite a few that accepted the kind offer. I wanted to leave and was handed more than six months salary to do so. Without that extra push, who knows whether I would still be watching the seasons change out of a classroom window. Perhaps I have something to thank the then Education Secretary, Michael Gove, for after all.

On my last day I left my headlights on. When I returned to the car the icons on the dashboard flickered and the engine groaned as it turned over. Then the lights went out. I sat in silence for a minute and contemplated how it had all ended. My last ever lesson was as dull as all the others recently. I'd stopped smiling in the classroom, laughing, making bad jokes.....caring.

Since that day there have honestly not been any pangs of doubt or second thoughts. Not one shred of my being misses teaching, which I find a little surprising, even though the warning signs of apathy had been flashing for many years. It almost makes me question whether it ever truly was my vocation in life. I have let it go so easily, like water slipping through fingertips. I am so glad I was a teacher, but I'm equally pleased to no longer be one. It was a time in my life that is gone forever, and all I have now are vague notions that I was good at it and enjoyed it, for the most part.

Last summer we moved house and I busied myself with a large renovation project. It distracted me for a while, enough time to realise that I didn't want to spend the rest of my life managing house projects, but it felt like I was treading water. My mind kept wandering back to a silly idea from decades before, a time when I still had silly ideas and life was simpler. Could it be that now was the time to finally pluck it from obscurity and make it happen?

# The Idea

Okay, it was more than just a silly idea. It was an utterly absurd one. I'm not averse to them. Sometimes it takes an absurd idea to move the whole thing forwards. I'm sure when Leonardo da Vinci sketched out his helicopter the men in white coats (or 15th century equivalent of) were standing by, sizing him up for a straitjacket (or 15th century equivalent of).

At the start of 2015, with our house project nearing completion, my absurd idea from 20 years earlier resurfaced and began to occupy my thoughts with increasing regularity - could I really watch horse racing at all of Britain's racecourses in eighty days? A bit like people who attempt to visit all the service stations on the M4 in one day (for there surely must be such people), the next question has to be "Why?"

The truth is that I didn't know why. I'd hoped that somewhere along the way, say for example on a service station on the M4 between Newbury and Windsor, I might have my revelation, but I didn't want to have that as a motivation for doing it in the first place. I would hate to discover after eighty days that I had actually pulled it off but felt somehow empty that I hadn't discovered the reasons why I was doing it. I'm sure the salmon doesn't try to analyse why he's swimming thousands of miles to spawn. It's absurd, but it just seems like a good idea at the time, and perhaps, in this age of campaign strategy and psychobabble justifications, that is reason enough to do these things. Let's just say I fancied it, in the way that I might fancy that 20/1 outsider in the novice hurdle at Fontwell.

The conversation with The Wife didn't go well. In the world of corporate personality testing she is a 'Blue'. In other words, she likes to plan ahead and know what's about to happen, and dislikes suddenly being put on the spot. For example, when the cooking of a roast dinner is nearing completion and she asks if she can help, the correct answer is "no thanks honey, it's all under control" rather than "can you just do the gravy?"

But after she'd had a few days to process the admittedly shocking news that her husband was a lunatic, as is the way with Blues, she came around to it. I could see the enormity of the task in her eyes. I was asking this beautiful woman to continue her demanding job that pays the mortgage and puts the chicken nuggets in the freezer, but then also assume responsibility for running the family unit. When she got back home after a twelve hour day she would now be required to do the cooking and the washing and the homework, and tend to the multitude of plates that a modern family has spinning without letting too many of them crash to the floor.

She described the discussion that we had, in her critically acclaimed guest blog, as something close to emotional blackmail. It is true that we both knew how much I wanted to live the ridiculous dream, and that I had a 'now or never' feeling about it. But I would willingly have postponed or given up entirely my fanciful notion if we had decided as a couple that it was not right for our family. Once she was on board she was fully committed to the project, and I simply couldn't have done it without her wholehearted support.

So I set about a period of planning. First to sort out, and the most obvious and pressing aspect, was the itinerary. I had 58 racecourses to visit. From Ayr to Brighton, and Ffos Las to Fakenham. I would say from Aintree to York in an A to Z kind of analogy, but Stephen Cartmell trumps me on that one, having already written an excellent review of his visits to all the racecourses, albeit not in eighty days. And anyway, York lets me down in that respect by not beginning with Z. I'm not trying to pick on

York in particular, all the other racecourses fail to begin with the letter Z as well, but seeing as York has gone to the trouble of being so far down the alphabet anyway, you'd have thought it might just have gone the extra furlong and called itself Zork. Think about the extra publicity, not to mention revenue, which would be generated for the city by appearing in all those other A to Z lists. York (or rather Zork) would now be the finishing post for tours of the country's football grounds, cinemas and bowling alleys.

Anyway, I can only work with the materials given, so Aintree to York it is. Except that it isn't from Aintree to York at all. The racing calendar just wouldn't allow it. In fact, I'd go as far as to say that the people responsible for the fixture list hadn't even considered the possibility that someone may want to go from A to Y. When I first had this absurd idea, a generation ago as a silly young man, I wasn't even sure if it could be done at all, alphabetically or otherwise.

The trouble is that there are some racecourses that very inconveniently only race over the jumps in the predominantly winter season, and likewise some equally annoying tracks that only operate flat meetings in the summer. It had to be a three-month stretch that straddled both disciplines, and some racecourses are very concentrated with their meetings in one part of the calendar. Cartmel, for example, only raced on eight days in the whole of 2015, most of which were late in the summer and would therefore have excluded a lot of the winter jumping tracks. Finding a sensible route through the fixtures maze made cracking the Enigma code look like child's play.

I used to teach a branch of my subject called Decision Maths which applies algorithms to real-life situations in topics as diverse as game theory and linear programming. Astonishingly, there is one problem in the module that does not really have an answer:- how can a travelling salesperson visit eight different towns and return home in the shortest distance? The might of modern mathematics can only come up with two separate algorithms that the true answer must lie somewhere between - not very satisfactory, at least to a mathematician.

To be honest, a computer could probably run through all the different permutations for the example of eight towns fairly quickly and give you a definitive solution, but start increasing the number of towns and the permutations grow exponentially. If you extend the problem to, say, 30 towns, even a computer that could check a trillion tours per second would take almost 300 billion years to find the answer by brute force. My proposed schedule included 58 different stops. We can quickly see why a single, definitive algorithm (a set of rules that anyone can follow to quickly find the solution) would be useful.

However, to this day, the Travelling Salesperson remains one of the great unsolved mysteries of mathematics, and as such attracts a prize of one million dollars to the first person to find the answer. However, if you were to stumble upon the algorithm (whilst having a bath, for example) I would urge you to patent it quickly (or whatever else you do to algorithms) as it is surely worth billions to industry. Just think of how many delivery vans hit the roads every day!

So the proposed itinerary was not a product of a perfect mathematical process, but of semi-rational guesswork and random fancy. 31 jumps meetings, 26 flat and one mixed, encompassing four Nationals, six evening meetings, an all-weather week and an enormous amount of miles. I would be able to tell you the exact number of miles, if only there were an algorithm for it, but my guess is that my chosen route was far from optimal. I was to witness the start of the flat season, the end of the jumps season (somewhat bizarrely, in different months) and the retirement of the most successful jockey, and possibly the most committed sportsman, to ever grace the planet.

Cheltenham on Friday 13 March 2015 was to be my superstitiously inappropriate D-Day, with an eighty-day campaign planned up to Fakenham on Sunday 31 May. In between lay the other racecourses arranged in as logical an order as I could manage. Of course I tried not to be in Perth one day and Plumpton the next (although I failed spectacularly in that respect), but occasionally a hefty journey just couldn't be avoided and there just wasn't that much slack in the schedule.

Epsom was particularly stubborn in having only one meeting in my window, but seeing as I chose to frame that window to stop just shy of the Derby, I forgave it its recalcitrance. In a way, Epsom made it easier in its declaration "Here I am, what are you going to do about it?" In fact, you could similarly say that Cheltenham, Doncaster, Aintree, Ayr, Sandown and Newmarket really chose their own position in the schedule with their high-profile fixtures that an ardent fan just couldn't miss, irrespective of the difficulty of fitting it into a coherent pattern. But assembling the rest of the jigsaw pieces around these star offerings proved much trickier, and finalising the route was like trying to put a fitted sheet that had shrunk in the tumble dryer onto a bed - just when I thought I'd got it covered something pinged out the other end.

For some reason Carlisle, despite generously offering five different dates to choose from in my eighty days, was devilishly tricky to pin down. I've nothing against the place (one of my happiest New Years Eve celebrations was in the Lake District) but boy did it prove a logistical nightmare. If I ever do this again (note to self, and The Wife:- don't do this again Neil) I shall start my planning with Carlisle. It ended up sitting mournfully marooned in the middle of my schedule, no neighbours to keep it company, and with neither convenient airport nor easy train line to speed my passage. I became quite fond of it, perversely, as it symbolised the lunacy of the entire charade. A 620 mile round-trip on a Tuesday in mid-April to go racing: what was I thinking of?

Then there were the other imponderables – Acts of God as the insurance companies might say (and I'm not talking about the odds-on favourite falling at the last). An outbreak of foot and mouth disease, for example, would be personally disastrous, just as it was to horse racing and many other industries back in 2001. And then of course there were the roadworks on the M1 and the deteriorating condition of my ageing car, not to mention the deteriorating condition of my ageing body. In the end I managed to find a reasonable schedule for the tour, but if illness or injury, weather or war were to intervene it could be game over in an instant, the equivalent in form figures of a "P" next to my name.

We all know that in the racing game there is no such thing as a certainty. If I were a betting man, I would have said the chances of me completing the venture were Evens. Therefore, if any kind bookmaker was to offer me 2/1 I should have taken it like a shot. The trouble is that bookies don't tend to offer 2/1 on evens shots, as Graham Sharpe of William Hill reinforced when I phoned him a couple of weeks before the off. Renowned for accepting unusual wagers, Graham was unimpressed by my quest. Just a small bet, I persisted, any winnings split between our two charities? Graham didn't like it, even at what I suggested was the very fair price of Evens. There was nothing in it for William Hill, he said, because it was a done deal. Of course I could watch racing at all the British courses in eighty days - where was the challenge in that? Little were we both to know how wrong he would soon be proved.

# Proposed Itinerary

1) Fri 13 Mar – Cheltenham
2) Sat 14 Mar – Uttoxeter
3) Sun 15 Mar – Ffos Las
4) Mon 16 Mar – Taunton
5) Tue 17 Mar – Exeter
6) Wed 18 Mar – Warwick
7) Thu 19 Mar – Chepstow
8) Sat 21 Mar – Bangor-on-Dee
9) Wed 25 Mar – Newton Abbot
10) Thu 26 Mar – Newbury
11) Fri 27 Mar – Wetherby
12) Sat 28 Mar – Doncaster
13) Sun 29 Mar – Ascot
14) Tue 31 Mar – Southwell
15) Wed 1 Apr – Chelmsford
16) Thu 2 Apr – Wolverhampton
17) Fri 3 Apr – Lingfield
18) Sat 4 Apr – Kempton
19) Mon 6 Apr – Huntingdon
20) Fri 10 Apr – Leicester
21) Sat 11 Apr – Aintree
22) Sun 12 Apr – Market Rasen
23) Tue 14 Apr – Carlisle
24) Fri 17 Apr – Fontwell
25) Sat 18 Apr – Ayr
26) Mon 20 Apr – Windsor
27) Tue 21 Apr – Brighton
28) Wed 22 Apr – Epsom
29) Thu 23 Apr – Perth
30) Fri 24 Apr – Plumpton
31) Sat 25 Apr – Sandown
32) Tue 28 Apr – Nottingham
33) Wed 29 Apr – Pontefract
34) Thu 30 Apr – Sedgefield
35) Sat 2 May – Newmarket
36) Sun 3 May – Salisbury
37) Mon 4 May – Beverley
38) Tue 5 May – Catterick
39) Thu 7 May – Worcester
40) Fri 8 May – Chester
41) Sat 9 May – Haydock
42) Sun 10 May – Ludlow
43) Mon 11 May – Towcester
44) Tue 12 May – Wincanton
45) Wed 13 May – Bath
46) Fri 15 May – York
47) Sat 16 May – Thirsk
48) Sun 17 May – Ripon
49) Mon 18 May – Redcar
50) Tue 19 May – Newcastle
51) Thu 21 May – Goodwood
52) Fri 22 May – Musselburgh
53) Sun 24 May – Kelso
54) Mon 25 May – Cartmel
55) Tue 26 May – Hexham
56) Wed 27 May – Hamilton
57) Fri 29 May – Stratford
58) Sun 31 May – Fakenham

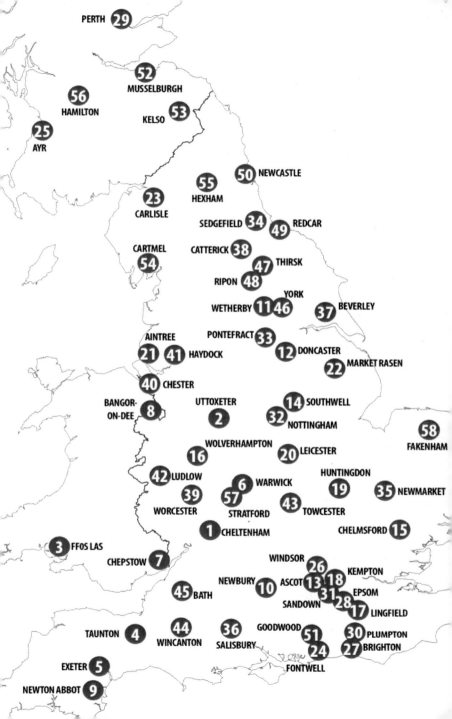

PERTH 29

MUSSELBURGH 52

HAMILTON 56

KELSO 53

AYR 25

NEWCASTLE 50

HEXHAM 55

CARLISLE 23

SEDGEFIELD 34 REDCAR 49

CARTMEL 54

CATTERICK 38

THIRSK 47

RIPON 48

YORK

WETHERBY 11 46

BEVERLEY 37

AINTREE 21 41 HAYDOCK

PONTEFRACT 33

12 DONCASTER

MARKET RASEN 22

CHESTER 40

UTTOXETER

8 2

14 SOUTHWELL

BANGOR-ON-DEE

32 NOTTINGHAM

WOLVERHAMPTON 16

FAKENHAM 58

20 LEICESTER

LUDLOW 42

HUNTINGDON

WORCESTER 39

6 WARWICK 57

19

NEWMARKET 35

43 TOWCESTER

STRATFORD

1 CHELTENHAM

CHELMSFORD 15

FFOS LAS 3

WINDSOR

CHEPSTOW 7

26 KEMPTON

NEWBURY ASCOT 13 18

BATH 45

10 31 EPSOM

SANDOWN 28

17 LINGFIELD

TAUNTON 4

WINCANTON 44

36 GOODWOOD

30 PLUMPTON

SALISBURY

51

EXETER 5

24

27 BRIGHTON

NEWTON ABBOT 9

FONTWELL

# Preparations

I have an admission to make. Before my quest began I allowed myself to be tempted over to the dark side, and I still feel somehow dirty and shameful because of it. I know, deep inside, that now I have made that transition I am very unlikely to go back to how I was before. That principled and upstanding man is now lost forever. Reader, I purchased a Satnav.

Yes, after years of waging an increasingly isolated campaign against the shiny little electronic aliens, I had to admit defeat and join the legion of numbskulls who have removed the part of their brain that deals with spatial awareness and replaced it with a patronising voice that deliberately mispronounces town names just to annoy you. This did not go unnoticed by my friends and family who, after years of me chiding them for surrendering their freedom, delighted in teasing me over my personal u-turn.

In years to come, when the shiny little electronic history books tell of the Satnav Apocalypse, I shall have played my part in the downfall of the human race. You see, we are raising a generation who are totally unable to read a map. Darwinian Theory dictates that in a few years time you could put a youngster in a room, remove their mobile phone, tell them that the Satnav is still locating the satellite, and they wouldn't have a clue how to get out of it.

And then, mark my words, a day shall come when Satnavs reign supreme (has anyone else noticed how most of them sound like the serenely malevolent computer, Hal, in 2001 A Space Odyssey?) by calmly directing all their unthinking puppet-pilots to "turn left through gate and proceed over cliff edge". I'm not sure how they then rise from the ashes to achieve world domination, but if they can work out the quickest route through London at rush hour, I'm sure they'll think of something.

I must point out that the only reason I allowed myself to be sullied by association with these dreadful contraptions is that the one I bought came with live traffic updates that promised to give the time-poor racecourse-tourist hours of his life back. I justified the decision by thinking that it may at some point save the whole endeavour from collapse, but even so, I was still begrudging of its presence, sitting all contrary on my windscreen as if to say "huh, thought you could live without me, eh Neil?"

The getting-to-know-you phase in February was like a new animal being introduced to a zoo enclosure. We eyed each other warily across the dashboard for a few days before getting properly acquainted. And of course during the early skirmishes there were several little spats. On our first major outing it proudly proclaimed "no traffic ahead" as I sat motionless in the usual jam near Stonehenge. Then I started fighting back, defiantly turning right when it wanted me to go left and immediately shaving minutes off my estimated arrival time - have some of that, cleverclogs!

So there was certainly a power struggle in the early weeks, a period of adjustment known in the trade as Post-Induction Satnav Squabbling, Pre Onwards Togetherness Syndrome (quite a handful I know, if only there were an acronym for it). It gradually wore me down, just through sheer persistence, and I am ashamed to say that I now stick it on if I am just popping to the shops, seeking reassurance that there is no hidden traffic jam at the end of the road.

I found a way of getting along with it because I had to, given that I would be spending more time in its company over the following three months than with my family. Even though we reached a workable truce, there were still dangers, including the video game that is 'Beat The Satnav' (it thinks I can't get there before 11:14, eh?) and an alarming feeling that it is actually some sentient autopilot driving the car for me, a hazard doubled if I am also using cruise control, but by the start of March I felt we had embraced a grudging acceptance.

My Ford Galaxy was not only replete with Satnav, it had even enjoyed its annual wash and hoover a few months earlier than usual. I had filled its footwells with bottled water, clementines and Wotsits, ideal grazing material for the calorie-counting traveller. I had checked the tyres, changed the CDs and filled its various trays with half-sized pencils. This project was not going to fail for lack of pencils, I proclaimed! Then, totally predictably, the car started making a weird noise (some sort of attention-seeking behaviour at the introduction of the Satnav, I suspected) and I had to rush it down to my local garage where they patched up the air intake.

I had booked trains, planes and hotels far enough in advance as to be prudent, but not so far in advance as to be cocky and tempt fate. I'd bought a lovely new iPhone6 with a super-dooper camera to chronicle the big moments, and a neat little dictaphone to record the banal detritus of racecourse conversations and motorway musings. The freezer had been filled with home-made lasagnes and enough chicken nuggets to sustain a small army. I even prepared an emergency drawer for The Wife containing vodka, sweet chilli sauce, Flash wipes and cash, all of which she gets through at an alarming rate. Everything seemed to be falling into place.

Then just nine days before the off, a routine ultrasound in London for my youngest son's long-standing condition turned out to be not so routine. We had attended many scans over the previous few years, and developed an ability to read between the lines with the often-guarded demeanour of medics. This was the first time that we had detected concern in the eyes of the doctor looking at the black screen, and a subtle change in the tone of the language used.

An invasive procedure on the Monday, the day before the start of the Cheltenham Festival and just four days before I was due to set off, proved agonising for the poor lad. The results of that test confirmed what we had suspected; all was not well. If you are a parent and you've been through similar, you will know that I would have done anything in my power to take away his pain and make it all better. But I couldn't, and I felt hopeless.

I also felt that it was not a good time to be sodding off around the country for eighty days. The Wife was brilliant. She persuaded me it was vital that things carry on as normal until we had seen the consultant and knew more, that a lot of time and effort had already been invested into this ridiculous initiative, and that it would begin as planned on the Friday. Without her unflinching bravery, and willingness to sacrifice herself on my behalf for three months, my journey would never have started. I owe all of this to her.

# Under Starters Orders

With less than 24 hours to go until I began my absurd journey, something that I had been dreaming of for years and planning for months, I was pensive. With my family in a state of flux I now wonder whether I would have started at all were it not for the fact that there was something comforting about my opening destination. It was a town that The Wife and I had lived in for the first seven years of our marriage, containing a racecourse that I had attended more than all the others put together - Cheltenham.

We lived on Cleeve Hill, the backdrop to so many great Festival scenes over the years, in what was, in hindsight, a ridiculous house to buy. It had downstairs bedrooms, sunken bathrooms, and a back garden that was so steeply sloping that it was rumoured to be a winter training ground for the British ski squad. What it also had, and what probably initiated the quirky purchase, was a jaw-dropping view of the distant Malverns and, if I went on tiptoes in the top bedroom, a narrow slit of a view revealed about five yards of racecourse running rail.

The Wife and I would go racing in the early carefree and childfree weekends of the 1990s. I remember her joyously jumping up and down when that fine old mare Dubacilla ploughed through the mud at a January meeting to win at 8/1. She had £2 on it and a random chap next to her in the stand, who was also roaring home the winner, had £200. I honestly think The Wife was happier than the other chap. It's funny the things I can remember, when I often nowadays stand frozen and lost in a room, unable to piece together why I went in there. Despite its slightly eccentric nature, I loved that house, and we raised Eldest there. His earliest memory is watching the hot air balloons drift up from the valley below, skimming the rooftops to such an extent that we felt we could almost reach out of his bedroom window and touch them, the serenity broken only by the roaring bursts of fire from the burners.

So, amongst the multitude of decisions to be made with the planning of my itinerary, there was only one that was set in stone from the outset – I would start at the Festival on Gold Cup day. I found it ironic that I was to start my quest at Cheltenham, for in a sense it is the culmination of the jumps season, the destination for so many setting out on so many roads so many months before. I would be beginning my journey just as horses, trainers, owners and jockeys would be ending their season-long quest for sporting greatness. As such it represents not only a finale, but also for the majority of the special few who are actually good enough to make it to the Cotswold outdoor-theatre of immortality, the realisation of failure.

Aintree and Sandown (not to mention their flat racing compatriots of Epsom, Newmarket et al) must get dispirited by the dominance that Cheltenham holds in our affections. The only racecourse that can justifiably claim a share of the equine crown would be Ascot, but in a slightly different way.

The word itself, "Festival", used so prevalently nowadays by as diverse a cross-section of society as cinemas to market stall traders, really only means one thing to most horse racing fans. When we talk of "The Festival" we are talking about Cheltenham in March. The use of the word by so many other racecourses now to encourage enthusiasm for relatively inferior meetings lessens their own impact in comparison, rather than detracting from the real thing. What exactly is it, though, that allows Cheltenham to overshadow all of its competitors?

Recently, various sources have agreed that jump racing in general, and the Festival in particular, dominate betting turnover for the horse racing year. The Aintree

Grand National remains the chosen flutter for the once-a-year punter, but the Levy Board revealed that just two of the top ten betting races in 2014 were on the Flat, whilst five of them were at the Festival. Some of the individual bookmakers have published statistics that are even more skewed towards Cheltenham.

Ultimately, though, it's more than just competitive racing producing fierce betting heats. It's something intangible that tugs at the heartstrings of any racing fan. As the flag falls on the first race of the Festival there is a strange noise to be heard at the foot of Cleeve Hill. It is a mixture of an ecstatic roar and a collective sigh of relief, representing the joy that this beautiful thing that we have waited for across twelve long months is finally upon us. In stark contrast, however, the most common noise heard over the next four days of intense sporting drama is the harsh tinkle of shattering dreams.

We, as punters, take a personal grief in the failure of our horses, and for those as addicted to the jumping game as I am, the hopes that we cherish are held not just for the few minutes of a race but for the many months preceding the Festival. It is truly something to say that you spotted the champion before anyone else did, and maintained your belief through the season-long possibility of injury and illness, the inconvenience of changing plans from trainers and owners, and the overwhelming probability that the apple of your horse racing eye was simply not as good as you thought.

I know this from bitter experience because I invested four years of my life in pursuit of one horse (paradoxically named One Man) that I knew, just knew from the moment I first set eyes on him, would become a champion. And he did. The fact that it was in the Champion Chase rather than the Gold Cup merely added to his legend. The fact that his triumph came after two stinging disappointments at previous Festivals only made it sweeter. The fact that the biggest wager of my early punting life came on the first of those Gold Cup defeats was irrelevant.  For on a fine March afternoon in 1998, One Man repaid my faith in him (as well as a little of the financial investment) with his stunning success in a championship race over a distance previously thought too short for him.  However, it was far from a monetary victory.  In some ways now I wish I hadn't backed him when he won, because the intrusion of financial considerations somehow sullied the pure joy of that moment - a joy that contrasted so starkly with the heart-wrenching devastation of a month later when One Man died at Aintree.

Perhaps over the eighty days I would find out why I still loved a sport that, despite all the incredible highs it has bestowed, gave me such a savage low that day that I wondered at the time whether I would ever stop crying. But as I've already said, I would have been wrong to have this as a motivation for doing it.  I was looking for winners more than answers, and if either came along then that would be a bonus.

It was also quite fitting that I started at Cheltenham because in a way that is where it all started for me some 25 years before.  My obsession with the sport was born on Gold Cup day in 1990 when the most preposterous of horse racing fairytales unfolded just as I was beginning my equine education.  Being a new devotee, and naively crediting myself with more knowledge than could possibly be acquired in a few teenage months, I 'knew' that 100/1 shots didn't win Gold Cups.  I also explained this to my friend who had never been in a bookies before, giving him the full benefit of my new-found wisdom in a lengthy exposition on odds and what little I knew of the form book.

Jason listened patiently, and then declared "Yeah, but I just like the name Norton's Coin."

It was the first and only time (I'm tempted to say "first and last", but horses have a habit of not reading the script) that a 100/1 shot has won the Gold Cup, and it is a race that I will never tire of watching, again and again, in the cine-camera of my mind. It stands as a supreme monument to what can happen if you dare to dream. There was surely no reason for Welsh hill farmer Sirrell Griffiths to enter a horse that had finished last, beaten 39 lengths in the King George three months earlier, but he did. There was surely no reason for jockey Graham McCourt to think he could ever win, but he did. The rest, as they say, is ludicrous.

It would seem that, amongst all the broken glass of fallen angels that lie on the tarmac of Cheltenham's betting rings, hope is still alive. Even the most rampantly optimistic of dreams can come true if you allow yourself to put sense and reason to one side.

Norton's Coin stalked the leaders, took closer order as one by one they faded (including favourite Desert Orchid) and in a final, exhilarating thrust, with the commentator's voice soaring and the horse and jockey urging and straining and almost throwing themselves at the line, just prevailed over the unfortunate Toby Tobias. Jason and I danced around his living room like lunatics, like only the young and innocent can dance, not yet knowing that it wouldn't always be that easy, not yet knowing that we wouldn't always taste that glory, and not yet knowing what pain the sport could bring. Those were the days when Jason still had hair, I could still see my ribs, and each new day was an adventure to unfold. They seem a long time ago now.

So on that Thursday evening, just hours before setting off to meet my destiny, I felt as though I was standing on the brink of something extraordinary, or at least moderately strange. Half of me felt vaguely heroic, like Laurie Lee walking out one midsummer morning into the great unknown, and half of me felt rather sheepish and silly, as I imagined all the people that knew me thinking "Shouldn't he have grown out of this sort of thing by now?"

I suppose it was man's innate urge to achieve the seemingly impossible that was driving me on, the thought of looking back from my rocking chair in fifty years time and saying "I was the first!" – Hillary and Tensing, Armstrong and Aldrin, and now myself, a latter-day explorer redefining the bounds of human endeavour. Yes, either that or the fact that it was very hard to turn down the opportunity to go racing for eighty days.

I'll admit I had butterflies. I was almost apprehensive about the 2015 renewal of the pinnacle of the jump racing calendar. It could easily have been the thought of leaving my family for extended chunks of time, or the crystallisation into a stark and prickly reality that this absurd venture was really happening. Or perhaps it was just the fear that Gold Cup day would not live up to that sublime moment a quarter of a century earlier. I didn't know, but I would soon find out. The starter was mounting his rostrum.....

# Part 2

*And They're Off*

# 1) Cheltenham

## Day 1 - Friday 13 March

I'm not sure what I had expected of the opening morning of my odyssey. Would I wake feeling like I was part of a cereal advert, bouncing into the new day like a spring lamb? Perhaps I'd rise from my bed in a forthright manner, steely and determined as I marched towards my destiny?

As it was, I woke normally, with a glug of stale bedside water and the familiar gnawing of backache to remind me that I was tall, overweight and 43 years old. I hadn't really had time to digest what was going on, and what was about to happen. One of the many aspects of planning to get jettisoned as unnecessary in my last-gasp push for the starting line was the 'sit down for an hour and appreciate what you are about to do, Neil' moment. The morning of Day 1 certainly wasn't the time for reflection as I wolfed down my breakfast, put the bins out, and finished my imperfect packing by forgetting my binoculars.

I would be home again in a little over 48 hours, but it did feel somehow significant. Youngest was still off school, recovering from his general anaesthetic at the start of the week. Truth be told, we were all in a bit of a daze, and I felt like a rat of a parent leaving the sinking ship. But I'm a man, I can pigeonhole. Show my son that it's okay, life goes on, we shall all get on with it. Stay positive. Yes, nothing to worry about son, Daddy is still doing his silly tour of racecourses. So I hugged him and The Wife goodbye and got in the car.

When I picked up Paul from the station he was wearing a silly hat, Scottish in theme to reflect his heritage and occasional sporting leaning (although his supporter's matrix is confusingly muddled depending on which sport he is watching – I've never seen him support Scotland in the cricket, for example). So I got my silly hat out too and felt a bit better about everything. The first time you wear a flat cap in public you feel a little self-conscious, but after a few minutes you kind of grow into it. By the end of the day it was second nature, and we certainly weren't alone. Perhaps Paul and I have reached the age when we just don't care, consider it a sensible precaution against the British weather, or even find it somewhat stylish? Paul reported that it was hosing it down in Cheltenham, which reminded me that I had left my waterproof jacket at home. So after a brief detour (and still without my binoculars) we set off in earnest to experience all that Day 1 of my odyssey and Day 4 of the Festival had to offer.

To promote the Jules Verne theme of my quest, I shall name Paul my Passepar-one (do you see what I did there?) Over the last quarter of a century we have spent many fine days racing, and many more elsewhere. I couldn't have wished for a better companion with which to commence my journey. Paul's opening salvo was to savage a Ginsters sausage roll all over my freshly hoovered car. He had recently lost an alarming amount of weight on the 5:2 diet, but it was clearly a day of feasting rather than fasting.

There was a slightly surreal air to proceedings that morning. The drive to Cheltenham went spectacularly well, but there just didn't seem to be enough traffic on the roads to signify something momentous. If this was the most popular day our sport has to offer it didn't show at 9:30am on the M4. As Paul and I slipped into the usual banter, I waited for the starting gun to sound in my head.

As we swept north from Swindon along the A419, Jason called to wish me luck. I impressed Paul, who often looks at me with a mixture of disdain and pity at my lack of savvy with new technology, with the skilful use of my new hands-free kit. Jason, in true Norton's Coin fashion, requested £10 on an outsider in the Gold Cup. The horse in question seemed to be "Oscar's Just Shat In The Middle Of The Playing Field", which was certainly a new one on me and probably beyond the limit of characters allowed when naming a horse. It could also have confused spectators when Simon Holt was commentating on the race.

It became clear that he was walking his dog, a beautiful streamlined lurcher by the name of Oscar, and actually wanted to bet on Home Farm. We had a debate about backing him without the favourite, a concept which Jason, a man of impressive if erratic intellect, still found confusing despite 20 years of attempting to understand it. I explained that Home Farm would still have trouble winning if we were betting without the first 15 favourites in the 16 runner contest, which only added to the confusion and did nothing to dissuade him from his selection. The conversation then descended further into chaos, if that was possible, with Jason's suggestion that horses should run in Lycra, like athletes.

After the call was over, I pondered briefly whether I should stand the bet myself and pocket an easy tenner, but this guy had a long history of finding outrageous winners, so I resolved to secure him better than the 100/1 that was forecast in the Post and see whether the bookie laughed as I placed the bet.

As we shimmied along the Leckhampton Road from the Air Balloon roundabout the weather could best be described as 'dreech'. A low mist clung to the contours and the temperature gauge on the dashboard claimed a refreshing 3.5 degrees, a long way from the balmy conditions that had ushered in the Festival just 72 hours earlier. There was something muted and introspective about the day, rather than the exultant and joyous opener that I was hoping for. Perhaps the grey skies were deadening the vibrancy, or perhaps the inanity of everything had finally caught up with me?

I remember reading the book about James Cracknell and Ben Fogle rowing the Atlantic, and even a gold medal winning Olympian seemed slightly lost at the start of something so overwhelming. As they rowed out of the harbour with 3,000 miles to go, there was a vaguely hollow feeling at the absurdity of scale. It's as though you can sense your own mortality, like watching a tiny but huge jumbo jet make a trail in the sky at 30,000 feet, or an ant trying to cross a motorway.

We arrived at The Battledown B&B, a splendid but fiendishly expensive Edwardian offering on the eastern edge of the town. Paul and I, having been somewhat taken aback at the cost of last minute accommodation for Festival week, had dallied with the idea of throwing a couple of sleeping bags in the back of the Galaxy and setting up camp in the car park of the Rising Sun, the marvellous pub on Cleeve Hill that is a thriving factory of Festival fervour in the middle of March.

Frankly, we agreed, we would be highly unlikely to remember going to bed that evening, so could save the extortionate fee. Then our respective other halves stepped in and told us to stop being so stupid and pay the money. The Wife said that this ridiculous charade was not going to fail on the morning of Day 2 because I had tried to sleep the night in an eight-year-old Ford and done my back in again. Whisper it quietly, but I think she was right.

I searched for a way to get back in the Festival groove and so we headed for a quick pint in the Kemble, our traditional opening pit stop. The tiny pub was heaving, as usual, but the service was swift and friendly and there was a shared understanding amongst the patrons that we were in it together, all kindred racing folk. Some of them looked jaded, as though the first three days of Festivities had taken their toll, and they supped at their beer like they were methodically reloading ammunition for the last big push.

Paul and I began the pilgrimage up to Prestbury Park. As we wended our way down Fairview Street, Glenfall Street and Albert Place our numbers grew, foot soldiers in tweed and jeans. By the time we reached Pittville Lawn the crowd had swollen to legion status, sustained by stalls selling breakfast baps and cans of Guinness. Even before we reached the roundabout at the racecourse entrance, the corralling had begun, and basically didn't let up for five hours. Contrary to popular opinion, you can swing a cat within the environs of Cheltenham racecourse on Gold Cup day, but only if you are standing on the track itself, and that wouldn't be very sensible. Queues to place a bet were long, to go to the loo even longer, and to get a pint in under 20 minutes was a feat rarer than a novice chaser winning the Gold Cup. I felt unable to settle in any one place and no territory felt truly comfortable.

Here's the thing: I could have enjoyed the hubbub of the walkways and turnstiles if I'd had somewhere to call my own once inside, but the concrete stands and swathes of tarmac were strewn with racing refugees like me, trying to find comfort in a quiet corner or at the bottom of a pint of the black stuff. I could have booked a seat in the grandstand for another small fortune (the Club ticket cost £75 as it was) but felt that was taking the piss.

Cheltenham was undergoing a £45 million facelift, and the season was always going to be a difficult one of transition for the National Hunt flagship. In fact, much of the earlier media feedback had been positive, but the crush of Gold Cup day was markedly different to a convivial press day in February or the genteel ambiance of a hospitality unit. Even the main enclosures earlier in the week must have seemed relatively calm compared to this. Despite there still being construction work in progress and large sections of some grandstands out of action, the attendance on Gold Cup day of nearly 69,000 was significantly more than the first three days and also up on previous years. Believe me, as someone who was on the ground that day, it showed.

Apparently, extra space had been created at the North entrance, an open piazza dotted with benches and smiling racegoers basking in the relaxed atmosphere, but we never found it. Perhaps at future meetings management should employ people with large signs, like the ones on Oxford Street advertising golf sales, to direct oppressed racegoers to quieter spots? They could employ traffic-flow consultants, and have big screens with coloured maps of the facilities to indicate congestion?

I suppose if I had stumbled upon several winners things may have seemed different (an undeniable truth about the tidal wave of emotion of a day at the races), but as always the racing was fiercely competitive and I didn't get a sniff. When I backed Mullins he had a shocker, and when I backed outsiders it was a race for the favourites. My big fancy of the week, Beltor in the Triumph Hurdle, was anonymous to the point of me wondering if he was a non-runner.

We met up with Ivan, a member at Cheltenham for longer than I had known him, which is a long time. He was the guy that mentored me through my teacher-training year, and had retired a few years back to follow his dual passions of horse racing and Norwich City FC. We've had some spectacular days at Prestbury Park, including one memorable afternoon when he had four winners, I had five, and our friend Chris went through the card. I'd have settled for just one on the opening day of my journey. He confirmed our malaise with proceedings by divulging that he was thinking of not attending next year. The problem was the sheer number of people trying to do too many things, in too short a time, in too little space.

The bar under the new half-completed grandstand had the charm of an airport departure lounge when the planes are delayed. Perhaps it was unfair to judge an unfinished article, we thought, and so tried the Arkle bar across the way and soon had to give up as a five-deep throng progressed agonisingly slowly. We moved away from the course to check if the See You Then Bar or the Guinness Bar were different. They weren't. Paul, a keen observer of social trends, commented on the meteoric rise of the ridiculous beard. Fresh young things everywhere, mostly male, were sporting an array of bold styles. It was like anyone under the age of 30 had been given a free, stick-on facemat with their Tattersalls ticket.

We watched the second race on a giant screen, perched on some plants overlooking the paddock. We weren't alone – thousands of others were doing likewise, trying to find an island of comfort in the maelstrom of humanity. We didn't even bet on or watch the third race, other than glimpses of action on a small Tote screen that had seemingly had a light-reflecting film added. This was the heart of the matter - we were paying a king's ransom to be herded like cattle and watch racing on not-very-good TVs.

Let's get one thing straight – I love Cheltenham. I love the theatre and the drama. I love the glorious setting and the unique racecourse. I love the variety of the people and the bravery of the horses. How I have loved the horses over the years! This place thrives on its history, and no place has a history quite like Cheltenham. In fact, when I die, I have always fancied the idea of my ashes being scattered on this most hallowed of turf. And yet (you knew there was an "and yet" coming, didn't you?), I didn't love Gold Cup day at the Festival. The pinnacle of the sport left a slightly hollow and uncomfortable feeling.

The feature race itself at least provided some welcome respite in the form of a scintillating performance by Coneygree, in only his fourth run over fences, that provoked cheers in those of us that hadn't even backed the eight-year-old. Some had questioned the wisdom of his trainers, Mark and Sara Bradstock, for aiming this talented but inexperienced chaser at the summit of the jumping game. As it was, his rivals were the ones that looked out of their depth, and one by one they fell by the wayside in the wake of his scorching pace. The Hennessy winner Many Clouds was only sixth, favourite Silviniaco Conti seventh. The two previous Gold Cup winners, Lord Windermere and Bobs Worth, were both pulled up. Home Run, whom I'd managed to secure 150/1 about (the bookie in question was too busy to even smirk at the bet) didn't stand a chance. But even Coneygree's reception into the winners' enclosure seemed tepid, as if smothered by the torpid blanket that still shrouded Cleeve Hill from view.

Finally, the last race of the day, not just for us but also of AP McCoy's Cheltenham Festival career, was upon us. AP was received warmly as he cantered to the start, and even more so as he came back in, a slightly unlucky fourth. The winner was almost forgotten in the public's clamour to recognise this admirable over-achiever.

We joined the slow-motion human train that departed the course and funnelled its way across beer-sticky concourses and mud-strewn side streets. Paul hit the nail on the head when he suggested that for that entrance fee he had expected it to be easier to enjoy the day. And he was right. Enjoyment of a day at the races is not just about winning (witness our warm appreciation of a Gold Cup winner we hadn't backed), it is about having the time and the space to ponder, and talk, and watch, and digest, qualities that were so noticeably lacking from Cheltenham on Gold Cup day. Killing the goose that laid the golden egg, Paul called it. There must come a time when the numbers decrease, either by natural selection or artificial constriction, although worryingly Cheltenham supremo Ian Renton has said that he thinks 70,000 is about right.

We headed back to The Battledown, a sanctuary far from the madding crowd. Suddenly, spending more on a B&B room than I did on my first car seemed like a very good idea. Paul has a habit of becoming 'uninterested in proceedings' in the latter stages of a big day such as this, and over the last couple of decades I've developed various little techniques to manage his evening and keep him awake. The best strategy used to be to prevent him from sitting down, in order to keep his alcohol-induced narcolepsy in check, but recently he had managed the extraordinary feat of falling asleep whilst standing up, so I decided to take a different tack. I allowed him to nap for a couple of hours whilst I began the daily process of writing, a discipline that simply could not fail over the coming months. A laptop, a lamp and the gentle snoring of an old mate in the quiet of a Cotswold bedroom ushered in a new routine, and one that, truth be told, I inwardly relished in my new and expansive post-teaching world.

During the 1990s, Paul and I moved from Exeter to London to Cheltenham in the space of five years, clinging to an evolving friendship in the traumatic post-university landscape of growing up. So after my writing was done, and with my Passepar-one suitably rejuvenated, we decided on a stroll down amnesia lane and headed into town on an unplanned ramble around some old haunts from the years we shared in this fine part of the world.

As it was we didn't get far and found ourselves unable to escape the clutches of our second watering hole, The Strand, where a local band called Masterplan were belting out the crowd favourites. Kindred spirits danced and drank the night away, an eclectic patchwork quilt of clothing and cultures that horse racing seems to meld together like no other sport. I sensed that my Festival, and indeed my journey, was finally starting, miles from the racecourse and hours after the last race. It was still crowded, but it felt relaxed and fun.

When I die I would still like my ashes to be sprinkled at the final fence at Cheltenham, and by then I won't care about the queues and the crowds, but I feel as though my scatterers will deserve an easier opportunity to attempt it than Gold Cup day.

# 2) Uttoxeter

## Day 2 – Saturday 14 March

I love a National. They are rich with opportunity: for horses to get into a race that would otherwise be run off their feet, for the underdog to triumph against the classier animals, and for the odds to be upset. There is something epic about that element of survival as a big starting field is whittled away to a handful of finishers.

I remember a horse trained by Henry Cole called Just So, unkindly referred to in some circles as Just Slow. He ran in the Grand National in 1994 and was just touched off by Minnehoma. It was my first Aintree marathon since leaving university and I impressed my new colleagues with my horse racing 'expertise'. I had told them at the start of the week, when it started raining in Liverpool and showed no signs of stopping, to lump on the stout stayer each way at 50/1. They duly did, and seemed mildly disappointed with me at work the following Monday that it hadn't won.

It was an old-fashioned Grand National, with only six finishers and more than half the field running from out of the handicap. Just So was himself carrying more than a stone and a half above his correct mark, a truly heroic performance. It was his moment in the limelight, his 15 minutes of fame, and he came up just a length and a quarter short, pipped in the shadow of the post after more than four and a half miles!

Anyway, the point is that Just So ran all his races, mostly over extreme distances, in the same manner – getting behind early on, making late headway, but usually staying on just a little too late to trouble the winner. Nationals allow this type of horse to claim their slice of glory – those with little pace but abundant stamina, and not just a little heart and guts. Just So never made the placings again and was retired the next season, but some of us still remember. That's the thing about horse racing – somebody, somewhere, will fondly recall the horse whose career highlight was finishing third in the selling hurdle at Fakenham in 2002.

Rising on the morning after a Cheltenham Gold Cup can be difficult. Not just the Guinness-fogged head with hazy recollections of the night before, but the inner emptiness of knowing that it will be another 361 days before the Festival party starts again. This year, however, was different. Not only was my horse racing odyssey just beginning, but I also had a personal pilgrimage to attend. In true Just So fashion, I was going to get a little behind early on by taking a detour to The Wife's childhood home, before hopefully staying on late to make the first race at Uttoxeter which was hosting its own version of a marathon trip with the Midlands National.

We've been married 18 long years, and in that time I've come to realise that the one thing we have in common is that we both got married on the same day. I'm kidding honey, and I'm also borrowing a joke from an old friend without his permission. My sweetheart grew up in a little village called Bramshall, but precise details were sketchy. I was looking for a house with a big garden, and a field nearby that has a bull in it, or at least had a bull in it 35 years ago. I don't really know how long bulls live for, but if it was the same bull as back then I wanted to have a word with him about scaring my wife all those years ago, and even I, with a BMI that makes doctors frown, would have a fighting chance of outrunning it.

Over a delicious breakfast at The Battledown, Paul and I started chatting to Alan from Preston who had been in Cheltenham all week. He was surprised by our views of the over-crowding yesterday and explained his strategy of finding somewhere and sticking to it, a strategy which had found him next to a burger van on a mound in the middle of the course. He seemed tickled by my project and I could see he thought about it seriously when I suggested Uttoxeter might be on the way home for him.

The short journey to drop Paul at the station was strewn with red lights, of which Cheltenham seems to have a staggering array. These are provincial red lights too - no hurry on a sunny Saturday morning for these guys. Paul's ten o'clock train was in doubt, a 2/1 shot I would say, as we stop-started our last half a mile to the station. He then told me it was actually at 10:01 and all of a sudden the chances of making it went odds-on in running. If it were written up in the results pages, our two-mile trip would be described as "started slowly, behind early on, rapid progress from 2 out, stayed on well, won a tad cosily". Hopefully that was a good omen for my selection in the Midlands National later that afternoon.

Even so, there was no time for long farewells as my Passepar-one flung himself from the moving vehicle in the station car park and sprinted for the platform. Not returning homewards with Paul made the challenge seem real for the first time. I thought back to an earlier conversation we had shared over breakfast about whether I considered my project business or pleasure. As I travelled north through the interminable M6 roadworks I wasn't sure it was either. Then a road sign divulged the alarming news that Newcastle was only 18 miles away and I panicked slightly that the Satnav had cocked up, before realising that it wasn't the Geordie version.

I passed a horsebox and decided I would back the first runner trained that afternoon by the name on the side, Alexandra Dunn. Sometimes you can over-analyse the form, and I didn't have a Racing Post yet anyway. This was similar to a technique I had employed, to some effect, in the 1990s when I used to frequent Wimbledon dogs. There was a busy suite of six gents' urinals near the traps, and I would choose my dog for the next race by counting the urinal that became free as I queued. If there was no queue and two urinals available it would be a dual forecast, and three empty spaces became an all-ways tricast.

I phoned The Wife to update her on my progress and see whether she had yet run out of either vodka or sweet chilli sauce. The answer was no, but a slightly frosty tone hinted that neither of those two aforementioned commodities, as worthy in their own right as they undoubtedly were, were suitable substitutes for the cocoa that I had forgotten to get in the weekly shop. I protested that there was some Cadburys drinking chocolate in the cupboard, but she didn't seem to share my enthusiasm at tweaking recipes to suit the ingredients available. Blues just don't like to improvise, you see. However, even as a non-Blue I could understand her reservations. I once tried to cook her a birthday cake in my usual make-it-up-as-I-go-along style, only to discover as I cut in to the crispy exterior and a molten slurry poured out, that you really can't take such liberties with a recipe as far as baking is concerned.

As I sat in the car outside a house on a quiet street in Bramshall, wondering whether its garden was big enough or whether there was a bull-sized field out the back, the idiocy of my journey smothered me like a pillow. Could I really do this? Could I really be away from my family for so long over the next eighty days? I knew I was acting like a wimp. There are many family men and women who are obliged to spend large chunks of time away from home as part of their jobs, knowing that it's an indefinite routine rather than a three month sabbatical. There are explorers far more intrepid than I, who have fought for longer in more difficult circumstances, and defeated greater foes than the traffic on the M6.

As I pondered whether to start knocking on random front doors in a sleepy Staffordshire village, I became painfully aware that I had actually chosen to do it, and that it would be a more daunting undertaking for The Wife, who is usually in the office at 7am doing the day job so that I could entertain ridiculous notions like giving up teaching and going racing for eighty days. That she really wanted me to do it, despite all the extra pressures it would bring her, was testament to her grace and patience. Either that or she'd just had enough of me after 18 years.

My two boys, as well, my two brave, gorgeous boys, faced an extended period without their taxi driver and occasional father in their lives. I hoped in years to come they would not single out that moment as the one when they finally worked out that they were much better off without me in the way, messing things up and embarrassing them in front of their friends. If I would run into a burning building for them, and I know that I would and hope that I never have to, then why could I not have parked these silly notions for the next ten years, or better still have stopped living this Mitty-esque fantasy altogether, in order to make the next three months of their formative existences a lot easier, and perhaps a little happier?

I was bewildered by my choice. I hoped that over the following eighty days I would understand better my reasons for doing it. And I hoped against hope that, even if they never understood it themselves, my family would learn to forgive my frivolity. Anyway, on with the show, I thought. Day 2 was far too early to get mawkish and introspective, and there was a National coming up. I abruptly came to my senses, realised that I didn't have a clue what I was going to say to the occupants of the house I was parked outside, even if it did turn out to be The Wife's old home, and set off for the track.

I arrived in Uttoxeter in good time so stopped off in Tescos for a Racing Post and a sandwich. As I breezed through the entrance I was presented with massed ranks of flowers, waiting patiently for their onwards journey to Staffordshire windowsills. I realised that with everything else going on I had completely forgotten it was Mothers

Day, and phoned up my Mum to make my sincere apologies. She understood, as mothers do, that I had a lot on my mind. So much so, in fact, that I was actually apologising for missing something that hadn't happened yet because I was a day early. Guilt morphed into embarrassment as I mumbled something about "wanting to be upfront about it".

The Alexandra Dunn trained Black Narcissus was a well-backed outsider in the first when I arrived at the busy and cashew-shaped racecourse for its biggest fixture of the year. I'm sure it wasn't my £5 at 18/1 that prompted the odds to halve by the off, but there must have been some shrewd money out there to invest in the mare who had finished 8th, 7th, 15th and 16th in her four runs so far that season.

Whoever else was on the bandwagon, we didn't have long to learn of our collective fate. Black Narcissus was obviously inspired by the cryptic suggestion on her horsebox – Dunn Racing. She whipped around at the start and refused to race. Somehow, it summarised my qualms perfectly – was I, too, 'done with racing' only a day and a half into my eighty-day journey? I had expected that somewhere along the line I would have a "what the hell am I doing?" moment, but I hadn't expected it to be on Day 2. Perhaps it was best to get it out the way early on, before it had time to fester, I mused as my Narcissus nemesis sauntered casually back towards the stables.

The course seemed to suffer from the Cheltenham ailment of too many people and not enough space. Queuing was impossible to avoid, unless you had come racing to not do any of the following:- bet, watch the race, eat, drink, or go to the loo. I wondered whether racecourses were always this crowded and I'd just never noticed before because I usually had friends to distract me. I couldn't remember the last time I'd gone racing on my own, and resolved to avoid it wherever possible in the future.

I followed Alan's idea from breakfast and found a spot by the paddock away from the crowds. It was the Tommo Show as Derek Thompson, previous stalwart and ever-jolly frontman of Channel 4 Racing, held court and gave assembled interviewees a gentle and jocular inquisition. At regular intervals a bucket would be passed around the crowd to collect losing betting tickets from which Tommo and guests would then select lucky winners to receive, yes you've guessed it, free bets. I was too embarrassed to chuck in my Black Narcissus chit.

It was soon clear that it was tough work out on the track, as usual, on the traditionally testing ground. Many, including most of mine that afternoon, were pulled up. In the second race won by 20/1 outsider Barafundle only three of the nine runners finished the three mile novice chase.

As AP McCoy came out for the fourth race, flanked by security guards to easy his passage through the adoring galleries, I made a mental note to avoid backing his mounts for the next six weeks as they would surely, given the huge outpouring of public warmth during his extended retirement tour, prove to be atrocious value. Accordingly, Beg To Differ then won the handicap hurdle, a heavily backed 11/4 favourite, under a typical McCoy never-say-die ride.

The sun broke through as, strangely, Amazing Grace was sung in the paddock before the big race. As McCoy got the leg up on another well backed favourite an old man called up to his hero half his age "Good luck Tony!" without acknowledgement. He was sat alone on one of the stools lining the parade ring, flat-capped and grey-moustached, wrapped up against the cold in a variety of beiges. Clasping his walking stick in one hand, he held up the other in a frail thumbs-up gesture and tried again. "Good luck mate!" Still no response as the ever-focused McCoy adjusted a stirrup. Both of their luck was out – the well-fancied 5/2 favourite Catching On fell early.

I fancied Foxbridge, a progressive eight-year-old who relished soft ground and seemed to like being held up early before finishing with a flourish, not dissimilar to dear old Just So. He ran a good race but finished fifth. I scampered across the horsewalk before the tired runners trooped back in and headed for the car park. My race was run as well. I yearned to be heading home, but with Ffos Las the next day and an overnight stay booked en route to the Welsh outpost I felt as though I had to stick to the schedule.

My room for the night was back on Cleeve Hill in my old local, The Rising Sun. It was as close as I was going to get to the feeling of going home, so set off in earnest. On my last night in our silly house on the hill, eleven years earlier before we moved to a new life nearer London, I sat on the ledge for over an hour, drinking beer, writing poetry and watching the sunset colours bleed to the horizon in a rampant final exultation. Things seemed so different back then. Nowadays, I still drink beer but the poetry has gone, along with my vista to the west.

I raced the light back down the M5, turned off along once-familiar roads and experienced my only winner of the trip so far, savouring the last few minutes of a glorious Technicolor show from the car park of the pub before the sun slipped below the Malverns.

# Not Ffos Las

## Day 3 – Sunday 15 March

The Rising Sun is a lovely pub, and after its busiest week of the year the bar staff were still smiling and the place had a relaxed vibe in the aftermath of something momentous passing through town. It has a failing however, or at least it had during my stay – the wifi is appalling. I asked in the bar after I arrived on the Saturday evening.

"Oh yes, nobody's been able to get on all day!" said the breezy barmaid helpfully, before adding "It's not us, it's the cloud."

I presumed she meant virtual rather than real. Without a 3G signal either, I was marooned from the electronic world with no means of posting my Uttoxeter blog. I suppose there are worse places to be marooned than a comfortable pub with stunning views, but that wasn't the point. I wanted to keep to a schedule, maintain the structure before everything unravelled on Day 3. Little was I to know quite how unravelled things would get.

I didn't sleep well, and was awake to hear my Racing Post schlap onto the carpet outside my door at 7am. With breakfast not until 8:00 I jumped from my bed to luxuriate in an hour of unfettered form studying, something which bizarrely I hadn't managed to do thus far.

Disaster. In a small and personal sense, utter disaster.

Ffos Las did not appear in the Racing Post. Surely such an esteemed publication could not have forgotten about one of the few meetings on that Sunday? I grabbed at my phone and at last got some semblance of a signal. After an agonising wait for the page to load, my fate was sealed in a ghastly slow-motion reveal of pixels.

Abandoned.

If you remove the 'o' from the first word of the racecourse you will sense my mood. I sat deflated for a while before my fight came back. I must keep going, I thought, find a way. Friends and family texted soothing and positive messages: "all adds to the challenge!" and "#partofthejourney".

I rifled through my file to the by now well-thumbed printout of fixtures and quickly located some small crumbs of comfort – Ffos Las had four further meetings in my eighty-day window. Two were immediately ruled out due to clashing with some not-to-be-missed feature days, but two others gave me just a shred of hope: Sunday 12 April if I could successfully juggle Market Rasen without the house of cards collapsing, or Saturday 23 May in the middle of my Scottish Swing. It was possible that I could do a day trip from Edinburgh, in between racing at Musselburgh and Kelso, a day trip that, I would suggest, had never been done before in the history of human travel.

Relief coursed through my groggy veins. The whole thing was just about still doable, although severely creaking under the pressure of random quirks of fate after just 48 hours. Relief quickly boiled into anger as I thought back to the words of Graham Sharpe from several weeks earlier. A "done deal" he had said. Where was "the challenge"? Well challenge number one, Graham, is the British weather, it being an outdoor sport and all. And here on the morning of Day 3 the Gods of Probability were already taunting me with their chaotic powers.

I took my fixture list to breakfast to see whether I could work through the Market Rasen possibility and bumped into Parviz, the manager who used to welcome The Wife and I so warmly when we lived just 200 yards down the lane and popped in regularly. The intervening years had clearly taken their toll on both our memories, and he smiled blankly when I reminded him, recognition clearly blurred by the passage of thousands of customers between then and now. Either that or I'd put on about four stone since he last saw me.

I texted my boys to remind them of Mothers Day and popped into Cheltenham to buy some flowers for them to hand over, before driving home for a welcome bonus day with my family. But as I skimmed along an empty M4 I knew that of the two chances I had to complete this crazy venture, Slim was saddling up and about to ride out of town.

# 3) Taunton

## Day 4 – Monday 16 March

I'll let you into a secret. Despite my svelte appearance and youthful good looks, I actually turned 40 several years ago. I decided to mark the occasion, in traditionally modest style, by hiring a big house in Somerset and hosting a five-day celebration of myself. Those friends that had sufficient days holiday left at work and, more significantly, could be bothered to spend that time with me, were offered a trip to Taunton races at the end of the gruelling jolly and actual day of my fortieth birthday. It was a chance to clear the head and breathe in the crisp December air. Needless to say, it was a small and select band of brothers that joined me for the dénouement of the shindig.

I'm not proud to admit that after four nights of partying I was feeling the pace a little, and cannot remember much other than Jason's very plausible impression of Juha Kankkunen, hurtling through the narrow lanes of rural Somerset, that had me heaving on the driveway as I disembarked his Audi. Another stalwart to accompany me then was Simon who has since reminded me of the distasteful scenes at the end of the afternoon. The balcony of one of the private boxes on the top floor had been commandeered as a makeshift turret and its suited occupants waged war on the bookies below, not with the usual weaponry of fivers and tenners, but with ice cubes that had presumably been left over from what I can only assume was a 'convivial' luncheon earlier in proceedings.

As the ice cubes hailed down, Simon spoke briefly to one bookmaker who seemed to be receiving a significant portion of the incoming fire. He explained, whilst literally dodging bullets, that he had no idea why he was being singled out for the treatment, other than the misfortune of being closest to the requisitioned balcony. Despite asking the stewards (the neon-vested ones, rather than the horsey ones) to sort it out, this had been going on for quite a while. Perhaps the management just hoped that the louts would soon run out of ice cubes?

The spectacle did indeed reach a natural conclusion that was announced with a loud crash from the suite backing onto the balcony. Perhaps one of the yobs had fallen off a table, or hopefully slipped a disc whilst trying to carry an ice machine to resupply the ammo. So no innocent bystanders got hurt, and seemingly one of the hooligans got their comeuppance. It won't be the last time morons get drunk at a racecourse, and it didn't surprise me that it came from suits in a hospitality unit. Of course, I must point out that this is not a problem unique to Taunton in particular, or horse racing in general. Many venues try to attract the 'professional' demographic with disposable income and a thirst for expensive alcohol.

I need to be careful of hypocrisy, and not a little rose-tinted nostalgia here, but I can't help feeling that the well-meaning Racing For Change initiative of a few years back has been hijacked by creeping commercialism that manifests itself as deliberately attracting young men and women who have little interest in horse racing but a keen desire to drink themselves stupid. I have been known to drink at the races. I have been known to get drunk at the races. Incidentally, it is rarely in a suit, never in hospitality, and always with a Racing Post in my pocket.

And that last point is key - the reason I am there, rather than getting drunk in the pub, is my love of horses. Does racing really want to bus in caches of soused idiots in order to massage the bottom line of the profit and loss account? This seems a very misguided and, at best, short-term strategy to me. Goodness knows how parents with young children that day responded to the inevitable question "Mummy, Daddy, why are those men throwing ice cubes at the people?"

Therefore I didn't know quite what to expect on my return to Taunton. I hoped to find an absence of ice-cube hurling hooligans, certainly, but more than that I needed a good day. The first two days at Cheltenham and Uttoxeter were disappointing and the abandonment of Ffos Las had really messed things up. However, an unexpected Sunday at home had helped replenish some positivity and the thought of getting the train for two days rather than driving invoked a sense of the journey beginning again. At the very least, it allowed time for reflection, and some decent form studying.

13 unlucky bets into the tour and I really needed a winner. I considered an early switch in betting strategies, just to gain some momentum - perhaps some each ways on shorter prices, or backing more than one horse in a race? Jason once infamously backed the entire field at the Galway Festival many years ago, and believe me when I say that was one of the saner moments of the extraordinary four-day holiday. He may not have recorded a profit, but at least he got a return, a feat he so spectacularly failed to repeat in the pubs and clubs later that evening despite some outrageous persistence.

Thankfully, Taunton had a completely different feel to both the first two stops on my tour and my fortieth birthday. There was smiling, talking and helping each other with bags on the train down. When I arrived at the station three disparate groups immediately and easily coalesced to share a taxi to the course, as well as our experiences of the Festival.

We were greeted by friendly staff on the gate, and once inside the course the good times continued. There was space, that I could move around in, unhindered! Space to luxuriate in, even! If I wanted to go to the paddock, nicely positioned in front of the stands, I could walk in a straight line and view the horses parading without having to peer over somebody else's shoulder. When I wanted to get a (quite decent) pint of Tetleys, I was served within seconds and called darling. So I found a spot and settled, something that was so noticeably absent from the claustrophobic Cheltenham and Uttoxeter.

I didn't want to back the Nicholls hotpot in the first at odds-on, so found an outsider who ran creditably but lost, predictably, to the Nichols hotpot. I fancied a Pipe debutant in the second race and backed him early at 9/4, fearing his odds could only plunge, and retired triumphantly to the bar. On coming out just before the race was off, I was astounded to see that Perspicace had drifted out to 7/2, but my new-found bonhomie was such that instead of seeing this as a possible warning sign, I decided to lump on again at the enhanced price. Tom Scudamore guided the four-year-old to an easy victory, and I had my first winner of the tour. A decent one, too.

I celebrated by browsing the stalls selling books, cards and paintings, and was surprised to find equine artist Caroline Cook behind the till, busying herself with a commission that she was working on. I told her that my first racing print to hang proudly on my wall was one of hers from many years ago – One Man and Barton Bank jumping the last at a Cheltenham January meeting. She concurred "yes, that was going back a while now!"

We got chatting about my tour and discussed the financial side of selling prints at racecourses. Caroline was often at Taunton as she lives in Wellington, but had given up the bigger meetings. She too bemoaned the frenetic pace of the Festival, as well as the cost of hiring the space, which came with 'compulsory advertising'. Nowadays, with the changing face of retail, she sold most of her work online, but still did a fairly good trade with individual commissions. Her best-selling print was originally a Christmas card for the Injured Jockeys Fund, featuring six favourites from across the ages. I expressed my disappointment that One Man was towards the back of the line-up, and she smiled patiently as if to say 'if I had a pound for every punter who's said that'.

My themed choice in the fifth race, The Road Ahead, ran a very strange race. He was on and off the bridle before finally becoming interested in the final few furlongs and losing in a photo finish. When he unsaddled, jockey Sean Bowen, riding for his father, looked very upset – certainly more upset than I was, and he didn't have any money on it, or he shouldn't have anyway. Taunton wasn't Cheltenham but passions still ran high and a win was a win, which this wasn't by the narrowest of margins.

I shared a taxi back to the station with John from Chesterfield and his friend Mick who was clearly a Geordie. I asked what had brought them all the way down to Taunton for some frankly ordinary racing on a Monday afternoon, and John's eyes lit up.

"This is my last racecourse, I've visited them all now!" he said with obvious satisfaction.

What a coincidence! He was finishing his quest as I was starting mine. His tour had taken a little longer than eighty days, beginning in earnest three years ago after taking voluntary redundancy. He was a quiet-natured individual, and it was hard to pin-down his age as his grey hair contrasted with his youthful complexion.

I quizzed him on his journey. His favourite course was Ludlow; the trickiest was Kelso, "miles from anywhere." Then I asked him what he felt like now he had finished, and what he would do next. At that point John became less animated. It was almost as though he hadn't got a plan for what to do next, and was beginning to realise that he needed one. It was like he had climbed his Everest, but now that part of his life was done and everything else would seem slightly underwhelming in comparison. His purpose was gone, and the energy visibly drained from his face as he pondered my innocent question. He seemed slightly lost as he sat in the back of that taxi.

I wanted to chat further with these instantly likeable guys, have a beer with them and discuss past races and future plans, but the taxi had reached the station and I had a train to catch. Racing is like that though – thousands of strangers with thousands of different stories, flung together by their love of an unusual sport. Our connections are heartfelt and humorous, but so very random and transitory.

John and Mick would not be at Exeter the next day. Their race was run. In fact it was probably 500/1 that I ever saw them again, but I felt as though my journey had finally begun in earnest. Real racing folk at proper grassroots courses had brought out the best in me. That, and a winner of course.

As I entered the station a guy noticed my Racing Post and asked if I'd had any luck. One winner, I replied, but that was enough. What about him?

"Oh we had a horse running today" he said, "It came second." Which race, I enquired? "The second race. It ran nicely but got beaten by the new Pipe horse."

My win had been somebody else's loss. I said his horse looked a nice prospect, and asked about plans, but like John he also seemed unknowing of the next step. Perhaps that is the key to horse racing – enjoy the moment, you never know what the future may hold.

On the train down to Exeter that evening I reflected on whether I too would be like John in a few months time, triumphant but somehow empty that it was all over. When you have achieved a lifelong dream, what do you do next? Go back to the day job?

I texted Clive to update him on my first win of the tour. Clive is another of the university crew, a guy that I've been fortunate to know for more than twenty years and someone who I have shared experiences with at racecourses and, more often recently, poker rooms across the land. Clive is a true gambler, like me, because he always has hope. Not a month goes by without an email to tell me he's cracked it, found a new edge on the poker tables that will undoubtedly lead to fame and fortune.

When I told him that I was heading to Exeter he replied that Ben, his nephew and Economics student, was a drummer in a group called Bloom who were playing in the Battle of the Bands final at a club on Queen Street that evening. It would have been easy for me to hide in my hotel room and busy myself in writing, but I reckoned this was the sort of spontaneous direction my odyssey should be taking me in. The road less travelled by, as it were. And besides, Exeter was my old stamping ground, the place where I met Clive, Simon, Paul and, of course, The Wife.

I got a taxi up the hill from the station (some things had changed from student days) to my hotel and dropped my bags before heading out. The evening was simply superb. It started in The Rusty Bike on Howell Road, which I once knew as The Eagle Tavern run by Exeter City centre forward and local legend Tony Kellow. Gastropubs hadn't been invented when this was my local in the early 1990s but, as they go, The Rusty Bike is a pretty good one. On a Monday night it was quiet, with a friendly barman and a handful of well-behaved students playing a board game I didn't understand. I wolfed down a decent burger, slightly uncomfortable with the first solitary sit-down meal of my journey, and headed off into town.

Suffice to say that I was almost certainly the only person at the gig who was not asked for ID at the entrance. Ben found me in the gloom and he seemed relaxed before his big moment with the natural confidence of youth. I've known him for a few years and he's a great kid, the sort of lad that makes you positive about the future of our country. When the band went on they were simply mesmerising. I tell you this without one hint of nepotism: Bloom really are the next big thing. To compare them to Radiohead would be unfair on them, not Radiohead (interestingly, also a product of Exeter University). Their music is a joyous, bleeding mixture of old and new, radical and melodic, and it shone brilliantly in the dark, subterranean arena of the Cavern Club on a student-sprinkled Monday night. After their set I bought them a drink before becoming uncomfortably aware that I was twice the age of anyone in the place, including the staff, and making my excuses.

I retraced my steps down once-familiar cut-throughs and alleys. The city hadn't changed that much, but of course the people had. No longer could I walk into a random pub and find somebody I knew, an isolation only enhanced by the yawning chasm of the age gap between myself and just about everyone else I had encountered that evening. However, it had been a good day, and I still had the next day in Exeter as well.

# 4) Exeter

## Day 5 – Tuesday 17 March

I slept well and rose early the next morning but noted, as I sat in an empty breakfast room, that two disciplines were already slipping. Firstly, I had chosen to go out on the tiles the previous evening instead of writing, and needed to keep the balance. I resolved that there was simply no way I was going to get to the end of May and realise I'd had a bloody good time but had forgotten to write any of it down. The writing had to be my scaffolding, maintaining a structure in my post-teaching landscape.

Secondly, breakfast proved to be the first of many Full Englishes that I struggled to finish. Less than a week into my quest and the body was already showing signs of rejecting the rich and fatty diet it was being subjected to. Despite appearances to the contrary, my diet is relatively healthy – low fat, high fibre and mostly gluten-free given The Wife's wheat allergy. My one weakness is a fondness for a pint of beer, but other than that I'm perfect. I keep trying to tell everyone that my alarming BMI is because I'm big boned, and my persistent tummy is merely an unavoidable consequence of genetics, inherited from my father who, along with his many brothers, looked like they were auditioning for roles as Father Christmas. But nobody ever listens to me.

The landlady of the Raffles Hotel liked to talk, and as I struggled to edge towards the exit of the room she marched me on a circuitous route through the politics of the South West. Eventually I feigned an important meeting (which wasn't so far from the truth, in a way) and escaped to finish the writing and head up the hill to the campus.

I cannot begin to tell you of the amazing three years that I savoured in this fine city and university. If I tried the words would seem empty and lifeless compared to the glorious richness of those experiences some twenty-odd years ago. It has to remain a knowing glance and satisfied smile that is shared only between the people who were there, part of a club that you can't join if you are not already a member.

The place has changed a bit though. When I wandered through a spectacular new atrium at the heart of the campus that would not seem out of place in a five star hotel, I found purposeful young things engaged in calm meditation at laptop screens. This was also markedly different to my day, as I remember.

I continued into what used to be called Devonshire House and found myself in The Ram. I don't usually start drinking at 11:30 in the morning, but to fully embrace the vibe of my undergraduate years when frankly anything was possible, I unloaded my heavy rucksack and settled in with a pint and the Racing Post, listening to the distant chink of pool balls and young, excited voices.

For the second time in less than 24 hours in this fine city, I felt slightly out of place. It was like squatters had taken over my home and airbrushed me out of its history. As beautiful a place as Exeter undoubtedly remained, it was no longer mine, so I walked down the hill towards the station. I was fortunate to stumble upon an impromptu beer festival at the enormous Wetherspoons that was once known as the Imperial Hotel. Wetherspoons comes in for a bit of stick sometimes, but it does good beer at great prices and I could have stayed there all afternoon, finding a niche in the cavernous layout and sampling the extraordinary range of beers on offer. However, I had a greater purpose to follow, sort of, so onwards and upwards.

Unfortunately, I use the word "upwards" not in a striving or financial way, but in the sense that the racecourse is on a hill several miles from the city. I first visited Devon & Exeter (really more Devon than Exeter) in my opening term at university after I discovered a few like-minded guys on the degree course we occasionally attended. Back then the place was a complete dump - a wooden shed for a stand, a long bar underneath with all the panache of a motorway service station, and the far side of the course completely obscured from view because it dipped down into the valley after a few furlongs, the runners only reappearing after a minute or so just before the home turn. Those were the days before big TV screens relayed all the distant action, so goodness knows what shenanigans went on unnoticed in 'the dip' on the far side, out of view of both punters and stewards. We loved it. I used to go with two Jims and a Steve, who was the proper punter amongst us, with a habit of feeding the £200 jackpot slot machines in The Ram to prove it. I remember one day we almost collectively put the term's grant cheque on an animal named Galaxy High at the prohibitive odds of 1/3. This was a decent horse who was running in a dreadful race, but we chickened out and watched as it won by 8 lengths, a heavily backed 1/5 favourite.

When I got to the course I found that things had changed. New stands and shiny facilities adorned the venue that was now exhibiting the investment from the philanthropic Jockey Club umbrella it sat under. Like Taunton, Exeter had generous lashings of space to waft around in, and carried a relaxed vibe that immediately put me at ease. I sat at one of the many empty big round tables covered by pristine white tablecloths and buried my head in the form.

I was soon joined by Trevor and Mal, two localish retired guys who had the banter down to a tee so that it was neither forced nor aggressive between the double act, just endearingly funny. Trevor was the older and rounder of the two, ruddy cheeks smiling from a kind face, with wisps of white hair drifting aimlessly from his head. The scene when Mal had just collected Trevor's winnings from a previous Placepot couldn't have been scripted any better, the dialogue that interspersed the slow-motion transferral of cash laden with the gentle and perfectly-timed humour of old friends.

"No, no, no.....keep going.....no, more than that....." Trevor advised as Mal put the notes down in staccato fashion on the table in front of him, "bit more there, that's it.....now he's nicked me lucky pen, look!"

Mal took on the role of dogsbody for the afternoon, fetching coffees and lists of non-runners, whilst Trevor held court at the big round table, waxing lyrical on a vast array of topics. When Mal reappeared with the first betting slips of the day he advised me "now don't listen to a word he says!"

I scanned through the runners and riders and, to my astonishment saw that Black Narcissus was running in the last race. Just three days on from her shameful outing at Uttoxeter, she had the temerity to turn out again! All afternoon I had conflicting thoughts whirring around my mind. Why so soon after her aborted run? Why at all, with her dreadful form this season? Should I back her for old times' sake? What about the shrewd but not-so-shrewd money at Uttoxeter that had made her odds halve?

I had a winner in the first race, a horse called Quebec who had improved dramatically from his first run for being gelded. I decided not to follow suit personally. Even if losing my knackers improves my hurdling, I'm quite attached to them really. As I suppose Quebec was to his at one point. His victory in the seller sparked a bidding frenzy at the auction in the paddock afterwards, with bargain-hunters steaming in as though being gelded was the new wonder-pill, forcing his sale price up to £31,000.

After my initial success, the card progressed in slightly frustrating fashion. I was agonisingly close to backing easy winner Jay Are, but got put off by some frothing at the mouth in the paddock. By the horse that is, not the jockey. Or myself. It won pulling the proverbial cart.

And so to the last. The racing so far had really just been a preamble, with everything building up to this moment. I had been trying not to think about it and putting off the big decision, but I could procrastinate no longer. Time to let the head rule the heart. I wasn't going to let the Guinness of St Patrick's Day get in the way of making a rational decision. The favourite had a good chance; the 25/1 shot and fickle mistress Black Narcissus didn't. I had to lay down a marker early in the tour. This was not going to be a steady bleed of silly bets on outsiders. Not for me, I'm an ex-maths teacher, you see, studied the form and everything, even read the bits of the Racing Post that tell you the record of trainers and jockeys at the course. No, it was to be big, bold, sensible bets for me over the next eighty days, the sort that make the bookies give you a second glance. A large one on Horace Hazel, 2/1 was a fair price.

I don't think I need to tell you the outcome.

I sat in stunned silence as the taxi driver tried unsuccessfully to make conversation on the way back to the station. It took me until 17:46 by the big station clock until I could laugh about it. And when I finally did, they were big, cackling, guffawing laughs that made the people on the platform edge away from me slowly. They had to be, otherwise it would have been big, baby, blubbing sobs.

I knew then that she'd got me, forever. I would have to back Black Narcissus every time she raced, and I also reflected with an absolute clarity that after her easy victory that afternoon she'd never win again. It was almost like a divorce settlement, a monthly payment for which there was no hope of any personal gain, just something I was required to do.

# 5) Warwick

## Day 6 – Wednesday 18 March

Before getting the train up to Warwick I investigated possible solutions to the Ffos Las fiasco. Flights from Edinburgh to Bristol were unavailable for my selected date, the spare Saturday between Musselburgh and Kelso, unless I wanted to go via Antwerp. Er, not really thanks. And I didn't fancy the round trip, which Google Maps told me was in excess of 700 miles and 15 hours. Market Rasen would have to be shuffled to where Catterick was, and Catterick fill the spare Saturday, which in itself was quite a drive but not as bad as the alternative. Best laid plans, and all that, but at least the flimsy balsa wood raft on which my hopes rested was still afloat, although I wasn't sure it could withstand another storm.

I didn't feel like betting, but I knew I would. Black Narcissus had bruised me with her impudence, but punters are a hardy lot. Give us 24 hours to lick our wounds and the money merry-go-round begins again. For the early part of the journey I avoided the racing pages and read the news items. There was an intriguing debate about whether wind operations should be declared or not. A wind operation, contrary to popular opinion, is carried out on the soft palate of a horse with the aim of improving its breathing during a race. They can dramatically improve the chances of horses who have been struggling, and are now so commonplace that it was recently reported that the great Sprinter Sacre had nine wind ops over a four-year period. None of this was known at the time, but now that we had got wind of it (sorry), some trainers were arguing that it is no more noteworthy than knowing that the feed has been changed to a new supplier, or that new shoes have been fitted. Clearly there has to be a limit on the information that is required to be declared about a horse due to run, otherwise the whole system will collapse under the pressure of death by data and the punter will just receive white noise. But in my opinion, the ability of these procedures to dramatically improve a performance means, like blinkers, they need to be declared even if they don't go on to produce the improvement hoped.

Then there was also an interesting article on page.....what! Richard Farquhar was walking around all of Britain's racecourses, and by that I don't mean from the bar to the bookies to the stands and back again, but actually walking from one course to another! And he'd got t-shirts printed! And had got four columns in the Racing Post! My immediate jealousy at being usurped by this more organised rival seeped away as I read the article and discovered that he was taking 13 months rather than eighty days to complete his adventure – the slowcoach! More importantly, he was attempting to raise a total of £1.4 million to be split between Racing Welfare and Pancreatic Cancer UK.

I immediately felt guilty about worrying I would be put in the shade by a competitor on a frankly far more worthy and well-organised mission. But the timing was extraordinary, and it did show that for all my protestations about it being a 'personal journey' and 'living the dream', there was a small part of me that quite liked the idea of my project being a success. The thought of never having to go back to teaching, but instead eking out some sort of future in a bizarre sporting travelogue niche, was an attractive one even if it was a longshot.

As the train pulled in to the station, I suddenly realised I knew absolutely nothing about Warwick, other than it hopefully having a racecourse. It was very pretty, I discovered, as I eschewed a taxi and walked through the centre. I kept an eye out for the castle that the sign near the station had championed, but failed to spot it. You'd think you could see a castle in a small place like Warwick. Perhaps it was a little like Leeds Castle being nowhere near Leeds?

I entered the course for free, courtesy of my Cheltenham Festival badge and a reciprocal arrangement between the two Jockey Club racecourses. I was up already, sort of, but refused to count it in my betting profit and loss account. Punters may be optimists but we are realists as well, if that isn't a contradiction in terms. It was a weird course, I mused, on first inspection – a track of two halves, you might say. I surveyed it from the grandstand and found it almost entirely flat and uninspiring on the left, but just after the winning post runners encountered a steep hill and then a hidden descent behind trees. It's almost like they didn't get planning permission for the right-hand side, but I liked it. Horse racing would be boring if it was all run on athletics tracks, and anyway the horses might skid on the tight bends. Perhaps they could wear trainers, which would then have to be declared in the paper?

Continuing the theme of the previous two stops, there was a relaxed atmosphere and, again, space and time abounded. It was 50 minutes before the first race and easy to get a drink. This really was the way to do it. I got chatting in the bar to a lovely couple from Pershore and we agreed that the first race was not much of a betting opportunity. It contained a 2/7 favourite that I simply refused to back, a 3/1 second favourite that I didn't fancy, and a bunch of no hopers. But Cleeve Hill Lad caught my eye. Okay, it was because I used to live there. There really was no other reason. Well, I suppose the Tote's odds of £187 for the win and £87 for the place looked very attractive, even if there were only two places in a seven-runner race. The thing with backing an outsider on the Tote, of course, is that your small bet tends to have a big impact on the price, but the few bookies who were doing each way terms had him at 50/1 with only one fifth those odds for finishing second. So I found the nearest Tote window and had a little dabble. It transpired that the couple knew a man who part-owned a horse called Lady Rebecca.

"Lady Rebecca," I shrieked a little too loudly, but nobody in the bar seemed to mind, "she was one of my favourite horses!"

Bought as a yearling for only 400 guineas, she went on to win 13 races and more than £160,000 in prize money, including an incredible seven victories at Cheltenham. We reminisced about the tough little mare who, despite injuries, won the Cleeve Hurdle three times. I think I was present at all of them, and Ivan used to back her as though defeat were out of the question, which it usually was. For her final win he'd had a large one on her and we drank champagne afterwards. Believe me, you need to have had a big winner to drink champagne at Cheltenham. Happy days.

The couple told me they'd had a horse with Charlie Longsdon as part of the Pershore Pessimists syndicate (great name that!) called Doctor Collins. He had some problems and only raced twice, but they'd had fun watching him at Sandown and Newbury. He was now a dressage horse.

I wondered whether he was retrained at The Racehorse Sanctuary, the wonderful establishment that rescues, rehabilitates and rehomes the beautiful animals that are literally the lifeblood of my sport. Graham Oldfield and Sue Collins co-founded the charity in 2006 after long and varied careers in the equine world. Their website aptly summarises the ethos of the place, with a definition borrowed from the Oxford English Dictionary:- "Refuge or safety from pursuit, persecution, or other danger."

These are far from just words – it lives and breathes these sentiments. I visited just weeks before my quest began, and as I stepped from my car into an oasis of calm, the traffic-ridden journey through the Surrey lanes and villages melted away in an instant, and all I could hear were soft country sounds and the distant drum of hooves. The pair were open and friendly, and for some strange reason seemed genuinely interested in my crazy adventure. But my project seemed somehow facile and insignificant compared to the work of the Sanctuary and, anyway, I wanted to see the horses.

The first to be led in was Repton, a handsome chestnut gelding who was now 19 and had run 34 times in his career, winning on four occasions. Adjacent to his box was Zigaura, a bay mare who had a briefer but very successful racing career before breeding no less than ten foals. She was quiet and kind and let a relative novice pat her without objection. Next up was Mossy Morning, a grand old mare who had her own separate paddock nearby. Despite being wary of me, she was happy to approach Graham and Sue. She had every right to be wary. Her story, and a heartbreaking one it is too, can be found on the Sanctuary's website. She was 29 years old when I saw her, and died three months later, but what a beautiful spot to see out your days, and a damn finer one than the desolate place she had come from. I couldn't imagine why somebody, somewhere, did not want to cherish this beautiful horse, and felt so grateful that the Sanctuary had been there to step in.

We talked about the beginnings of their project, and their faces lit up as the conversation quickly turned to the heroic Moorcroft Boy, the horse that was given to them after his astonishing Scottish National win in 1996.

"He came third in the Grand National won by Minnehoma, and was leading over the last before bursting a blood vessel," recalled Graham. "The next season he fell in the Becher and broke three vertebrae in his neck."

"The fall was horrendous," added Sue, "there was a hole this big in the turf where his nose hit the ground."

His comeback from those life-threatening injuries is the stuff of racing fairytale. However, you can tell that he was more than just a Scottish National winner to Graham and Sue. He was the starting point, the catalyst for what was all around us as we stood on a fine Spring afternoon in the Surrey countryside. And he was also, by all accounts, a bit of a character. Fondness would be a vast understatement of their clear affections for this horse. He died a few years ago, a permanent resident of the Sanctuary, but I sensed that his legacy lives on. The facilities were incredible:- 25 boxes, two turf gallops and a long all-weather, as well as 100 acres of the landlord's land to explore. Work was to soon start on a new outdoor ménage. We toured the stables and I asked Graham how many horses he had.

"We've got 24 at the moment, but a waiting list of about 60." I was staggered by this news, but with an estimated 5000 horses leaving training each year, perhaps I shouldn't have been. Why did he not fill the 25th stable, I asked, when there is such high demand?

"We like to keep one in reserve for emergencies" of which, apparently there have been several over the years, last minute reprieves with literally hours left before the worst happens. "We would like to take more, of course, we would like to take them all, but you can't care for them properly".

This seems the essence of the place. Whatever happens here will be in the best interests of the horse. They will be expertly cared for and allowed time to get better and progress, and that will take as long as it takes. At the Sanctuary they have no time limits or targets.

Two more sauntered back in from the field. Mr Vitality raced in Asia, winning the Hong Kong Derby on his way to £6.4m career earnings. When he left the country 35,000 fans turned up at the airport to see him go. Yes, really! He was being led in with a friend who had won £1,400 in his career. They probably didn't care about the huge differential. Neither did I really. When I questioned why a rich man would want to get rid of horse that had won him such astronomical sums, Graham chose not to be judgmental. Remarkably, there seemed not a hint of bitterness that he was the safety net for owners who are unable or unwilling to pay for the upkeep of their horses any more. The visit was both reassuring and uplifting, but also just a little sad that they could do so much more if the funds were available.

Anyhow, I digress, and back at Warwick the first race was reaching a conclusion. Cleeve Hill Lad did well, staying on as the favourite went clear round the home bend. The second favourite took a tired fall at the last, but I think the Lad may have beaten him anyway. He finished second and I listened for the Tote dividends to come through – the place paid £22.80 to a £1 stake. Not quite the £87 of before the off, but a nice return from a silly bet in the first. Perhaps my luck was turning?

I decided not to bet in the second race – discipline eh, Neil? The third and fourth races were more interesting betting propositions, both handicaps over more than three miles on testing going, but also more tricky and I got them wrong. The favourite cruised home in the fifth and I was on him (not literally). I was just into the black again and celebrated in the gathering chill with a hog roast.

And then the last race. I could leave ahead, I thought, no need to bet. I went to look at them in the paddock but I'm no paddock judge. They all looked good to me. Do I lump on this favourite, I agonised? Third behind a Mullins winner on his debut in a bumper, and Mullins rules the world. He looked a bit jig-joggy, on edge? I thought back to Paul's sage "#dontlumponthelast" text this morning, after I'd reported the savage setback of Black Narcissus. I thought I could survive that beating, just about, but not two in two days, surely?

I walked back to the betting ring. What exactly did I want to find? If the odds of the favourite had gone up that would be more attractive, but slightly worrying that it was on the drift? Conversely, if the odds had shortened it would show confidence behind his chances but I would have missed out on a better price. I stood in the ring for a while, soaking up the atmosphere. I love the tension, feeling the moves before they happen, sensing that tipping point. 4/5 became 8/11. Worse odds. Messy odds. I urged myself to hold the line. Don't do it, walk away a winner. Keep the balance.

I didn't bet. Well done, Neil. Well done. It was really cold by then, hat and gloves time. I looked around and wondered why everyone else wasn't freezing. As they gathered at the start I remember thinking that I really didn't mind whether he won or not. I had made the right call not to bet, whatever the result turned out to be. He was pushed along from home turn and never looked like winning after that, finishing second. The warm glow of a good decision eased the familiar pain from my back as I walked a heavy rucksack back to the station through the freezing Warwick streets.

# 6) Chepstow

## Day 7 – Thursday 19 March

Chepstow was the landmark that signified Day 7 of my quest. One week in, and I'd lost many pounds sterling, and gained one pound in weight. I had to admit that my diet had gone slightly awry over the past week. It was very hard to turn down an inclusive Full English breakfast. Or a hog roast for that matter. The Wife, also known as The Keeper of my Discipline, suspected something was up a few days before. My beer-chin had returned, and two rows (that is exercise on the rowing machine, not marital disputes) had done little to shore up the slippage in my diet. In fact, I was quite pleased with only gaining a pound, given the extent of the slippage. So with that milestone under my slightly straining belt, I resolved to approach the diet with renewed vigour. From that point on it would be "celery, apples, walnuts and grapes. No cheese!" Hang on a minute, that sounds a bit like a scene from Fawlty Towers.

I felt for the first time as though I was getting into the swing of it. I was actually enjoying the writing and the discipline of having to post a thousand words a day, despite severely underestimating the vast swathes of time that it would consume. It wasn't even the writing itself, as slow a typist as I am, but my inability to post it for the wider world unless I had pored over every last word. Even then, I recognised that it was not entirely as I wanted it, and had to deal with those imperfections as the trip went on. In addition, the trains and motorways had been kind thus far, although I was sure that revelation would come back to haunt me at some point, and I was startled to discover that driving was quite nice when it was not rush hour and the motorways were working.

For the second time I passed a horsebox on way to the races, this time on the M4 just past the Membury services. Thankfully there was no name of a trainer on this one, so I couldn't be tortured by thoughts of "should I or shouldn't I?" all the way to Chepstow. It was £6.50 to cross the Severn Bridge and I couldn't work out if that was good value or not. It was certainly an uninspiring two minutes in the hazy gloom that lingered over the river. At the equivalent of £210 per hour, I thought that there were better things I could do with my money (you probably could too), but if the alternative was a large detour perhaps it was money well spent?

I was racing the Satnav to get there for the first race. The Satnav won and I missed it by a few minutes. I'd already had a blazing row with my hands-free kit which refused to call anyone, instead repeatedly questioning what I wanted to know about that person.

"I want to know why you're such a turd!" I screamed.

"I'm not sure why you think that." it retorted and that was the end of the matter.

So I had time to dally on the way in and examine a quite extraordinary creation on the roundabout by the entrance. Some very talented individual had fashioned a stunning sculpture of a horse jumping a hurdle out of nothing more than fallen tree branches. The juxtaposition between the slow-growing nature of the chosen material and the flowing speed of the subject was sublime. I should have asked at Reception who the artist was but by the time I'd got there I'd forgotten all about it and had slipped into horse racing mode.

The tall and affable Steve zapped my ticket at the entrance. I asked him who had won the first and he replied that he had on Indian Stream, except that he hadn't because he wasn't allowed to bet whilst on duty. I asked him about the second race and he nominated the favourite, It's A Long Road. Noting the coincidental link to my quest, I decided that would do.

In my rush to make the first race I had not stopped to grab a Racing Post, and so began the first of what was to prove a nationwide championship of hide and seek with the specialist daily. Rumours of one at the sweetshop were greeted with a blank expression from the chap serving there, as though I was asking for an exotic variety of confectionery. I was left with no option but to study form from the walls of the on-site betting shop, which I have always found a strange place to lurk if the real thing is happening just yards from the door.

It was a sunny day so I had taken my sunglasses from the car. I really needn't have. The stands at Chepstow are north facing and the shadow extended over most of the betting and viewing areas. Adding to the already glacial ambiance, the racecourse management had apparently decided to install invisible and entirely made-up chillers that blasted icy air through the betting ring. One local said "Cor - somebody's left the door open!" I like the gentle Welsh humour.

I got my bet on and decided that I needed to leave the dark side as quickly as possible to avoid freezing to the spot, so went out the back for a coffee. I asked the lady if, given the arctic conditions in the shadow of the grandstand, she had sold a lot that day. "Ten!" she replied indignantly, "I thought it would be quiet, but not this quiet!" Perhaps the warmth of the indoor Premier Bar was more attractive?

It's A Long Road was pulled up, and I hoped that it wasn't an ominous prophecy for my journey. I bumped into Steve again who had moved places and was now performing an indistinct role near the paddock. He approached me and apologised for his tip. He wore a moustache that suited him, all his own work I believe although I never asked, and revealed that he had been at the Festival for the entire four days. It transpired that he was working there as well, doing the shifts at his local courses of Cheltenham, Chepstow and Worcester after retiring a few years ago. He seemed genuinely interested in my bizarre project, and disappointed that he would miss me at Worcester's opening fixture of the season because he was committed to doing security at a gardening show. I quietly imagined Steve stopping all the pensioners trying to sneak in through a gap in the hedge, and breaking up fights over the fuchsias in his affable but no-nonsense manner. He fancied the favourite, again, in the third race. I wondered if this was his stock reply to any quizzing by punters. Nominating the favourite each time is likely to minimise the disgruntlement.

Chepstow really is an extraordinary rollercoaster of a racecourse. The home straight resembles a swooping slide at a water park, and the back straight is reminiscent of a climb up a Brecon Beacon. Chepstow clearly doesn't suit the namby-pamby, flat-track bully. However, it is the vertigo-inducing bend after the finishing post that intrigued me most. I'd watched it on so many Welsh National programmes over the years, but you only really get a sense of its dramatic plunge if you go and stand there and watch the tons of horse flesh thundering past.

I got a bet on the race, ignoring Steve's favourite to plump for a 33/1 each way on Billy My Boy, and ventured down to the bottom bend. It was nice down there, and also in the sun, which helped. As I waited for them to go past, a couple scrambled up from the horsebox area, clearly as keen as I was to see the famous bend, and found the frosty gale that hit them a bit refreshing, as I did. I asked them if they had a runner (they just looked like they did) and the chap revealed that they had Tugboat in the hunter chase.

"He'll love tanking up that hill." he said as the runners came barrelling towards us.

I felt like I was standing at the bottom of Coopers Hill in Gloucestershire when the annual cheese rolling competition was in progress, and was ready to duck behind a tree should one of the horses have built up too much momentum to make the turn.

"Got a chance?" I suggested after the field had flashed past, always looking for inside information.

"Oh, he's just here for the beer money!" said the chap, before disappearing sharply to shelter from the arctic wind. I wasn't sure whether he meant that Tugboat was an alcoholic who only consented to race on the agreement that any winnings would be swapped for ale in his nosebag, but either way, the vibes weren't overly positive.

Steve's favourite won a tad cosily, but Billy My Boy seemed to run very well in second to give me a cheeky return. I didn't really know, though, as I couldn't see the race. I was stood in a massive dip on a Welsh hillside. I didn't mind though. It felt a bit like Warwick yesterday. I love the idiosyncrasies of our racecourses. Every football match is played on a standard pitch (except if you were John Beck's Cambridge United of the late 1980's where the corners resembled a sandpit to give the wingers something to chase).

The fourth race on the card was interesting, a competitive handicap chase over three miles. The racecourse commentator claimed that Waldorf Salad was a prospect for next season's Welsh National. He was trained by Venetia Williams, who knows a thing or two about the race, and looked an impressive stamp of an animal. A big and scopey seven-year-old, he certainly appeared every inch a chaser, and possibly a bit of a handful too. He had to be mounted by Aiden Coleman out on the course, such was his enthusiasm on leaving the paddock.

Waldorf Salad was a good starter (geddit? starter? .....oh it doesn't matter) but he got tapped for toe on the home bend and then made a juddering mistake three out. The ground may have been a little quick for him so I decided not to give up on him just yet. Then Tugboat finished second in the hunter chase, beaten only a couple of lengths at 16/1. Perhaps he really fancied a drink that night, and he should have got a fair amount given the £304 he earned for his efforts.

As I left the shadow of the facilities at the end of the afternoon, the weak Welsh sun hit me like a soft, lightly-toasted marshmallow pillow. It was a welcome wash of warmth after several hours in the cryogenic chamber of the racecourse, despite it not having any noticeable effect on my core temperature.

I felt strangely triumphant on the trudge back to the car. I had got through the first week, minus a racecourse, with a large hole in my wallet and possibly a touch of mild hypothermia. But I had survived, met some interesting people and had some fun times along the way. As I swept back over the bridge to begin the long journey home, I made a mental note to take two important points from the day. Firstly, however sunny it looked when I was leaving home in the morning, pack some thermals just in case. Secondly, keep an eye out for Waldorf Salad in next season's staying chases. "It's celery, apples....."

# 7) Bangor-on-Dee

## Day 9 – Saturday 21 March

Friday 20 March was my first (scheduled) day at home and I relished the chance to make up for my earlier absences, doing all things housey to try and ease the pressure on The Wife who seemed to be coping remarkably well. I caught up on writing, tackled bills and emails, did the washing and shopping, picked up Eldest and friends from after-school activities, and cooked a family meal. We were settling down to watch some TV when The Wife asked,

"Where are you staying tomorrow night?"

I had never planned to stay overnight after Bangor-on-Dee because in the original itinerary, which had lasted all of 48 hours before the Ffos Las farce, it was going to be a day trip. But I had shifted Market Rasen to the Sunday and now needed a stopover somewhere in between.

"I don't know yet." I replied.

This didn't seem to cut it with The Wife, who ended our cuddle to attend to something more pressing, and obviously less frustrating, elsewhere. It wasn't like I was intending on sleeping in a ditch, and I hadn't forgotten about it either, but in the hundreds of loose threads that needed attending to that day, I hadn't yet got around to tying up that one. I was prioritising, and my priorities lay with making that day a success for my family. What I hadn't realised, of course, because we are such different people, is that The Wife would rather know for sure where I was staying the next night than have the dishwasher unloaded. It reinforced that the trip, which had so many opportunities for mishap and uncertainty, could easily be more unsettling for those around me than myself.

Not only am I quite a laid-back guy, but I have a keen sense of time management. To an onlooker, lying on the sofa with the family watching TV when there are hotels to book may seem like an odd choice. To me, it was a conscious decision that made me happier with the earlier choice I had made to embark on this ludicrous voyage.

"What exactly should I have not done today to make time for finding a hotel?" I enquired.

It may have come across as slightly supercilious, but I was truly bewildered at the situation, when I'd worked so hard for my family and missed out the bit that I thought was only for my self-comfort. It wasn't that I was entirely going to wing it. I would try and book something the next morning before setting off. Britain in 2015 must surely offer some solution for a weary traveller wending his way from Wales to Lincolnshire. But I didn't get to say that last bit, of course, because the conversation was over, and two over-tired partners drifted apart in the remnants of a spoilt evening.

I left a frosty atmosphere at the house the next morning at 10:05 for the drive to North Wales. The Satnav predicted an arrival time of 1:20 which I had managed to whittle down to 1:07 before stopping at Warwick Services and immediately handing back all my gains. All the way up the M40 I'd been tempted by the signs for fast food outlets, but I opted instead for a low-calorie sandwich and tub of fresh fruit. This was becoming a bit of a habit, sort of, and as an added bonus for my self-discipline, I got the last Racing Post. There was more dissent from my hands-free kit, however, on the long drive up. I think it was still sulking from our Chepstow spat. With false sincerity it informed me "I'm really sorry about this but I can't take any requests at the moment. Please try again in a bit." Like you'd got something more important to be doing, you piece of junk?

I arrived at the Best Western Cross Lanes Hotel, a pretty establishment on the way to Wrexham, with time to freshen up and order a taxi. I had managed to book a single room just before setting off. Perhaps I was lucky to find one at that short notice, but I like to think that you make your own luck with hotels, and parking spaces too for that matter, if you just have the balls to butch it out.

If you are a certified lunatic with too much time on your hands, and fancy following in my pioneering footsteps with your own pilgrimage around all the British racecourses, one thing you should note in your planning phase is that Bangor-on-Dee is nowhere near Bangor. They are distinct and separate, by about 70 miles actually. Bangor has a fine university and easy access to Anglesey. Bangor-on-Dee is much smaller and, this really is key, has a racecourse. Glad we've cleared that up, and just a shame that I wasted so much of my precious time on the wrong one.

I arrived at the racecourse on a sunny afternoon and investigated the facilities. The track didn't seem to sit quite right in its environment. The main viewing area faced a bend, and in the last few furlongs the runners finished straight towards the public. It's almost as though the racecourse was set up before they thought about where to put the facilities. Either that or an enormous Welsh sinkhole had rotated the once sensibly aligned track to an unhelpful angle. In an era prior to the advent of giant TV screens, it would have been almost impossible to work out what was happening at the finish.

With the Scoop6 rolling over for many weeks, and the promise of three-quarters of a million quid up for grabs, I tried to get my bet on. All I had to do was find the winner of six fiendishly tricky races spread across two or three meetings - how hard could it be? Admittedly, the odds of landing it made it similar to playing the Lottery, but it's more fun watching horses than little coloured balls.

However, I was confused. I was looking for a Tote window but there weren't any. I approached a cheerful lady at one of the many 'BangorBet' windows, who told me

I'd have to place my Scoop6 wager off course. With no 3G signal available, she was right. It was only then that I vaguely remembered something about some of the courses breaking ranks with the mighty Tote to provide their own on-course pool-based betting product several years back. The BetFred chain bought the Tote from the government back in 2011 and there have been rumblings of discontent ever since. The percentage take from the pool was increased, effectively introducing a betting tax on the common punter, and staff wages were slashed. It was like bookmaking but without the risk. Clever man, that Fred Done.

So no Scoop6 for me, but two winners from the first two races endeared me to the place, and all of a sudden I had a chance of making proper inroads into my earlier losses. The third race was a tricky handicap chase and I sought inspiration in the paddock. 9 kept looking at me every time he went round. 3 looked scrawny and went to post early. Then 8 started looking at me too! But 8 was looking at everybody, I wasn't sure it meant that much. Then 1 was looking at me as well, but 9 seemed to have lost interest. What did it all mean? In my confusion I decided on a scattergun approach and backed 1, 8 and 9 to small stakes at large prices.

The race was not very old when 1 fell and badly hampered 9 who was pulled up. 8 ran well but couldn't catch the scrawny-looking 3. The horses were making a mockery of my 'looked at me in the paddock' betting strategy. Can we have a rule from now on please, all horses that are reading this, that you are only going to look at me if you are going to win? Either that or I'll have to stop going to the parade ring.

New starting rules introduced earlier in the season had been generally well received, and indeed had produced an enormously positive effect on the usual melees on offer at our major jumping festivals. The British Horseracing Authority, or BHA for short, who govern the sport can justifiably pat themselves on the back for the successful initiative. However, nothing is perfect, and there are bound to be situations where it cuts both ways. The fourth race was a case in point. The well-backed Western Jo was being fractious at the start, but had gained some forward momentum and they were in a pretty good line to get going. The starter didn't let them go, though. He couldn't. Western Jo was coming in at more than "a walk or at the most a jig-jog". So, as the new rules dictate, they then lined up stationary on the tape and of course Western Jo was left about 20 lengths behind at the start. She finished second, beaten seven lengths.

The fifth race was the most intriguing of the day, surprisingly as it was a three-runner affair and the 13-year-old Westwire Toby, with form figures that season of PPPP couldn't win. But Shantou Magic, the odds-on favourite, was pulled up last time after breaking a blood vessel. If he was fit and well he should be well clear of the second favourite Askamore Darsi. I decided on a complicated strategy. One bookmaker was offering 33/1 on the dual forecast Askamore to beat Westwire. If the favourite bled again and had to be pulled up I was a big winner. But I also needed to back the favourite in case his problems had been sorted out. I didn't like betting at odds-on, but in that race it might just have been value. The only possible way I couldn't win was if Askamore won but Shantou was second. Or even, if Westwire won, which couldn't happen. It was like printing money! Wasn't it?..... Phew, it was.

Bookmaker Cliff Emery bravely stood all the money he could on Shantou Magic, constantly shouting "take 9 to 4" (i.e. 4/9 to the punter). I watched for 10 minutes and didn't see him take a single bet on either other horse. He then defiantly pushed the price out to 1/2. I asked him after the race, as I collected my winnings, if it was a big loser for him

"No, piss poor price weren't it."

This hardened veteran of the betting ring had seen it all, and was happy to pay out on a horse that was odds-on after bleeding last time, knowing that next time he may not. But for another hardened veteran, this time of the weighing room rather than the betting ring, his race was run and he hung up his boots for the last time. Tom Siddall retired after jumping off Westwire Toby, who had just finished comfortably last of the trio as expected, and left without fanfare. In 19 seasons in the saddle he accumulated 163 winners, a total which the also retiring, but to much wider acclaim, Tony McCoy beat with unerring regularity every year (bar one) to remain champion jockey over an almost identical timeframe. The comparison was stark, not just in numbers but in the harder to quantify currency of fame. Stop a hundred people in the street and almost all will know of Tony McCoy, but I suspect none would have a clue about Tom Siddall. He may not have been as famous, talented, or lucky as McCoy, but he was just as brave and without the Siddalls our sport could not function.

Before the sixth race I stood near a bookmaker just to soak up the action of the betting ring. Normally I would be prowling, searching out the best odds, and it felt a little strange to be stationary. I love the energy, the million twitches of a moving market and trying to profit by being ahead of the next wave to roll across the electronic boards. For a smallish course Bangor had a big and competitive ring, and the bookies weren't afraid of laying a horse. The chap I stood next to seemed totally unfazed by the deluge of cash for the second favourite at 2/1.

"Forty on one, tenner on one, twenty on one, fifty on one....." he called out to his guy behind the board with the computer, and he took it all without hesitation. Only shortly before the off, under incessant pressure, did he go to 15/8 and the barrage abated. The favourite beat the second favourite quite easily. They know a thing or two about horse racing, these bookies.

I skipped the last, leaving ahead for the third time in as many meetings. I began to wonder whether this 'quitting whilst ahead' approach was a strange form of betting cowardice, rather than shrewd investment approach. Perhaps the best opportunities were in the last races which I was now tending to avoid, and this might be a negative approach in the long run? Anyhow, I'd booked the taxi to get me back to the hotel for the start of the England rugby match.

The taxi driver was a nice guy. He'd been to Wembley with Wrexham FC twice in recent years, once to see them win the FA Trophy, the other to see them lose in the Conference playoff. He'd rather it was the other way around, he said, but they still get a good crowd there, plying their non-league trade. He didn't go too often any more – four young boys all into various football commitments seemed to eat into his weekend availability. I knew what he meant and as we skimmed through the Welsh lanes my thoughts turned to my own two boys who were without a father cheering from the touchlines that weekend. I hoped it wouldn't damage them long term, and in fact in the short term they probably appreciated not having a tall chap shouting at them, but I missed it, and I missed them. Watching them compete, challenge themselves and extract all the good things that competitive sport has to offer is one of the greatest pleasures in my life, and one that I strangely chose to forego for three months.

I found a sprinkling of interested parties in the bar when I got back to the Cross Lanes Hotel. A few of them were defiantly white-shirted England supporters, but the majority, including those who'd just come in from the Wrexham game in red football shirts, were most certainly not. The French, of course, took the opportunity of playing their best game of the tournament, just to spite us, and all the Welsh in the bar had found a sudden solidarity with their new Gallic cousins. The matter was confused slightly

91

when a real French couple wandered in and seemed puzzled that a twenty point loss for their team was really a massive win when it stopped the old enemy from winning the Six Nations title. Despite being widely celebrated for their nationality on arrival, they drifted off confused and uninterested.

The atmosphere was lively but warm. The only hint of aggro was from a young kid, no more than twelve, who shouted "you're not singing any more!" at the English contingent, when we weren't singing anyway. He was forgiven as an innocent learning his pub-banter trade.

So a pulsating game of rugby and a few beers in the good company of strangers brought the Six Nations, and the day, to a close. Physicality on the very edge of the rules coalesced with respect for both the referee and the opposition in a way that is hard to achieve in any other sport, except perhaps horse racing. In both, bodies are put on the line and the knocks are taken with stoicism and humour. Both have a raw, almost primal passion at their core, and both I love because of it.

# 8) Market Rasen

## Day 10 – Sunday 22 March

The Best Western Cross Lanes Hotel was a beautifully relaxed place to ease into a sunny Sunday morning, and served me an excellent Full Welsh breakfast. However, its one major drawback was that there was no sodding wifi again. I would have to stop en route cross country to post my Bangor blog, and when I was facing eight hours of driving that day, throwing in extra hurdles really did seem tiresome.

As the M6 seeped seamlessly into the M62 a sign warned "Bumpy Road Ahead". How prophetic that was for my journey later that evening. A few miles further on, after a sudden outbreak of roadworks, a shiny new sign proudly proclaimed that this was an upgrade to produce a new "Smart Motorway". I wondered whether people would drive along it when it was finished and say "ooo, don't you look smart!", a phrase uncomfortably reminiscent of school uniforms, bad haircuts and tedious family weddings. Then I passed an enormous wind farm on the M180 near Scunthorpe. There must have been 30 of the three-pointed whizzers, all merrily going about their business, and I was reminded of the innocent inversion of a situation that only children can manage when Eldest said on one of our first family holidays to Cornwall "what happens when the batteries run out?"

As I got nearer the course I passed through the unfortunately named Spital-In-The-Street, which seemed to be the gateway to proper Fenland Lincolnshire. Suddenly the horizon was all around and the skies ranged 180 degrees like a blue-tinted protractor. The light takes on a different quality over there, a purity that bathes the landscape in warm hues. I grew up in Cambridgeshire and whenever I head back home I get a sense of space like nowhere else in the world.

I parked easily, next to a small guy faffing with kit bags in his boot. Perhaps it was a cameraman sorting equipment, I thought, as I leapt from the car and dashed to the entrance. As I was paying, Tom Scudamore, of faffing-in-boot fame, was suddenly behind me and being ushered through. I kicked myself for being too hasty and missing a prestigious scoop – a brief chat or even full-on interview with a top jockey. I get too blinkered sometimes, if you'll forgive the horsey pun, too caught up in rushing from one thing to the next to notice events unfolding around me.

However, if there was ever an antidote the frenetic pace of life it was Market Rasen. I climbed an almost deserted stand to survey the scene, and what a marvellous scene it was, washed in a clear and serenely piercing light with simply wonderful views over the whole course. All three enclosures sat harmoniously together, tidy and replete. Facilities were spacious and sparkling, the bookmakers ring lively and friendly, and the paddock (which I was deliberately avoiding after the fiasco of the previous day) couldn't have been more handily placed. I know this seems a bit soppy, but everyone seemed genuinely happy to be there on a fine Sunday afternoon whether they were winning or losing.

Breathing in a new calm aura, I flicked through the paper to find that Scudamore had only one ride that afternoon, for the in-form trainer Nigel Hawke in the fifth race. Second in the jump jockeys championship, he had probably travelled further than I had to be in Lincolnshire for a shorter time, and the Racing Post forecasted his mount Mister Wiseman a 10/1 outsider of the sextet. A closer inspection of the form could not dissuade me – the horse had come even further to be here, 251 miles from Devon indeed, and had won at the course five times. Admittedly, it had run poorly on the last two occasions on softish ground, but had slipped down the weights as a result and was now back on both a better handicap mark and surface.

Much had been made in the media over the previous month, especially in the run-up to the Festival, about prize money levels at the top of the sport. This is a devilishly knotted rope to untangle, with many different strands. The Jockey Club owns Cheltenham along with 14 other tracks, including Market Rasen. It operates as a trust with no shareholders, and its profits are reinvested into the sport. Despite not being required to do so, it registers its accounts at Companies House, although these do not break down the figures course by course. The criticism in some quarters, including several top trainers who have been known to benefit from success at Cheltenham, is that the supposed £10 million profit from the Festival each year should be reinvested in boosting prize money for the biggest events, not propping up the smaller provincial tracks.

I could not disagree more. I feel that the lesser grade racing I had witnessed over the previous few days is essential if the sport is to remain healthy from grassroots level upwards. The top owners are in it for the prestige and exhilaration of having a runner, let alone a winner, at the Cheltenham Festival. Frankly, they can afford not to get much of their investment back. Don't get me wrong - I'm glad that they are there and the trickle-down effect of them effectively funding the sport brings numerous benefits, but racing is not just about the events that make it into the headlines, nor should it become that. If it were to, it would lose that possibility of fairytale, like football has over the years, and become a poorer sport for it.

Britain has the best racing in the world, and the fact that owners here receive a paltry 26p in the pound return on their investment makes it all the more remarkable that the whole house of cards is still standing. That it is, just, is in no small part attributable to the rich diversity on offer in the foundations of its lower tiers. Is the loaf of bread on the table too small to divide up? Possibly, as Hereford and Folkestone know to their cost. Is the solution to give the bread to only the bigger members of the family and let the runts wither away? Undoubtedly not, in my opinion. Our pyramid would hardly be seen in the landscape of modern sport were it not for the legion of smaller courses that make up the base layers. How many of today's devotees stumbled upon horse racing by chance, channel hopping between Bridge Over The River Kwai and Bargain Hunt on a Saturday afternoon? Not many I would suggest, and far fewer than were initially introduced to the sport when taken to a local track like Market Rasen.

Owners in other countries are more generously rewarded because they have state monopolies over the betting product. The cost of the leak in our system is not borne by the bookmakers, but by the owners and punters, big and small, who all get a raw deal out of their willingness to invest in our sport. The biggest prize on offer at Market Rasen on that fine Sunday afternoon was £5,198. That would pay the training fees for a few months, but not that many. The fact of the matter is that you don't own a racehorse to become rich.

The second race on the card, a handicap hurdle, was interesting. Ivans Back led and stayed on gamely over the last, but seemed to be tiring on the long run in. At this point a mature lady with cropped, silver hair came screaming from behind me towards the finishing straight. She had her arms aloft, galloping like a lunatic performing a rain-dance, and was making a guttural noise that came from somewhere deep in her soul. The gist of it seemed to be that she really, really wanted the leader to keep going. Alarmed racegoers parted quickly, worried they would be mown down should the lady attempt to hurdle the running rail and literally carry her horse over the line. It wasn't required. Ivans Back held on by a length to win at 15/2. Everybody enjoyed the spectacle, and it transpired that the lady was the owner. If you want an advert for racehorse ownership, at whatever level, it was right there. Somehow, for that lady I don't think it was all about the money.

By the time the fifth race arrived two things had transpired. Firstly, I was badly in need of a winner. Secondly, Mister Wiseman was priced up the 3/1 second favourite, nowhere near the generous 10/1 suggested in the paper. It seems I wasn't the only one to have spotted that the Wiseman had travelled far. I dived in at 100/30 and he won well. Again I left before the last race, in profit for the fourth meeting in a row.

If you forgive the fact that the horses are not the fastest in the land, I'm not sure you can ask for much more from a day's racing. They are all superstars to somebody. I had a warm glow on my four-hour drive home, at least until I hit the M1 anyway, and therein lies the track's only problem. Market Rasen is not very easy to get to, or indeed get back from, as my homeward journey attested. If this fine racecourse survives because of its place within the Jockey Club family, then this can surely only be a good thing for racing as a whole.

As I slowly juddered down the M1 I thought back to the question Paul had asked on the morning of Day 2 and had repeated on the phone on the way up to Bangor-on-Dee. No, I replied, it still didn't seem like a job, it seemed like I was going racing again! I've done real jobs, many and varied, as I'm sure you all have. Jobs seem like hard work because they are. This seemed like I was doing a tour of all the British racecourses and writing about it, which I was.

That was a true and full summary of the situation until about 6pm that evening. With the Friday night tiff not fully resolved, I wanted to get back to make a 7pm dinner date with my family and settle into my first proper break but, because of the usual M1 shenanigans, The Satnav was cranking up the estimated delay with each crawling mile south. Astonishingly, although I'd never realised it before despite numerous journeys along those stretches of roads, a clever button on the Satnav told me I was not due to pass a petrol station between Luton and my driveway. I had also not filled up since leaving for Bangor-On-Dee, but was confident I could get home. The Galaxy has a pretty big fuel tank, but the trouble with traffic jams is that they are not a very fuel-efficient way of travelling, and so as I shuffled past Luton I was fighting a losing battle on both the diesel and time fronts simultaneously, charted on separate electronic displays that my eyes nervously twitched between.

There were brief glimmers of hope on the rare occasion I managed to reach a decent speed and my dashboard display suggested the estimated fuel remaining to be just above my Satnav distance home, but all hope was lost on the M25. The queue for the M4 started two miles before the junction, and although this was the slightly shorter of the two options for my journey it would also be drastically less fuel efficient, so I ploughed on desperately hoping for a traffic free exit onto the M3. I didn't get it. By this stage the dashboard was reporting zero miles of fuel left and the dial on the gauge had no more red left to sink through. I was six miles from exiting the M3 and finding possible redemption.

It was seven minutes of the utmost concentration – try to be smooth Neil, no braking. If I wiggle (Formula1-esqe) does the gauge alter? How far can I glide before coming to a standstill? Was it better to use more fuel to reach a higher speed so that when it ran out I would glide further? Where was the easiest place to pull over, given there's no hard shoulder in the roadwork section? I can't see any emergency phones, so is there any mobile signal?

Somehow, I made it. After a nerve-wracking detour of an agonising extra mile, I pulled into the beacon of hope that was a garage and decanted 70.8 litres of diesel into a fuel tank that has an official capacity of 70. It must have been very, very close. However, what with all the faffing, driving at an economical rate and mile upon mile of roadworks and stationary traffic, I comfortably missed dinner. This was a dinner of redemption, to rebuild after an argument and take the pressure off The Wife. This was a dinner of anecdotes, that I had found a lovely racecourse and wanted to tell my boys of my adventures so far. This was a dinner of celebration with my first proper break coming up nine days into the tour. And this was a dinner that I missed because of the sodding traffic on the motorways. So yes, Paul, I thought as I finally cleared the traffic and hammered it home with a full fuel tank, it now seemed like a job.

# 9) Newton Abbot

## Day 13 – Wednesday 25 March

Two days at home restored my positivity and I felt ready to go again. It was amazing how ingrained I had become over the years to traditional working patterns, and the lack of a proper two day weekend break had begun to disrupt the usual rhythm and wear me down. Another reason to be cheerful was that I was catching the train and wouldn't have to face the bloody motorways for a few more days.

I noticed on the Tuesday evening that Black Narcissus was running again in the last race at the South West outpost in what would be her third outing in just eleven days. There were various good reasons to back her that I won't bore you with, and many obvious reasons not to that you already know. But I didn't want her to dominate proceedings again, like she had at Exeter. I didn't want to have a Black cloud hanging over the afternoon, agonising over whether to put my faith in this cruel temptress one last time, so I got the decision out the way early and backed her with an online account, to a good sum, at 9/2. Job done, and I could concentrate on the rest of the day.

In the February of 2014 a savage storm battered the Devon coastline and destroyed the track at Dawlish. Yet as I travelled west past Exeter on a calm and sociable train to Newton Abbot, there was little evidence of the destruction that was wreaked. Instead, there was a sense of rebuilding – the human spirit to overcome and persevere was omnipotent. Me too. I felt rejuvenated after the break and on a sunny Wednesday spirits were high. The Wife and I had acknowledged our differences and the boys remembered briefly who their father was. I wondered, to the soothing rocking motion of the train, if my mood was inextricably linked to the vagaries of the weather. The first two ports of call on my maiden voyage were visited in a shroud of clinging cold and deadening cloud, and I suspected I may have judged both Cheltenham and Uttoxeter unfairly, although both were undeniable crowded. The journey along the coast was particularly pretty, with the sun breaking through the clouds and dancing on the ripples of the English Channel. Ivan had told me many years ago of the beauty of this line, and he was not wrong.

With an hour until the first race I ventured up to the Paddock Restaurant where a sign for the carvery elicited a Pavlovian response in me. I weakly justified the roast beef to myself on account of the carrots and cabbage, and the fact that I had walked past a hog roast outlet to get to it. And amazingly good it was too. The head chef was carving and overseeing the operation in an efficient but jovial mood, and to process that number of hungry punters in the rush before the first race whilst maintaining such quality was a rare achievement, and one that would make other racecourse offerings seem shameful in comparison as the tour continued.

Buoyed by a hearty lunch, I headed to the bar and asked for a Tribute, but the barmaid ignored the obvious chance to celebrate my many and various qualities, and poured me a pint of bitter. I settled next to a couple and got chatting. They hoped I'd sat down to give them a list of winners, but with the state of my betting profit and loss account I quickly dispelled that myth. I told them of the Black Narcissus debacle. They were knowledgeable racing people, and we discussed her chances of racing over further, as well as her occasionally obstreperous approach.

"She's by Westerner" the lady said astutely, although I wasn't quite sure what that meant. I have enough trouble keeping up with the form to worry about breeding, in a horse sense anyway. Perhaps Black Narcissus had special dispensation to act truculently because of her lineage? Suitably refreshed, we wished each other luck and I headed towards the betting ring. I'd had time to study the form properly on the way down, and there really is no better way of finding winners. Hard graft in the monochrome pages of the Racing Post is the pre-requisite, and anything else is a shortcut as far as I'm concerned.

The ground was meant to be good to soft, but the drum of the hooves as they landed over the last hurdle in the first race was startling. I was then banking on it being good ground or faster, and thought the top weights could be in with a shout. The afternoon progressed in predictable fashion – a nice winner, a few near misses and a couple of my selections running as though they were two drunk racegoers in a pantomime horse costume. A typical afternoon, in other words. But really this was all a supporting act to the main event, the warm up band before the Black Narcissus show sprang into life.

I broke my paddock hoodoo for the only time that day to see her appear and, like most females, she kept us waiting. Perhaps I was becoming slightly obsessed, but I was convinced that everyone else around the parade ring was waiting for her as well. She was certainly the name on everyone's lips in the hushed conversations that I eavesdropped. Many good form judges gathered around the rail were worried she was just staying on through tired horses at Exeter last time, and surprised to see that Conor O'Farrell was not back on board.

I really thought that Black Narcissus would either refuse to race or win. In the event she did neither. She jumped off fine, travelled much better than previously and looked comfortable throughout. Perhaps that was the problem – it was too slow a pace, and Newton Abbot seemed a tight track suited to the speedier types. On the final circuit the jockey Rhys Flint decided to move forward and force the issue. I could see why, given the steady pace and her ability to stay, but she had won so well at Exeter coming from behind. I don't think there was too much wrong with the idea; perhaps it was just the wrong race for her. She didn't look like winning from two out and finished third.

I had managed to avoid backing her again on course, and that at least was a saving grace, but I walked back to the station not really sure what the future held for me and this moody mare. Three and a half miles on testing going with some fierce pacemakers and a start nowhere near the stands, oh and odds of 25/1 or more, and then I might be interested, old friend.

On the train home I flicked through the rest of the day's racing results and was shocked to see the win of Mercy Me on the Lingfield all-weather. A 16/1 winner wasn't perhaps all that unusual, but when the horse that had come second, Triple Dip, was the 1/20 favourite in a four-runner contest, it represented quite a turn-up for the books. I had suffered my first losing meeting in five, but this must have been nothing compared to the misery of those who had backed the 1/20 jolly.

So the reconstruction of my bankroll was still a work in progress, but punters have an ability to endure and see things though in the long run, much like the brave men and women who rebuilt the Devon coastline. Rome wasn't built in a day. In fact, the train line to Newton Abbot took two months, which was about what I'd got left.

# 10) Newbury

## Day 14 – Thursday 16 March

Sometimes you have to ask yourself what many and varied twists of fate have led to you be in a certain place at a certain time. Just six months after stopping teaching, on a bright and very breezy Spring afternoon, the collision of a million thoughts, chance encounters and strands of circumstance resulted in me being ushered through the grand entrance to the Royal Box at Newbury.

To give myself some credit, it wasn't entirely down to fate. The royalty in question was Julian Thick, CEO of Newbury Racecourse, whom I had emailed to ask if he would talk to me. For some reason he agreed, and offered half an hour of his time freely and willingly, as though my absurd project was in some way worthwhile. I marvelled, not for the first time, at how open and generous racing folk are. Communications Director Andy Clifton had left a ticket for me at the entrance and accompanied me up the sumptuous staircase to meet Julian.

I was interested in the only racecourse plc in Britain and, in particular, its independent status when half of its counterparts are part of either the Jockey Club or Arena Racing Company conglomerates. Both Julian and Andy had previously held prestigious positions in the Jockey Club, including time at such luminaries at Cheltenham and Aintree, so knew their stuff and had seen both sides of the fence. Was it beneficial to be part of a group, I asked?

"Economies of scale are quite tricky with racecourses," Julian said, "but clearly the advantage of being part of the Jockey Club is that it has two major festivals."

Andy added that being independent made them more "agile, open to change", and changing it certainly was.

Newbury was two and a half years into a joint venture that would bring 1,500 new homes to the racecourse, along with a significant investment in the infrastructure and facilities.

"The challenge is doing it sympathetically and in a supportive way to the racecourse," said Julian, who cited similar examples from county cricket, but was quick to acknowledge that this route to financial security was only available to those venues lucky enough to be in an area of the country that is in desperate need of housing. "If you're Wincanton, for example, there's limited opportunity."

Andy concurred and, unsurprisingly given his recent stint at the Hong Kong Jockey Club, described it as framing the course.

"The thing in our favour is that this view is not going to be affected," he said, gesturing to the tree-lined backdrop to so many dramatic Hennessy moments over the years, "We took Clare Balding and the Channel 4 cameras up to one of the penthouses and they couldn't believe the view!"

But part of my journey was about examining the way the sport itself is changing as it struggles to evolve in the fierce competition for modern audiences, and the new generation who have the attention span of a demented goldfish. It is a struggle that had infamously seen another notable CEO quoted as saying that he operated a hospitality venue with some horse racing tagged on the side. If that is the prevalent view then I am officially worried for the future of my beloved sport. I accept that racecourses are luxuries in terms of space, and that hundreds of acres of green land need to justify their existence, especially when many are sited in built-up urban areas. So, I've no issue with building apartments or hosting conferences. My worry, I explained to Julian and Andy, was that this process of evolution would crush the essence of the racing itself, such that I would rather see it perish in the backwaters of eccentric British minority pastimes rather than flourish in a gaudy metamorphosis of what it currently is. Would this urge for change actually detract from what we have, so that we may gain one million new racegoers by 2020 (one of the many ambitious proposals from the BHA) but in doing so would lose two million of the existing base?

"We're a business" Andy put it bluntly, "and if by putting on alternative entertainment we can attract more people or a slightly different audience to come racing then for me as somebody who loves racing that can't be a bad thing. I wouldn't want to be involved in anything detrimental to the industry."

"We've both worked for Edward Gillespie," continued Julian "and one thing he was really good at was 'evolution not revolution'. At Cheltenham there would be a number of things that would be different from year to year. Some of it didn't work and it was quietly dropped, like the music coming back into the winners' enclosure, but others have been accepted."

"Like the fourth day of the Festival?" I suggested.

"Yes. I would say it really was 50:50, and a lot of those for it would be for purely commercial reasons, but most of the doubters would now say it works," Julian said, before adding reassuringly, "one of the reasons people fall in love with racing is the tradition, the prestige, the history of places like this and that's something we would give up at our peril."

Continuing the theme of change, I offered them both a magic wand to change anything they wanted in racing. Julian came back as quick as a flash "The horse that was fourth in the last race at Cheltenham because my Placepot would have come in", and Andy quipped "what, apart from my salary?"

They may have sounded slightly flippant, but these really were the best answers I could have wished for. These guys were in it for the love of the sport, and this showed deeply in the humour and warmth in which they discussed it. I would hate to think of the people in charge not wanting to have a bet, or seeing the racing as merely a means of getting people through the gate.

"Flat racing needs a steady flow of Frankels, something to take us from the back page and give us our moment in the sun, which jump racing has through the Grand National," continued Julian, "we need something stellar that attracts peoples' attention and gets them through the gates. Once we've got them here I think we give them a good time."

"The world is personality-driven at the moment," offered Andy, "and people at an impressionable age have got to have heroes to look up to, human or animal. That's why fans of jump racing are more loyal because they get to follow those heroes for longer."

"Being in the parade ring and the winners' enclosure working when some of the great champions are led in and seeing the atmosphere and emotion of the owners and the jockeys and the crowd – it's priceless."

As it turned out, the half hour was more than an hour and I savoured every minute. Both Julian and Andy came to horse racing simply as fans of the sport, and genuinely seemed as appreciative as I was of the opportunities afforded us. Suffice to say that I left the Royal Box feeling that Newbury Racecourse in particular, and horse racing in general, was in the hands of good people who have its best interests at heart.

I met an old friend before the first race, one of the guys from university who used to accompany me to Devon & Exeter races. Jim and I had spent two years on the same course and it would be fair to say that we were both disaffected Economists who struggled with the inanity of the syllabus. One particularly memorable nadir was the endless, blackboard-rotating nonsense of the Neyman-Pearson Lemma (no, I don't know what it is, or does, either) which lasted for a full 60 minutes of meaningless hieroglyphics.

It must have been 23 years since I had last seen the bloke, yet the time rolled away in a warm handshake and I realised we were essentially the same, just slightly larger versions of our old selves. It seemed absurd to try and catch up on personal news over a quarter of a century, so we started chatting about racing and my journey so far. Almost immediately Ivan appeared and I introduced him to Jim as the guy who taught me how to teach, 18 years earlier.

"Didn't do a very good job, did I?" Ivan offered.

"Well, knowing him 25 years ago," Jim replied "if you got him to teach for almost 20 years I think you did a very good job!"

And with that two strangers bonded by gently taking the piss out of the common link, and the afternoon unfolded before us like a sepia tablecloth. Andy had kindly given me a tip for the first race which won nicely and we retired to the bar.

Ivan was not impressed by the only ale on offer being Doom Bar. He has his funny ways, and I like most of them, but I'm a fan of Doom Bar, and used to holiday near the then tiny brewery in Cornwall, so challenged him. "Is it because it's taken over the world?"

"It's exactly that!" said Ivan, before struggling to find the right word for its astonishing growth and domination of bars across the land. "Ubiquitous" Jim suggested, and we agreed on that, and cleverly threaded the word back into strands of conversation throughout the afternoon. Jim has a nice way with words, which is quite useful in his profession as a sports commentator, I suppose.

After a good start with the betting I again failed to 'train on' through the card. Some weary selections found one too good into the fierce headwind down the long home straight. Ivan insisted that we went to a different bar to try some proper ale by the name of Barman's Armpit, or something similar. It was okay, but I preferred the Doom Bar.

Jim left early to go to work. He does 60,000 miles a year and had a back operation a while ago to prove it. I was staggered by this figure. My trip computer had racked up 1,200 in two weeks, and I was already beginning to get bored with the roads. 23 years was a yawning chasm to overcome, but we did pretty well with the backdrop of a day at the races to guide us. New friends or old friends, ones you see regularly, and some you haven't seen in a generation. Somehow it doesn't matter. Racing gives a flow to proceedings that enables easiness, and without it I would struggle to replicate the pro forma it gives for a damn good get-together.

Ivan and I backed another loser before heading to a pub he knew near the station and planning out a strategy of when he would be joining me. I was considering driving to Bath on 13 May, but quickly revised that idea when Ivan said he would be in attendance.  For reasons I can no longer recall, we got talking about the former Liberal MP Shirley Williams. Some new ales amused us for an hour, and they were certainly better than the Armpit.

# 11) Wetherby

## Day 15 – Friday 27 March

I took my usual service station fare to the till and plonked down my travelling life in front of the smiley teenager – a prawn sandwich, a tub of mango with a plastic fork in lid, and a large bottle of water. At M&S you are still served by teenagers, but they look at you and smile rather than look through you and sneer.

We exchanged pleasantries, and at the end of the transaction I internally winced as I uttered the word "Fantastic!" as she handed me my change. It's not really fantastic at all, is it Neil. Not like sipping champagne in a hot tub under the Northern Lights, or a 20/1 winner in the first race. It was just a financial transaction where I ended up with less cash and more mango than I had before.

I suppose the point was that it was the most fantastic interaction I'd had on that journey. Spending long chunks of time on the road made the little things become big. I had already started talking to the car, myself, and even The Satnav, which I'd had another disagreement with on the way up to Wetherby. When I deliberately entered 5EH at the end of the postcode instead of the correct 5HE, just to see if it was concentrating, the stupid machine took me to a very handsome stud farm. There were certainly horses, but no racing, and no bed for the night either. I castigated it for not spotting the obvious error and we got to the hotel shortly afterwards in an icy silence.

In my rush to do the bins that morning I had forgotten that it was 'Wear A Hat Day' at Wetherby to raise awareness for Brain Tumour Research. This was a serious oversight as I have a burgeoning collection of silly hats that I have accumulated over the years, and was thinking of either my Tyrolean Goat-Herder number, or the three-tailed and therefore plattable one from Australia. Either of these would, I reckoned, have helped me meld seamlessly into the crazy hat-party atmosphere that would be cranking up at the track.

When I got to the racecourse, a little later than planned due to the postcode mishap, I discovered that the hardy locals had not exactly embraced the theme. Most were hatless, many coatless, and indeed a large proportion of the ladies were dressed as though they were going to a wedding. A summer wedding on a tropical island, by all accounts. I'm all for making an effort, but only when it comes to studying the form, and the concept of wearing the bare minimum on one of the coldest Marches in history was baffling.

I'm happy to accept that I'm a southern softie, and I'm probably showing my age, but some of these youngsters could have been catching their death out there by the windswept A1 if there wasn't so much alcohol to warm them. I usually bought premier tickets on my tour, so that I could sample all that a racecourse had to offer, but my first foray into the premier enclosure was not pleasant. Suited, drunken, shouting idiots made this an instantly walk-throughable venue, and I sought refuge in the much more down-to-earth Paddock enclosure. There is a peculiar inversion at some tracks where a pricier ticket gets you a dicier atmosphere.

My first bet failed by a short head. I'd backed it partly because of the young claimer Joe Colliver who was showing a very healthy profit to level stakes that season, but Vasco D'ycy got going just fractionally too late. An unusual scene then played out as I watched an elderly lady tilting and rolling one of the rubbish bins for a good five minutes. She looked too well dressed to be scavenging for food, and I wondered if she was attempting to discover the next winner in a bizarre Yorkshire ritual akin to reading the tea leaves. Eventually her husband turned up, immediately spotted the winning betting ticket she'd managed to throw away, and they went off to collect the money.

Mr Burbidge in the fourth race secured me a positive position on the day, but for some reason it was the fifth race that interested me most, a National Hunt flat race with little prior information available. What form there was suggested Shantou Village (surely a relative of Shantou Magic from Bangor?) had a cracking chance, but I didn't want to back it at Evens with 12 other runners that were so unexposed. Instead, I searched for an outsider, and found one.

There was simply no reason to back the unraced Gray Wolf River, a horse that appeared so small whilst circling the paddock that she bore an uncanny resemblance to a rocking horse being dragged around on an invisible trolley. She was certainly more grey wolf than racehorse, and when the jockey mounted she threw an awful tantrum, as though she'd been squashed by an elephant. Her race number of 13 and extreme odds added little encouragement, and anybody that backed her would have to be considered a certified lunatic. Accordingly, I went in at 125/1 to small stakes.

As I waited for the off, with more drunken zoo-noises emanating from the premier stand behind me, I pondered whether the handicap system should be adapted to allow for the size of a horse. Certainly any EU court would decide that the other horses twice her size held an unfair competitive advantage.

It was hard to see Gray Wolf River for most of the race. It was like trying to spot a needle in a melee of moving haystacks. Or, perhaps, a small grey wolf in a bunch of horses. As they thinned out a bit on the home straight she reappeared in about 10th place, and stayed there. Shantou Village won nicely. Again I left before the last, but this time it was entirely justifiable. The final contest was literally a two horse race, and one of them was 1/12. After the huge odds-on upset at Lingfield a couple of days ago I wasn't touching that with a bargepole.

So with Black Narcissus robbing me again on Wednesday, and another losing day at Newbury, I was back to recording a profitable day, but my winning meetings were small and my losing meetings were big. Moreover, Wetherby racecourse had been a desolate place, and not just because of the weather and the proximity to the A1. My only interactions that day had been perfunctory ones with staff and bookmakers, and I felt pensive at the prospect of another solitary two-day trip. When I got back to the hotel I FaceTimed my family and felt better but somehow worse, especially when The Wife asked me to hold the phone further away because my face was too enormous to fit on the screen. Naturally I complied, but felt she had gone too far when she asked me to put a paper bag over my head because I was still upsetting the boys.

Perhaps being with friends at Newbury had rammed home the lonely nature of being on the road? Perhaps it was the loutish undertones of the premier enclosure? Perhaps it was that my longest conversation of the day was with a small box that sat on my windscreen? As I took the comfort blanket of the Racing Post down to the restaurant and asked for a table for one, I felt as though I needed a good day at Doncaster to right the ship.

# 12) Doncaster

## Day 16 – Saturday 28 March

The Mercure Wetherby is described as either "contemporary" or "functional", depending on the website you visit, but despite the lack of aesthetic charm I had slept well in room 212 and was pleased to see a pristine copy of the Racing Post outside my door. With renewed dieting vigour, I breakfasted in my room on complimentary coffee sachets and pre-packed cereal.

The morning brought news of Youngest's sterling performance in an epic 2-2 draw against the unfairly-gifted Knaphill Jedis. Afterwards he was recognised with the Man Of The Match award, and I was 200 miles away chasing some very strange dream, rather than there on the touchlines cheering him on. Again I felt a little silly, but I'd started this thing so ploughed onwards towards the next stop of my ludicrous tour.

The paper reported that the championship for flat jockeys was to now run from Guineas weekend at the start of May to Champions Day in mid-October. Well, I know very little about flat racing, having made the difficult decision about 15 years ago that it was an expendable part of my increasingly busy and child-strewn life, but even I know that the flat season starts with the Lincoln Handicap from Doncaster at the end of March. I can understand the desire to bookend seasons that seem never-ending as one rolls interminably into the other, but I do have to question the wisdom of dropping the Lincoln as the landmark that declares the flat season is upon us. Another casualty in the evolution of British horse racing, and I'm sure it won't be the last. Mind you, before I get too nostalgic for the good old days, I should point out that the Lincoln wasn't always run at Doncaster. Racing has already survived umpteen changes over the last couple of centuries and I'm sure it will survive more. To me, it's all about whether it loses its essence in the process.

It was literally blowing a hooley (whatever one of those is) as I scurried into Doncaster racecourse. The hall at the bottom of the Lazarus stand was cavernous, but had a good atmosphere. The management had done well to create a good vibe with the enormous area split into many themed sections, and queues at the many and various bars were virtually non-existent. There was a palpable sense of excitement about the place at the prospect of a new season, perhaps elevated further by the Scoop6 which had rolled over again from the previous Saturday at Bangor-on-Dee and promised even greater riches. I put on a small perm (betting combination, that is, rather than curly wig), doubling up with two selections in the first and last races – you never want your Scoop6 to fail in the first or last.

"I've got the winner here, you know!" I said to the lady behind the Tote counter, waving my betting slip. She just smiled and said "Next please."

I headed up from the warehouse on the ground floor to explore the rest of the facilities, and was naturally drawn to the food court near the top of the building. With plenty of time before the first race I was delighted to hunt out a proper homemade pie, rather than one of those individual fancies with a disc of flaky pastry floating on top. It was a big rectangular beast from which generous chunks were cut, the filling oozing into the space left behind and then scooped onto the plate as well. I went for the chicken and ham, just like I used to get at home, with mash, vegetables and extra gravy from a big jug. Suddenly I felt happy again. Food really is a marvellous thing, you know, and I could always tell The Wife I'd had a salad - she'd never know.

With stomach filled and form studied, I headed back downstairs with renewed enthusiasm for my task, and was genuinely surprised to see starting stalls for the first time since my journey had begun. It would be easy to justify my choice of the first eleven fixtures on my schedule being jump meetings by pointing out that the jumps season is loaded towards the softer ground in the winter and spring months, rather than the firmer conditions in the summer. But in truth, I chose jump meetings whenever I could because I prefer them.

There is something truly breathtaking about seeing a horse taking a fence at speed. It is something I have tried to explain to others on many occasions, but it's one of those things that you can only explain to people who already understand – preaching to the converted, as it were. On the occasions when I do try to explain I usually end up reverting to a moment many seasons ago, a supporting race at the Cheltenham Festival. I can't remember the horses involved but they were seasoned chasers and this was probably their last chance to book their place in the annuls of horse-racing history, their only shot at greatness. Three of them came to the third last, the fence at the bottom of the hill, and the TV camera took a low perspective from the landing side of the fence so I could only see the bobbing heads of the jockeys approaching the fence, and was not quite sure when they were going to see the final stride and launch themselves upwards. Everyone in the bookies was staring at the screens and holding their breath.

These three horses flew the fence together, line abreast, tons of straining horse flesh with jockeys faces grimacing, the pain and desire etched into their faces, and it was just such a beautiful sight and the whole of the betting shop made that wonderful noise that can only happen with horse racing, a cross between a cheer and a strangled roar, and these three wonderful horses landed together and kicked for home. They were still together over the last two fences and up the final hill, with the commentators voice rising, and the horses necks straining up the hill, glistening with sweat, and the jockeys pumping for all their worth, squeezing and urging their mounts forward, every last ounce of energy expended, almost trying to physically throw their mounts at the line, and everybody in the bookies going absolutely beserk.

As I stood there after the race had finished, in the afterglow of something magnificent, I knew that I would never forget that race, and I knew even then that in years to come I would be using that race as an explanation, a justification almost, for my love for jump racing. And I probably knew then as well that the people I was telling it to would listen patiently, nodding in all the right places, and then say something pathetic like "yeah well football's always been my game of course", and I would realise that they hadn't understood at all, and I may as well have been talking to a brick wall. Looking back now, I should have written down the names of the three horses, or at least remembered which particular race it was, but I didn't.

With one fence left to jump, class goes out the window and it comes down to which horse can raise itself one last time. I suppose there's something almost human about the jumps, the way these obstacles have to be negotiated if you are going to succeed, and it's not just simply about going faster than anybody else if you don't have the skill and courage to, literally, overcome the barriers that block your path.

The other aspect to it, and the reason I virtually gave up on the flat many years ago, is that the jumpers stick around for a while. The old favourites tend to reappear season after season, whereas a good flat horse is invariably worth more at stud than on the racecourse and is therefore retired before I've had the time to get properly acquainted. It makes studying the form harder, as the slate is usually wiped clean every year and I have to begin again from scratch, whereas I love seeing the jumpers returning at Cheltenham, Haydock or Newbury and working out if they've improved over the summer. When I look at the racecards they are more inviting because I already have several keys to unlock the puzzle.

In the first race of the new flat season at Doncaster there was little form to go on as a small field of two-year-olds battled up the home straight. I watched the replay again and again but still couldn't work out how my selection, First Bombardment, got beaten. A short head, they said. The flare of a nostril, if anything. He came to win the race and then just wavered in the last few strides. It could just have been young horses getting tired, but I also wondered whether it was the fierce headwind. In the second I backed the favourite and he just prevailed, but it looked like hard work out there. It was also hard work to see what was happening for the first half of the race because a big bunch of trees in the middle of the course was obscuring the view. Somebody said they had tried to get rid of them but the council objected. I wondered if it would have been the same story if they were in the middle of the Rovers football ground?

The hooley from earlier had intensified rather than abated, and trackside resembled a wind tunnel. I wouldn't have been surprised to see a car manufacturer testing a new design on the straight mile. The next three races were like something from the Tour de France. Arrowheads formed around front-runners who inevitably dropped away tamely in the closing stages. Astaire looked like he was going to win the Cammidge, but Naadiir swooped late from last to first, the invisible slipstream slingshotting him past the favourite, and my Scoop6 predictably failed in the first race despite my doubling-up strategy.

Doncaster was a nice course, but because of the wind I started getting that Cheltenham feeling of being unable to settle anywhere. I'd had enough of the constant buffeting for a while, so went back to the cavern where there was still a buzzing atmosphere. People were a lot drunker, but enjoying themselves. If you give a polar bear a concrete enclosure he will get bored and start a fight, but there was enough to distract the polar bears here. Staff worked hard to keep the place tidy and cheery. Punters seemed happy and mingled easily. Perhaps it was just that they had got enough space? There was still evidence of the summer wedding outfit, but it was not as cold as at Wetherby, so I was not as concerned for their occupants' safety. It was definitely a day for hairpins, though, and any toupee-wearer would have been ill-advised to venture beyond the sanctuary of the Lazaras Stand.

I needed my own personal comeback, in a betting sense at least. The two big handicaps were next, and I gave random number generator Jason a call. I needed an each way double – small outlay but big returns if it came off in two fiercely competitive races of more than 20 runners each.

"Easy," he replied, "3 and 14."

I quite liked his two selections, which was worrying, and placed the bet with an online account. This was Jason's last chance, mind. I was beginning to think he was just plucking random numbers out of thin air.

In any other running of the Spring Mile, Buckstay would have been produced brilliantly to win, but as he hit the front in the last furlong he began to paddle into the heart of the hurricane. Think back to when you were at school and it was windy in the playground and you flipped your coat up in the air and tried to lean forward. You did used to do that, didn't you? Chatez was another last to first winner, but Jason's number 3, Halation, came fourth at 14/1 and the each way part of the double was still alive and running onto the favourite of the Lincoln in the next.

The Lincoln Handicap was actually run in Lincoln until the course closed in 1964. In that year Mighty Gurkha triumphed at 33/1 in a field of 45. Surely, I thought, it must be easier to pick a winner 51 years on with half the runners, but it didn't feel like it. My feelings were astute. I backed Lincoln to win the Lincoln at Lincoln Bookmakers. This really was clutching at straws, or a similar analogy might be ripping up banknotes in a gale. Lincoln won the first half of the Lincoln easily, but was then a spent force. Gabrial drifted alarmingly in the market before the off, but was one of the few horses to keep straight on the course and was another winner to come from behind. The third home, Moonharib, seemed to stall within sight of the post as though he'd been sailing too close to the wind, and then started changing legs and tacking from side to side. GM Hopkins, the favourite and second leg of our double, was tenth. Bankroll resurrection would have to wait another day.

I was glad to return to the sanctuary of the car and begin the 200 mile drive home, and to while away the time as the stretches of tarmac disappeared under the wheels of the Galaxy, I decided to grab the Racing Post from its now traditional spot on the dashboard and mentally calculate the accumulated odds of the six Scoop6 winners. Wow, over a million to one, and frankly better than the offering from the pool-based Tote bet where a single £2 winner (and there was no guarantee that it would only be a single winner) would receive about £600k. I decided that, rather than continuing to line the pockets of Fred Done's organisation, I could obtain better returns for the same astronomical odds by simply placing an accumulator with whichever bookmaker was offering the best prices.

Then I started looking back through the racecards and form pages, trying to find some hidden message that I had earlier missed, and fathom out where I had gone wrong. Again I had let a decent betting start to the day drift away from me, and by the end I was simply gambling, grasping at coincidental names and the purity of a friend's randomness. If I was going to get myself out of the increasingly deep cash hole I would have to stop betting like an idiot and find the time to do things properly. Either that or pay for inside information. I closed the Racing Post and was about to return it to its usual resting place on the dashboard when I noticed some numbers at the top of the front page – 212, from my room number in Wetherby. I quickly reopened to the centre spread where the racecard from Doncaster still sat mutely, and my eyes frantically scanned the pages of the two big handicaps: Chatez was number 2 on the card, Gabrial number 12.

The each-way double, that I had entrusted to the unbiased chaos of Jason's brain, would have paid out over a grand on 2 and 12 if only I had spotted the blindingly obvious code, written in big numbers at the very front of my punting bible: Room 212. Users of the M1 that evening may have noticed a windswept chap laughing hysterically to himself in an empty car as he headed south.

# 13) Ascot

## Day 17 – Sunday 29 March

If any other course can justifiably lay claim to the crown that totters on the head of Cheltenham, it is Ascot. Its major festival has a greater attendance than Cheltenham's, it offers more prize money than its rival, and I'm sad to say that its impressive new grandstand offers a better racing experience when it gets busy.

I also have a long history with the place, not quite as long or illustrious as with Cheltenham, but significant nonetheless. It began in 2006 when a flatmate and I organised a jolly to the King George, a day so stiflingly hot that several people fainted on the overcrowded train. There was a Guinness bar there that was being tended by just one man, a small and cheery chap who maintained his positive disposition despite a queue longer than at a bookies when the favourite has won the National. He would ask every single customer what drink they wanted when he only served the black stuff, and each pint, true to the TV advert of the time, took a very long time to pour. It's funny what you remember, isn't it. I can't remember who won the King George on that sweltering day, but I can remember this guy obliviously smiling his way through a stream of hot and impatient racegoers.

Later, I took my two boys there in an era before they realised that they could dissent when I said "Come on, we're going racing" (it is, after all, free for kids at most racecourses and a much nicer place to take them on a Saturday than, say, a soft-play centre). It was a low-key winter jumps meeting and I let Eldest pick the horses whilst Youngest ate expensive sausage rolls. He secured four winners from four races, some at very tasty prices, before getting bored and wanting to go home to watch Power Rangers. We then discovered that neither of us had the last winning ticket, and went to the ring inspector to report the loss. He was a friendly chap who owned a leg in a horse called Philson Run. It was entered in the Grand National later that season, but he urged me not to back it ante-post at fancy prices because it needed really soft ground (as it was, it ran a cracker to finish fourth on good ground). The nice lady bookmaker paid us out anyway as she remembered the two boys. I let Eldest keep £5 of the substantial winnings, which some of my friends described as miserly, despite the fact that I was stumping up the stake money. You would have thought that afternoon may have endeared the sport to them, but both my boys are conscientious objectors to horse racing, perhaps because it consistently ruined their Saturday afternoons when Channel 4 Racing was on at the same time they wanted to go on the Playstation.

Recently we even lived within a stone's throw of the racecourse, renting a place in between selling our old house and moving into the new one. I would go running in the middle of the course and began to truly appreciate the stiffness of the last half-mile. It looks fairly flat on TV, but go to Swinley Bottom and try running up to the finishing post. It's testing, even without a jockey on your back. It was during that brief spell that I discovered the other side of the coin of living near to a sporting Mecca, namely the traffic chaos that ensued every summer during the Royal meeting when almost 300,000 descend on what is actually quite a small town. I narrowly avoided arrest when vehemently disagreeing with a policeman who wanted me to go on a two mile diversion to get to my driveway just 100 yards away.

More recently still, the biggest wager of my life came at Ascot, on my birthday last year. I was with Ivan and Simon, who both looked askance at the depth and resonance of my screaming as The Young Master approached the last.

He didn't let me down, and responded to my urgings all the way to the line (something which he failed to repeat at the Festival a few months later).

Anyway, back to the thirteenth destination of my whistlestop tour, and after what seemed like only a handful of hours after climbing from the car at the end of a long day's driving from Wetherby via Doncaster, a big bunch of the usual suspects were due to meet at the course for the Prince's Countryside Fund Raceday. I was getting a lift, which was much appreciated after the last two days, as was the company. Following a misunderstanding on the tickets, I panic-changed into jacket and tie to jump into the car with the immaculately turned-out Andrew, Maura and girls. The website promised a variety of family activities including, somewhat alarmingly, the opportunity to "give children an appreciation of where their food comes from." Our lunch came from The Stag on the High Street, and the children did indeed seem to appreciate it.

I offered my goddaughter Charlotte a £5 note to either put towards her savings for a laptop, or gamble on the horses. She opted for the latter – that's my girl! This seemed a simpler arrangement than the exchange-traded horse-racing derivatives that her father had offered her in a complicated loan scheme, but she coped with both situations admirably.

Over lunch conversation turned to my ludicrous challenge. The direct interrogator that is youngest sister Annabel fired two questions at me. I just about got away with the opening "What are you doing?", although it was said with a slightly disdainful tone if you ask me, but was completely flummoxed by the piercingly simple follow-up of "Why?" Day 16, and I was still waiting for my epiphany.

New ideas for my next quest included eating a hamburger in all the different states of America. Andrew dubbed it "A Round Neil In Eighty Days" – hilarious that guy. Doesn't he understand the food demons I fight against on a daily, even hourly basis? I even ordered the roast chicken in the pub instead of the roast pork to avoid the crackling and save calories! We were joined by Brian and son Jack who ordered after us but were served first. This was not a good omen for the betting later on. Jack, quite matter-of-fact, told me Special Agent would win the first.

We met Clive and Simon at the track. Simon has his own unique history with Ascot, having become uninterested in proceedings in the latter stages of Ladies Day a few years ago. His homing-pigeon instincts got him to the station where he would attempt the journey home to Wimbledon. He awoke some time later, after some encouragement from the train driver who had parked up for the night, and asked where he was. "Wimbledon sidings, Sir" was the reply. It was his only winner of the day, mind.

Charlotte chose Paddy The Deejay in the first race who ran well but was beaten by the Queen's horse Special Agent. This was young Jack's first time horse racing, and I sincerely hope that he doesn't chase the ecstatic high of that first win for the rest of his life. As it turned out, he didn't have to wait more than half an hour for his second hit. Clive and I had backed the unusually-named Thomas Crapper a few times at Cheltenham, and last time out he put up a really good performance at the Festival. That was good enough for us in the second race of only four horses, but not good enough to beat Puffin Billy in a photo finish. Jack's eyes danced wildly with the excitement of his second winner.

Following hot on the heels of Doncaster yesterday, that was the fourth photo finish out of four that had gone against me on my tour. At least we then got our money's worth out of the loss with some obvious toilet humour about "another bet down the drain" and regretting "having a large one on the Crapper". Tammy joined in on text, in between panic-texting her bets in to me: "I knew you'd have to get that joke out of your cistern".

After more than a dozen meetings, the form-lines were

just beginning to connect together like frozen synapses in the thaw. I scoured the next race for some information from the preceding fortnight and tried to sound insightful to Clive and Simon as I said "This Jeanpascal in the next, won very nicely at Warwick you know". I forgot to mention that it was a three-runner slog in the mud, and that I was going to desert him today to back the Pipe horse in first-time blinkers. Unaccountably, when I caught up with them they were eagerly holding a ticket at 33/1, to a not insignificant stake, on Jeanpascal. I knew these guys well enough to not feel one shred of guilt when it ran a truly awful race before being pulled up.

After disappearing for a while to enjoy the family fun on offer, Andrew reappeared proudly sporting a flat cap of his own, a traditional but strangely jaunty number chosen for him by fashion-savvy middle-sister Lucy. Somehow he seemed to carry it off rather well, and I suggested to Maura that she get him a pipe for his birthday. He really seemed to be throwing himself into the theme of the day. Later, he showed off a shooting target with five neatly clustered holes around the bullseye. We were all suitably impressed until he explained that it was really a shooting range for children that he had commandeered, and the target was about ten feet away. I sincerely hoped this was not connected to the earlier promise of "giving children an appreciation of where their food comes from."

We all decided to follow Andrew's lead and took a quick break from the racing, but sadly the falconry display wasn't quite as exciting as a few years before when an owl mistook a young child that was dragging the bait for the bait itself. It got a whack from the brave lad that it was attacking, and flew off in a huff to sit on top of the grandstand for half an hour. Health and Safety seemed to have neutered the event and it consisted of just a single bird of prey that was only marginally disruptive and wasn't allowed to hunt the children.

Towards the end of the afternoon my assorted

comrades failed to stop me buying a lurid yellow polyester scarf, supposedly in the colours of my beloved One Man (at least that's what the sign said). This was exactly the sort of situation where I needed my friends to step in and stop me making an arse of myself, but these are the same friends that said I looked stylish when I tried on my flat cap at the end of a Sandown meeting the previous year. And the same friends that I had earlier stitched up with Jeanpascal. Fair enough. On the way out Simon was denied a free chocolate bunny on account of him not being a child. I could have begged to differ, but it was time to go home. Another winner-less day saw my betting deficit grow even larger, but when you are with friends it doesn't hurt as much.

# 14) Southwell

## Day 19 – Tuesday 31 March

Southwell heralded the start of my all-weather week. There were certainly all types of weather on display on the drive up, but one constant was the wind, which seemed to have abated little since Doncaster. Recycling bins whooshed into the middle of the road at the drop of a hat and if you dropped your hat that would also have been in the middle of the road in an instant.

More ominous than the development of a UK hurricane season, though, was the news that a case of Strangles had been confirmed at Marco Botti's yard in Newmarket. Strangles is a potentially fatal bacterial infection of the upper respiratory tract of horses, causing enlargement of the lymph nodes in the throat, which can impair breathing. A major outbreak could have spelled disaster for my quest if racing was shut down, not to mention the agony for all the poor horses affected. It seemed like an isolated case, but I remember everything looking contained in the foot and mouth outbreak of 2001 just days before the Cheltenham Festival was lost due to the sheep grazing in the middle of the course.

Part of me was unconcerned about outside events, my fatalistic view of the tour growing in tandem with my concern for Youngest. He seemed quiet, and the frequent goodbyes made him unsettled. The Wife and I were trying to remain calm until the appointment with the consultant, but kids are great at picking up on vibes. He, like us, knew something wasn't quite right. He needed support and nurturing, and I was sodding off. Again. At least that morning he was coming with me part of the way to Southwell. It was the first day of his Easter holidays and, with The Wife at work and Eldest still at school, he was being driven to his Granny's house in Hertfordshire. On the way we began an epic contest of The Car Game, but even that old faithful drifted into silence as we circled the M25.

I dropped him at my mother-in-law's, but as usual I was pushed for time and dashed straight off. My poor little boy stood forlorn in the kitchen as he was deserted again. I felt like a parent leaving their child on the first day of school, desperately wanting every step of my retreat to turn back and scoop him up. I spent the remainder of the journey to Nottinghamshire just turning things over in my mind and feeling worse in our predicament with every passing mile.

However, I was meeting Jason at Southwell, and his unusual brand of thinking demands total involvement, so I would soon be snapped out of my doldrums. Things happen when Jason is around, things that you just can't script. One morning the previous summer, I laughed so much that I didn't know if I could stop as he skippered us, in the loosest sense of the word, on an old gaff rig on the Norfolk Broads.

We were hiring Japonicas for the weekend, beautifully restored but fundamentally brick-like sailing vessels that were used in the olden days to transport grain around the Broads. At 30 feet long and several tonnes they were not exactly nimble, but if the wind got up they could be exhilarating to manoeuvre in the narrow waterways due to their sheer momentum and capacity to sink lesser craft unfortunate enough to be in the way.

Jason was our self-appointed skipper. Admittedly he had more sailing experience than the rest of us on the boat put together, but then so did most of the windmills that punctuated the flat Norfolk landscape. In situations like this, though, you need somebody to take charge even if it is the guy who has written off more cars and bikes than anyone else on the planet. I've often thought it's better to have something occurring that had the potential of going savagely awry, rather than nothing happening at all, and he at least talked a good game at the helm, barking orders at his inept crew like some salty old sea dog.

We had survived relatively unscathed until the Sunday, although due to the light and unpredictable winds that morning, on several occasions Jason had lost "Steerage!", as he used to holler at us. That was the cue for Clive to frantically fumble at the controls of the motor, attempting to start it and regain control as we loomed to whatever impending disaster was only seconds away, usually involving young children in unfeasibly flimsy dinghies. Jason would invariably have to leave the helm to attempt to get the engine started, Clive would swap and lunge at the tiller that would be flapping around wildly, and Simon and I would be employed at the front and sides of the floating hulk trying to fend off trees, boats, and jetties whilst shouting warnings at those ahead of us and apologies to those left behind in the wake of something chaotically destructive passing through. Throughout these frequent episodes we would be trying to avoid the main boom on our veering vessel, which swung violently from side to side like some demented dinosaur tail intent on batting into the water at least one of the clowns that was failing to master it.

We'd decided that it was highly likely that someone would die, and should therefore be permanently under motor, which was not as easy as it sounded in these ponderous beasts. The propshaft was offset which made turning left quite tricky dependant on the current and wind, and very tricky in an emergency situation, many of which still presented themselves with alarming regularity despite the absence of sails. This of course wouldn't have been an issue if the boaty brigade adopted the eminently sensible protocol of driving on the left, but reduced to hugging the right in a 30 foot barge on an ironically-named Broad meant that the only way to turn around was to defy nautical convention and go clockwise. Jason, for reasons we still haven't got to the bottom of despite a full inquest, consistently chose to either ignore or forget this, and attempt the officially correct but virtually impossible task of turning anti-clockwise.

Approaching Potter Heigham bridge we had to moor briefly in order to lower the roof (which Jason had unfathomably instructed us to raise only a mile beforehand) and the mast. I jumped jauntily off the side, missed the rope that was chucked at me, and was left stranded as Jason attempted another ambitious turn to retrieve me. Again, he went anti-clockwise against the bias of the offset prop and succeeded only in ramming the side of the channel head on, literally yards from somebody's waterside home, with such force that I thought the entire Norfolk Broads network was about to shatter like a crystal vase, spilling its fear-ridden waters into the Fens all around. Jason looked undeterred by this minor setback. Simon and Clive looked scared shitless and clung on for dear life. Never one to give up easily, and with the Japonica rebounding dangerously backwards towards thousands of pounds of gleaming yachts, Jason engaged full throttle again and gave the bank in front of the exact same home another tremendous thump.

To this day I can only hope that the poor owners were out, because if they had been inside, slowly drifting into their genteel riverside Sunday morning, they must have come to the conclusion that they were either under attack from some misguided bombing mission or experiencing Norfolk's biggest ever earthquake. It was like Jason was skippering a giant malevolent fox that had been let loose into the previous serenity of a henhouse. Viewing the carnage from 50 yards away, stranded on the opposite riverbank, was like watching an aquatic version of It's A Knockout staged with real battleships.

Finally moored, Jason then decided that a clip at the prow needed to be unscrewed in order to lower the mast,

131

despite the rest of us doubting whether this was necessary due to this thing being rusted solid and looking like it hadn't been unscrewed in years. However, Jason was adamant that Simon and I should find a pair of pliers whilst he had another cigarette to settle his nerves, and after only half an hour we returned triumphantly and managed to get the reticent thing to release, at which point Jason decided we were right and it didn't need to be undone after all. As the debacle reached the grand finale Jason then stepped back into the open hatch of the expectant sail store for the second time that morning, and I was literally reduced to a blubbering wreck. In order to stop hyperventilating, I was told to lie down in the darkened coffin-like innards of an ageing gaff rig and, as Clive aptly put it, get a fucking grip.

It was our first major get together after Jason had given up the demon drink, a fact that the good people of Norfolk should be mightily thankful for, because the results could have been infinitely worse if he were still at the bottle. We shared one of life's exquisitely rare moments where I laughed so much I didn't know whether I would ever stop, and it was comforting that our relationship and shared passion for high jinks could remain unscathed in the post-booze era.

Back to the windy Tuesday of Southwell, and Jason was slightly delayed on account of going to a cashpoint in the pretty market town of Southwell and realising he'd lost his wallet. Or left it at work. Or it had fallen out somewhere in the car. Then his hat blew off in the car park and took his glasses with it and a scramble amongst advancing cars ensued, like a real life version of Frogger, or as the youngsters now know it, Crossy Road. The shack at the entrance was shabby, but other than that everything was pleasantly surprising. We had paid £4 extra for the Premier enclosure, but nobody seemed to be checking badges or attempting to separate racegoers and I quite liked that.

As I knew literally nothing about all-weather racing I intended to make the week a cornucopia of absurd betting strategies. I was deliberately leaving my Scrabble System (patent pending) for later in the week as I reckoned Jason would come up with something unusual. He didn't let me down, of course. His artist's eye was drawn to the geometric design of the carpet in the upstairs bar, and he quickly devised a method of throwing a pound coin at the diamond patterns so that where it landed denoted the number of the horse to back.

The mathematician within me instantly hailed this as biased. Surely we were going to aim for the middle diamond each time? Jason was unfazed, claiming any selection criteria were bound to be biased. He had a point, although I'd once seen him rolling dice at Cheltenham, which must be pretty damn close to unbiased. His pound coin landed on the third diamond, mine the fifth. Job done with our bets in the first race. I felt strangely liberated by the betting approach for the week. With no knowledge to fall back on the pressure was off and I enjoyed a sense of freedom in ignoring the form pages and relying on something totally beyond my control. It was pure gambling.

However, the irony of literally throwing money away on his ludicrous idea hadn't escaped me, as it hadn't for a couple sitting nearby. The old boy seemed rather taken with the spectacle and nudged his wife who smiled.

"It's never let us down once!" I protested, before admitting "It's never won us anything either."

They claimed to be complete novices in the horse racing game and had no idea who would win the first race. I wasn't sure whether that meant they thought we were professional punters who had devised an ingenious and foolproof way of making millions, or were just being kind.

Jason literally bolted a Diet Coke before marching off to get the bets on. The betting ring had eight bookmakers, less punters, and no prices at all for the first race, which was due off in nine minutes. No rush at Southwell, clearly. One bookie was offering odds at Huntingdon, and Jason seemed tempted before I distracted him with a visit to the paddock. Without any expectations, I was pleasantly surprised by the whole set-up. The facilities were clean and spacious and we could easily get a drink, see them in the parade ring and place a bet. There was also a fine array of eating options which hadn't gone unnoticed by either of us. Julian Thick at Newbury had been quite complimentary about the frequently derided offering of an all-weather meeting, and I could see why.

I was pretending not to look at the horses after my earlier paddock fiascos, but Jason liked the look of number 1. I urged him not to start panic-betting in the first and stick with our thoroughly-thought-through strategy of throwing coins at a diamond carpet. As we walked back to the ring, Jason spotted a traditional sweet shop and dived in for a bag of foam shrimps and bananas. I wondered if this guy I'd known for 35 years had some weird form of undiagnosed ADHD. The bag was gone within three minutes, and so began an afternoon of quite extraordinary eating. I managed to stop him before he hoovered up the last two to see whether he could successfully complete a blind taste test to distinguish between banana and shrimp.

"Ah, no problem," he asserted "I've got a very keen palate." It was clearly a random guess at yellow, but he got it right. Flukey git.

We got our bets on and number 1 won of course, unbacked by either of us after my disciplined stance in the paddock. Jason was intrigued by the tractor race that followed, and wondered if he could bet in running on the outcome. I suggested that the choreographed raking of the track was unlikely to produce a fair betting heat, but he still seemed interested.

The magic carpet had let us down in the short term, but a system can only be properly judged in the long term, so we returned to the same spot in the bar to select our bets for the second race. Jason decided that it was the coin that was at fault and changed to a fifty pence piece. It certainly bounced better, and it gave us a clear verdict – we were both to back number 2, the odds-on favourite.

Jason again liked number 1 in the paddock, and this time couldn't be dissuaded from backing that as well. He seemed unperturbed that this was the 66/1 outsider in a four horse race, but remember that this was the man who backed Norton's Coin to win the Cheltenham Gold Cup at 100/1 on his first ever visit to a bookies. I was worried that this was sullying the purity of our system, but he waded in anyway with a fiver. The odds-on favourite finished last of the four. Misu Mac, the 66/1 outsider of four.....won. Yes, really. More Norton's Coin-esque jubilation.

The couple from the bar upstairs smiled as Jason joyously waved around his wad of winnings. I wondered if they were going to misguidedly employ the magic carpet technique themselves, thinking it was a quick way to sure-fire winnings. As it was literally minutes since he last ate, Jason was keen to celebrate his winnings in Rosie's Pantry. I told him I'd already had lunch, but he said he had too, and marched off. As we stared at the really rather appealing selection of home cooked dishes, I caved in and he treated me to a very fine sausage and mash, just so I could keep him company, you understand. I hate to see a man eat alone. We both ordered coffee in some deferential nod to discipline.

We got chatting and realised it was too late to either perform the carpet ritual or go to the paddock before the third race. A rushed and random bet revealed that we really needed a system, and as the carpet had let us down badly so far, as the fourth race approached we searched for inspiration. Ominous, brooding black clouds whipped towards the racecourse, and the big screen flickered in the charged atmosphere. I decided I couldn't let Caged Lightning go un-backed at 9/2.

Just before the off there was an artificial sandstorm, as bits of the track were whipped across the betting ring and stung in the eyes of crowd. Then a vicious downpour was hurled at the course as if an invisible tornado had arrived. We scurried to the sanctuary of the stand, but the bookies were left to literally hang on to their boards and satchels, and bear the brunt of the onslaught. It was nice to see them get a hammering, even if not from the punters. Eighteen days before I was ambivalent to bookmakers, seeing them as just part of the machinery of the sport that I love, but I had to admit it was becoming more personal.

The storm-smeared camera tried to focus on the recall man, the poor guy who had to stand marooned in the middle of the track in case of a false start. This is not an enviable task at the best of times, facing tonnes of galloping horse flesh with nothing but a neon flag and white coat to protect you, but at that moment it seemed especially tough as he leant into the storm all alone. Jason loudly applauded his bravery.

Despite the weather, they were off okay and the horses seemed to cope with the conditions better than us. Out of the maelstrom Caged Lightning appeared to win cosily and salvage some cash, if not betting pride. It was my turn to treat Jason, but as it was less than an hour since his second lunch he declined the hog roast, and instead opted for a modest tray of chips. This guy somehow weighs about four stone less than me. I assumed he must have a tapeworm.

We returned to the paddock before the fifth race, but the magic had gone, along with the carpet. Jason selected three losers and a bag of Rhubarb & Custard from the sweet shop. On the way back to the car park we were stopped by the horses returning from the course to the stables. Jason chose this moment to examine his wad again, whilst still within the confines of a category 3 hurricane. One fumble and he would have been unable to chase the notes across the horse walkway. They would have been lost forever and probably wedged in a hedge several miles away. He clung on, just, as indeed Misu Mac had a few hours earlier.

On the way back to my mother-in-law's house I drove past the now familiar windmills by the M1, turning over time. A variety of stunning rainbows appeared from the spray, and my wandering mind mused on why they are always shaped in a semi-circular way. I really should know why the process of refracting light through rain results in a curve. Jason went home with his pot of gold, but he tends to make his own luck somehow. Perhaps mine was just over the horizon?

# 15) Chelmsford

## Day 20 – Wednesday 1 April

You can see Chelmsford City racecourse from a distance, and that is quite useful because if you accidentally head to Chelmsford to go racing you will discover that the track is actually eight miles away. As I approached, the floodlights stood tall and legion like sentinels, sitting incongruously in the arid Spanish-style surroundings. Finding the way in was tougher, but after an aborted attempt at the owners and trainers entrance, I parked up and asked the guy selling the Racing Posts if he'd got any tips.

"Not yet, but when Tracksuit Dave arrives he'll have some. He give me an 8/1 winner last week!" I was intrigued.

"Yeah, you can't miss him. Wears a tracksuit," really? "and he walks like this...." and at that point the guy did an impression of a cross between a bear and a wardrobe, shuffling along. I was beginning to wonder if this was all some elaborate April Fools routine, but he seemed genuine enough. I asked if Tracksuit Dave was a professional punter.

"Yeah, he's famous. Lovely guy too. Knows all the TV lot. He's got Tommo's phone number!" Well, a friend of Tommo is a friend of mine, I thought, and made a mental note to look out for tracksuited wardrobes during the afternoon.

The buildings were sparkling and fresh, crouching like villas in a desert-scape. It was the first racecourse I'd seen where all the facilities were in the centre of the course. On first glance it appeared like an efficient use of space, but I actually got a strangely detached feel as I could only view the final finishing straight and ended up watching everything else on the giant screen. That in itself wasn't so different to many courses, but it was very difficult to get a sense of perspective. It was like going to an art gallery and only looking at the bottom half of each painting. It was also slightly bereft of bookmakers. Just four stood lined up at the end of the hall by their electronic boards, like they were auditioning for a quiz show, and most punters seemed to be betting at the copious BetFred counters dotted around.

This is the operation that rose from the ashes of the ill-fated Great Leighs, and it only recently resumed racing after a five year hiatus at the venue. In the last decade, the Darwinian theory of racecourse evolution has overseen the demise of Great Leighs in 2009, due to financial problems just nine months after opening, and then in December 2012 the closure of both Folkestone and Hereford when Arena Racing Company pulled the plug on their long careers. When I first started planning this ludicrous journey many years ago there were 59 racecourses, and then briefly 60 with the arrival of Great Leighs. 60 had a nice ring to it, especially for a maths teacher. The Babylonians back in 2000 B.C. used a base 60 number system, some of which is still with us today in the way we measure time in minutes and hours.

The closure of three racecourses may seem like quite a turbulent recent history, but in fact if you take a wider perspective it is nothing new. No fewer than 97 British racecourses closed their doors in the twentieth century, a rate of attrition that makes recent events look rather staid. Harpenden is now a cricket club, Shirley a golf club, and Gatwick needs no introduction. Chelmsford itself hosted a two-mile oval track until 1935. Even my beloved Cheltenham used to race on top of Cleeve Hill rather than at the foot of it, and for many years staged only flat races.

It was only at the end of my fixture list trawling to produce the 2015 iteration of my ridiculous charade that I noticed I had 58 rather than 59 on my list. Yarmouth had literally gone missing. Puzzled, I scanned beyond my eighty-day period to find its first meeting of the year in late June, and I knew that it was gone from my venture. With all due respect to the town where I spent many happy family holidays in my youth, there was no way I was shifting the window later in the year and missing the Cheltenham Festival in order to squeeze in Yarmouth.

The track began a full programme of fixtures as early as Easter Monday the previous year, and the website of the ARC-owned racecourse shed no light on the sudden sea-change in policy to hit the coastal outfit. Initially I suspected that money was the main culprit again, although I'm not going to pretend that racecourse aren't businesses like any other that have to find opportunities to be as profitable as possible. You don't find many ice cream vans operating in January, I reasoned, and perhaps the East Anglian outpost had simply decided to concentrate its efforts on the more lucrative summer months? It wasn't until my chat with Julian and Andy in the Royal Box at Newbury that I discovered it was relaying the track after some issues the previous season. As it was, I was right not to shift the whole shebang a few months later because the inevitable delays meant that Yarmouth didn't reopen its doors until late August, and went on to experience further problems with the track after that.

So, I had to accept the situation for what it is. 58 was not as round a number as 60. Yarmouth, Herford and Folkestone would be missed, and in an ideal world it would have been nice to have ended with the Derby. However, just as any race is merely a snapshot in time, a result of the horses and conditions and vagaries in play on the day, my odyssey was a reflection of the harsh financial realities and twists of fate that existed in the spring of 2015. When I set off on my tour there were 58 courses open for business, and to use a ghastly Americanism, it was what it was. This was my own personal Gold Cup, and it was a shame Arkle wasn't in the line-up but I would try to win it anyway.

Before reopening officially at the start of February, Chelmsford underwent a 'soft launch' to test run all the systems, and it was generally well received by the interested parties. An astonishing £15 million was invested, but by all accounts the actual surface received none of the sackfuls of cash and came in for some criticism, with jockeys reporting that it was riding slow and loose. The Polytrack topping had been lying dormant for too long and had significantly degraded. Not surprisingly this resulted in Chelmsford having the smallest average field size of all the all-weather racecourses.

Scanning through my newly acquired Racing Post, whilst keeping an eye out for Tracksuit Dave, confirmed that again small fields were the order of the day with just 43 runners for a seven race card. This was going to make the chosen betting strategy for the day, the ludicrous each-way double, a tricky proposition. Not that ludicrous, you may think, especially when compared to throwing coins at a patterned carpet, but I was planning on using them with short-priced favourites. I would never back a 6/4 shot each way as I wouldn't get my money back for a place, but put two of them together in an each way double and all of a sudden it becomes a decent proposition. Even if they both just place you get your stake returned, and there's always the hope that they both win for big bucks.

The trouble with the Chelmsford card was on which races to employ this tactic. The first two had seven runners, which didn't really suit each way terms, so I went for a sizable double on Vejovis at 5/4 in the third race and Poppy Bond at 2/1 in the fourth. With that sorted, I bought a drink from eager staff at a sparkling new bar, and settled on a stool to study the form. Tracksuit Dave was even mentioned on the racecourse tannoy, and I expected this prodigal son to soon be parading through the facilities to general acclaim. I found a lovely winner in the second under the guidance of jockey Kieron Fox, who had a 60% strike rate when teaming up with trainer John Best. He gave Ninety Minutes a peach of a ride and it won well. I know it's easy to say in hindsight, but the winner had form over one of the other market leaders, who themselves tied in closely with many others in the race. With the stable coming into form as well, I was very surprised it was as big as 5/2. I toyed with the idea of stopping there – even if my each way double proved fruitless I would be ahead on the day. But I was beginning to dislike this somewhat heartless approach, and it certainly wasn't going to reduce the burgeoning betting deficit, so I ploughed on.

Vejovis was disappointing in the third race and the each way double was immediately sunk. I caught a glimpse of Tracksuit Dave. He wasn't as big as a wardrobe, and looked a genial enough fellow, but a busy one too. He seemed to know everyone, and my chances of catching a word with him seemed slim.

There was nothing wrong with Chelmsford City at all, but I just wasn't feeling it and after two more losers I headed for the exit. Like Southwell, it had a relaxed and diverse crowd, and it was easy to do want you wanted to do. It's a geographical exaggeration to describe it as Chelmsford, and some bright lights doesn't make it a city, but it's a nice enough little track and racing needs the Chelmsfords to succeed. I had actually enjoyed the feel of the first two days of my all-weather week, and was looking forward to Wolverhampton.

As I was held at the crossing until after the horses had left the track, I had time to think about Youngest, all quiet and lost as I left him that morning. I had already secured cheap advance train tickets for the next day from home, so drove back directly rather than via his Granny's. If I were a better man I would have gone back to be with him. It was the first real time on the journey that I seriously considered jacking it all in. Why don't you just stop this faded fantasy, Neil, and return to the real world where

142

your son needs you? It was the age-old conundrum of parenthood. My instinct was to scoop him up and hold him forever, but in doing so I would suffocate his development, and indeed his transition to a new life, whatever that would hold. I couldn't work it out. If I stopped would that actually make him more worried about his predicament? And would that matter anyway, if he had me and I had him? That conflict festered inside me, all the way back around a busy M25.

# 16) Wolverhampton

## Day 21 – Thursday 2 April

Day 3, of both my all-weather week and my unusual betting strategies, and it was time to wheel out the Scrabble System (patent pending) and dust it off after a long period in hibernation. It had been too long, old friend. When I started betting on the horses I was naive enough to think there could be a system that would direct me along an easy street to big winnings. Naive, but not stupid enough to think that system would have anything to do with Scrabble. It just diverted me for a while, before I became properly acquainted with the form book.

So here it is. You should feel privileged that you are getting this inside information for free, without having to phone a premium rate number or deposit large sums of cash in my Nigerian uncle's bank account. You will need to provide your own pen though: Score the name of each horse according to the Scrabble values of the letters. Ignore any horses with odd totals. Of the even scores, you are ideally looking for 16, 18, 20 or 22 points, but, and concentrate now because this really is key, the name must include at least one letter of four points (the more the better really). It's a long time ago now and I can't remember exactly how I discovered this beautiful scheme, or the foundations of its intricacies. It's just something that has always been there, along with the horses.

Scanning through the card at Wolverhampton in the morning produced some wrinkles in the selection criteria. Some races had no qualifying horses and others had many. If you are a disciplined sort, don't bet in the races with no qualifying names. If you have several to choose from, you could back them all, or alternatively (and this is the really inspired bit!) guess. As Jason astutely pointed out, almost every system will have its bias somewhere.

The cross-country train via Oxford was very busy, and as my right leg went to sleep (the bane of tall people on public transport when you can't stretch out) I surveyed the social scene playing out in the carriage. An old couple were huddled together, eating almost constantly but hardly saying a word to each other throughout the entire journey. I thought back to a phone call with my folks the previous day when I heard that my Dad had fallen down the last four steps of the stairs and was fortunate to sustain only cuts and bruises. I felt a pang of sadness that the latter period of life is almost a regression to the state of being at the start of it, except that old people aren't as cute as babies, and when they fall over they don't tend to bounce as well.

After working out the Scrabble scores, I turned to the news pages and learned of the sad passing of Ron Muddle. He, too, was old, 97 in fact, and had enjoyed a pretty good innings by all accounts. His is a name that many racing fans will be unaware of, but without Mr Muddle it would be unlikely that I would have been in the middle of an all-weather week. He had bought, redeveloped into all-weather venues, and then sold (at a tidy profit, mind you) three quite different racecourses, including today's destination. Even in his late 90s he was apparently contemplating the purchase of the now defunct Folkestone. I was quite glad he didn't get around to it – it would have been a long way to drive to squeeze in another piece of the jigsaw. The most touching part of the tribute in the Racing Post was a quote from the man himself, describing his transformation of Lingfield, "we had to work with what we had and, on top of that, I knew bugger all". Quite similar to my situation, I thought as I sped north.

I got a taxi from the station to the course, but the driver decided to drop me instead at a deserted Holiday Inn hotel. It was eerily quiet, and as I stepped from the cab

I literally could not see another soul. The only clue that there might be a racecourse hiding somewhere was a small sign saying "Grandstand". I followed this round the side of an equally unpopulated car park and eventually came upon an empty parade ring. A sudden panic bristled through me. Had it been called off at the last minute? Had I got the wrong day?

Then I spotted a tiny hut to the side, and after the attendant took my money and ushered me through, I began to spot the first signs of activity. As I entered the course a smattering of racegoers drifted easily between paddock, bookies and bars. I later learned that the official attendance that afternoon was 448, and from being on the ground that day, think that may have been generous. It's hard to know how a course can function like this in the long term, although in the short term it seemed to function perfectly well.

The system offered a clear verdict in the first - Leoncavallo. Purists might argue that it would be very hard to fit this on a Scrabble board, and that it's a name and therefore not an allowable word either, but they would be missing the point. For the avoidance of doubt, this is a ridiculous system that has hardly anything to do with the popular board game, is extremely unlikely to produce any long-term profits, and is one step away from throwing darts at a Racing Post. Glad we've got that out the way, and while we are at it, the author accepts no liability for any injury caused whilst using this system, and the value of your investments can go down as well as disappear altogether. Caveat over, and on with the action.

The paddock was covered entirely by rubber matting, but they'd coloured part of it green to represent grass. Not a grassy colour, but a green to tie in with the Holiday Inn windows that overlooked it. I wasn't sure it worked. The jockeys walked past me as they came out to mount. I know it's an obvious thing to say, but they seemed so small and fragile, and the contrast with the finely muscled

146

powerhouses they jumped onto was stark. I was painfully aware (and frequently reminded by my 'friends') that I was overweight, but this was at the other extreme of the spectrum and, surprisingly, slightly shocked me.

Leoncavallo was backed from second favourite to favourite and won nicely. Scrabble system: 1 from 1. Who said it was a ridiculous system that was extremely unlikely to end in profit? The second race produced no clear pick, but the two closest matches were both outsiders, Twice Certain at 20/1 and Miss Minuty at 40/1. I went for the former on account of the trainer's surname being a match, and I chose wrong. Perhaps I should have heeded my earlier advice of just blindly guessing; you can overcomplicate things sometimes. As they rounded the home turn it looked for all the world like Miss Minuty was going to get up and spring an almighty surprise, but the winner just held on. There was a guy in a red, stable-logoed jacket screaming just about as loudly as I'd ever heard anybody scream on a racecourse, and that was really quite loud. He was urging the grey outsider on, but she failed by the narrowest of margins.

Afterwards, I went for a drink in the Premier bar where I overheard the owner of Miss Minuty talking to connections about the race. As they dissected the action, I detected a slight deflation, a sense of what could have been. The 40/1 shot had run a great race in second, but crucially she wasn't a winner, and that makes a big difference in this game. The guy in the red jacket joined them later and his sense of loss seemed even more acute. I thought back to how a friend was inconsolable after the second week of the National Lottery when it started way back in 1994 - he got five numbers and won over two grand, but knew he would never get that close again. It was the same with trainer Ted Walsh after Commanche Court came second in the 2002 Gold Cup.

For the third race there was again a confused output from the system, so again I allowed the trainer's name to point the way – favourite Ninepointsixthree. I waited in the small indoors betting ring, sensing that the odds would lengthen. As they did, the guy next to me asked if 11/8 was better than 5/4 and I struck up a conversation with him as we both went in at 11/8. It transpired that Ken was a regular at the course. He was the owner of a building business but, evidently, there were frequent gaps in the busy schedule for him to go racing. We got chatting about my challenge, and Ken cut to the chase immediately,

"Have you had a winner at every one?"

A true punters question that, and I had to admit that I hadn't. The conversation was paused by the finish of the race. Ninepointsixthree had quite a lead but the second favourite was closing. Our horse just held on. Perhaps he was just a bit lonely out on his own and needed some company? That's a sentiment I'd certainly felt over the previous couple of weeks. We went to collect our winnings, and the system was showing a tidy profit.

I was beginning to lose my negative pre-judgements about the all-weather tracks. They offer a decent day out and are not troubled by the inherent baggage that the wildly popular meetings bring. So what if the quality of the racing is not that of an Ascot or Epsom? I would argue that the essence of horse racing is about competition, and it's very hard for a punter in the stands to know how fast a horse is running. Most racegoers don't really care about that; they are only interested in whether their selection is running faster than its opponents. And the fare on offer did seem competitive, certainly more so than some of the small field jumps races that I'd seen earlier on the tour.

All-weather racing seems an artificial version of the sport because its surface is exactly that. However, it could be argued that any racing surface or obstacle has been prepared in some way. Grass is manicured and watered and drained to make it safe and inviting, and fences are more forgiving than hedgerows and dry stone walls. The essence of any sport is that it is a contrivance, a movement away from a natural state. Tarmac circuits, gravel traps and tyre walls in motor racing do not grow naturally, after all. The trouble that Wolverhampton has is not that the track is artificial, but that everything else is too. The paddock is false, the bookies stand indoors, and the only grass on offer is taunting you from its splendid isolation in the middle of the track.

The next race looked tricky, and was made trickier by the complete absence of a system match. The disciplined thing to do in this situation would have been to not bet. Accordingly, I threw five pounds down the drain on a 50/1 outsider. It seemed that we couldn't all be Jason. Silverware in the fifth race was a match, but didn't run very well. The sixth race, however, had the clearest choice of the afternoon. Dark Profit scored 20, as did his trainer. Time for a big one. I caught up with Ken before the race. He fancied the favourite Sugar Boy, as did most people it seemed, but they didn't have the mighty Scrabble System at their disposal! Neither apparently did Dark Profit, who was unaware that he was a sure fire winner. It was close, but the favourite just got up to deny me a big payout and the system a triumphant return from retirement.

The train back was busy again, but people looked out for each other. A teenager offered up his seat for some grandparents who were struggling to contain four energetic young girls, and I was reminded of the profession I had left and the goodness of young people. In general, train travel encourages a camaraderie and sense of society, whereas the car is an insular and competitive way to go. But the cracks started to show on the tracks that evening as many people were forced to stand and the squabbles and screams of the granddaughters began to grate. Everyone was relieved, not least the grandparents, when their journey was over. My journey was still in its infancy, but pleasant as the day was, I too was thinking of the relief when it would be over.

# 17) Lingfield

## Day 22 – Friday 3 April

I drove up to Wimbledon to meet Simon for our two-day London jolly. Simon had taken the precaution of preparing a picnic for our trip, which seemed to consist solely of Marks & Spencers ready-mixed alcopops. He had done a lot of research on the matter, he explained, and although slightly pricier than the Tescos and Sainsburys versions, the higher alcohol percentage meant you got a lot more bang for your buck. Foresight like that can take you places; often unusual places if you are drinking 8% Cosmopolitans that taste like cherryade.

The day started unravelling early with news that the tram to Croydon was to be replaced with a bus at Reeve's Corner. More disconcertingly, my latest game in the nationwide series of Racing Post hide-and-seek had proved unsuccessful. Simon's local newsagent thought it only came out on a Sunday. If he was right, it was an unusual move for the once popular daily, but I didn't think he was right, even though I couldn't find any evidence of it coming out on a Good Friday in the Wimbledon and Croydon environs.

As we alighted from the bus and walked through the Manhattan of South London, as Simon described it, past the famous furniture store that was burnt down in the riots of 2011, a lady handed me a booklet that asked on the front cover "Whatever Happened To Discipline?" It was a good question, and one that I made a mental note to answer later in the day.

Eventually we boarded a train, and it was Lingfield bound. At approximately 1:34, two cans into his M&S liquid lunch, Simon lost volume control as he recounted a story from his recent building works. I'd never seen him so animated, but builders can do that to you. Then, for a reason I can't remember, we swapped curry jokes. Simon took the prize with his "I was in the curry house the other day and the waiter comes up to me and says 'Curry OK?' and I say 'oh alright, but just one song and then leave us alone'."

There was an astonishing amount of prize money on offer for the All-Weather Finals Day. The introduction of this fixture in 2014 was greeted warily, as is the way when anything new is introduced to a sport as traditional and, some might say, resistant to inevitable change as this one. I'm all for cherishing its history and traditions, but in a few years time I'm sure the general scepticism will have melted away and going racing on a Good Friday will seem as normal as going to Sainsburys on a Sunday. And it had certainly gone down well with the punters who made it a sell-out last year, prompting me to make Lingfield one of the few courses where I booked my tickets early.

It's easy to be disparaging about new initiatives, but change can be for the better, as long as it's not altering the recipe for Creme Eggs, or only publishing the Racing Post on a Sunday. There were quite a few dissenting voices about the fourth day of the Cheltenham Festival, but those noises have now gone quiet. I'm not saying that every new initiative works, but like any other sport and business, racing needs to tread the fine line of evolving without losing its essence.

The biggest debate, unsurprisingly, is about the money. Should the big boys get richer by plundering the juicy prize pot in excess of £1 million for the afternoon's seven races, or should the cash be redistributed to many smaller meetings at grassroots level to prop up the frankly derisory prize money shared by all the stakeholders at the bottom. As usual, I suspect the best solution lies somewhere in the middle, and I hope that doesn't sound like fence-sitting. It's hard to justify such astronomical sums at the top echelons of the sport when owners and horses are leaving the sport in droves at the lower end. My first two days on the all-weather trail were populated with frankly ordinary animals, but owners and punters (few though they were at Southwell, Chelmsford and Wolverhampton) got excitement from the sheer spectacle of racing. Most of those people, I would suggest, weren't in it for the money (if they were, I would suggest they were at best optimists and at worst completely deluded) but for the thrill of winning. However, there must come a point when as an owner you say that there isn't any money left; it was great whilst it lasted but that's enough.

It was the same for me in my previous career. I didn't go into teaching for the money, and I didn't leave teaching because of the lack it. But the fact that I didn't get a pay rise over my final five years in the profession (effectively a pay cut after inflation) made it easier to walk away.

On the other hand, it was undeniable that the megabucks and hoopla had attracted people and horses that otherwise would not have been spending their Good Friday in the Surrey countryside, Simon and I included.

Field sizes were down on the inaugural year, with the smaller trainers seemingly put off by the increased entry fees for the richer races. However, the flip side of the coin was that better horses were being attracted to the surface, which at least nullified the criticism of all-weather racing always being poor quality.

This raises a bigger question over the role of all-weather racing in general. Many critics see it only as a slightly contrived way to provide betting shops with high-volume, low quality racing on the cheap. Some argue that the USP of British racing compared to other countries, especially America, is its diversity. Races are not all run on mile-long oval dirt tracks, and are better for it. You know this is a contentious issue when Simon Bazalgette, chief executive of the Jockey Club which itself runs a successful all-weather track at Kempton, calls for a "sensible vision around what is right for the sport in the long term". At a time when racing is trying to promote itself to secure its future, is the best way forward to rip up perfectly decent turf tracks such as the one at Newcastle, and replace them with what could be seen as a dull and homogenised alternative? He was supported by both the National Trainers Federation and the BHA, so there is hope that in ten years time we will still be able to distinguish the action from Britain and America by means other than the commentator's accent.

Because of the tram fiasco we arrived after the first race and headed to the paddock where they were rumoured to be selling the Racing Post on a Friday. The rumours were right, and I felt a lot more settled into the day with my paper security-blanket. As we waited for the runners to appear for the second, staff entered the parade ring carrying signs and stood in random places, as if in silent worship of the Gods Of Probability. I wasn't sure what it was all about, but it was strangely reminiscent of a BBC2 weirdo drama.

Simon was intrigued by the concept of a pre-parade ring, and suggested the introduction of a post-race heckling ring where losers could be roundly abused. If such a place were in existence, we would certainly have been frequenting it that afternoon. Simon had selected the unusual betting strategy for the day: horse 1 in race 1, horse 2 in race 2, and so on. It was simple, I gave it that, but we discovered as the day progressed that it was also spectacularly unsuccessful and seemed to be just a method of haemorrhaging cash.

Simon is a tall chap who spends a lot of his life banging his head. True to form, he managed to find a low-hanging beam to walk into. We staged a Crimewatch-esque dramatic reconstruction of the incident for the benefit of the camera, with loose designs on suing the racecourse management for changing my once eloquent and intelligent friend into a drooling imbecile by the end of the afternoon, but fear they would have (rightly) argued that it was the Kronenbourg rather than the bang to the head. Despite the throng, there were plenty of places to settle and get a drink easily, which we used to full advantage through the afternoon.

In the fifth race, despite giving myself several good talkings-to over the previous few weeks about betting at odds-on, I couldn't be dissuaded that Tryster was a good thing and steamed in at 8/15. It won, but not like an 8/15 shot, and as I picked up my winnings I castigated myself for being so silly. As the Croydon pamphlet had sagely predicted, whatever happened to discipline? Then, as I walked away with the cash, I was pretty sure I got dipped. A trained hand was in my back pocket but quickly realised it was a wodge of post it notes and to-do-lists rather than the money I'd just collected. In an instant the hand and its owner were gone, melting into the crowded tarmac before I'd had time to turn around and punch whoever it was. It was the only time in the entire venture that I sensed any sort of criminality, and it felt like the Croydon pamphlet had exacted its retribution for my lapse of discipline.

For the sixth race I was therefore determined to bet only at what I perceived to be the correct price, and waited resolutely in the betting ring for 5/2 rather than 9/4 on Portamento. I sensed a market movement. There was not much money at 9/4 and I just wanted to get on with it rather than wait around for what I saw as the inevitable 5/2. On pitch 1 stood Lingfield stalwart Barry Dennis, ex-henchman of Channel 4 Racing. Here was a guy who had seen it all and would do the right thing.

"Hi Barry," I greeted him, like a long lost friend, "will you give me 5/2 on this favourite?"

"5/2!" he screamed, "I don't like beggars, now move out the way."

With that he gruffly ushered me to the side in order to serve a deserted piece of tarmac behind, just at the moment that his board flashed up 5/2.

"Go on then, 5/2" he said ungraciously, holding out his hand to take my money. In hindsight my correct response was to tell him that I didn't like beggars either and walk away, but I had become fixated on the price and so meekly took his offer. It would be all the sweeter, I reasoned, when I came to collect my winnings in ten minutes time. Portamento came sixth, beaten by a 20/1 outsider.

After the last we lingered in the food court area. I acquired a box of noodles that was so enormous that it defeated two grown men. Perhaps it was the chips that I'd added to the melee? Mark my words, though, combining carbs will be the next big thing on Masterchef, and in my opinion there's very little in the culinary world that can't be improved by adding chips. Except, perhaps, a bag of chips.

One thing that was beyond doubt, though, was that the day had been a resounding success for Lingfield, and probably horse racing too. A packed crowd had enjoyed themselves, some of whom may have become new converts in the process, and a handful of owners had gone home a lot richer with increased funds to hopefully reinvest back into the sport.

We stopped on the way home for a pint in the Prince of Wales near the station. As usual, the veil of alcohol encouraged both clarity of thought and honesty of expression, if only we could remember the startling insights the next day. After that there was only one thing on the minds of two men out on the Wimbledon tiles on a Friday night - yes, a game of Scrabble. Simon eventually won an epic encounter by the narrowest of margins after placing 'vapor' in the corner over the triple word score. I vehemently protested as the game was being played in England, not America, but he produced some spurious book to say it was allowable. The definition of vapor, apparently, is "a vapour". At last, he had secured his first winner of the day, but he surely couldn't be happy with the manner of his victory?

# 18) Kempton

## Day 23 – Saturday 4 April

And so my all-weather swing (NB: no swinging involved) ended with Kempton, or Kempton Park as they like to call it, the venue that had provided the televised backdrop to so many of my Boxing Days over the years. I had been to the course once before, in the mid-nineties with work friends when we'd decided at the last minute that an evening meeting was on the cards, and left our accountancy training early to make the first race. Frustration won at 5/2, a horse we collectively plunged on because we had been studying the topic of frustration in contract law earlier that day, as well as it neatly summarising my disaffection with the world of auditing that would later spur me into teaching.

Everyone crashed at my place afterwards, strewn about the living room like refugees with only the Racing Post for makeshift blankets. The next morning I achieved the remarkable, if not entirely appreciated, feat of making coffee without boiling the kettle. Even back then I think the idea of visiting all the British racecourses in eighty days was lurking somewhere in the back of my mind. I explained my change of career back then as going from one end of the Meaningful Spectrum to another. I saw auditing as essentially worthless (as well as terribly dull) and couldn't accept the idea that it was fine if all the numbers in a set of accounts are wrong, as long as they weren't (supposedly) too far wrong. Teaching, however, was entirely worthwhile, inspiring the next generation to give themselves a vast array of options in life, like becoming auditors if they wanted. As I continued my absurd tour it seemed like the pendulum was swinging violently back the other way, if not quite as far as 'worthless' then dangerously close to 'pointless'.

Simon's newsagent had acted swiftly on our consternation that the Racing Post now only came out on a Sunday, and had managed to secure us a copy a day early. Now that's what I call service. We came to terms with the day over a leisurely breakfast in the pub. Simon ordered the aptly-named 'Large Breakfast', in the middle of which he fashioned a well to pour his half bottle of house red (ketchup), before proceeding to savage the poor thing to such an extent that it looked like it had been put through a blender. I opted for the 'Healthy Breakfast', which contained only half the calories, and celebrated my discipline with a side order of chips.

As younger men, Simon and I once famously failed to exchange a single word during the last seven holes of an incredibly hard fought golf match at Tewkesbury Park (I won, 1 up on the 18th green, thanks for asking). However, we've both matured since then, and grudgingly spat a conversation at each other across the remnants of our breakfast, despite Simon's disgraceful behaviour the previous night over the Scrabble board. Shamefully, he was still claiming victory and would not even consider repaying the five pound note that I screwed up and hurled at him in a fit of pique after the game. Then he went off into one about how Superdrug's version of the Berocca restorative was less than half the price of the real thing, and the ingredients were exactly the same!

"Really? So you're telling me that own-brand products are cheaper than the real brand? Fascinating." I teased him, to his obvious indifference.

The Wife had borrowed The Satnav, so we relied on Simon's contraption to guide us to Kempton. Interestingly, despite the ongoing power struggle with my own plastic box, I was strangely relieved that I would not have to plot my own way there. How things had changed over the last three weeks. However, I'd not yet tuned into the new device and ignored most of its urgings until Simon realised what was happening and adopted the role of mediator.

When we arrived at the car park a bizarre scene played out. I handed the man on the gate my fiver and, unaccountably, he gave me a tenner in change. Was I a bad person for saying "thanks very much!" and driving on? Perhaps three weeks before I wouldn't have done that, but I was viewing the project more like a war of attrition by then, and decided not to look a gift horse in the mouth. Kempton would somehow get it back from me later on, I reasoned.

As it didn't go too well at Lingfield, financially at least, we considered immediately leaving and re-parking several times just to replenish our bankroll, but time was moving on and we were due to meet Tammy, Ant and their girls inside. Jason had declared at Southwell that no betting system could be truly unbiased, but he'd never seen Tammy in action at a racecourse. Her unique brand of randomness would provide the betting strategy for the last day of my week-long trial, and probably the best chance of winning. Once inside the gates Simon peered inquisitively in through the big window at the front of the weighing room and discovered a herd of colourful jockeys. It was like he was viewing animals in a zoo enclosure, but there was no informative plaque to tell him what strange species he was examining.

We couldn't find Tammy before the first race and so had to fend for ourselves. Simon backed a 16/1 winner, which he cleverly secured at odds of 14/1. He seemed in shock. Then Tammy appeared with her family and an assortment of betting slips in hand. She had backed the winner too, but that wasn't difficult when you've had six different bets in a five horse race. I was in need of a haircut and had forgotten my racing cap, and Tammy said I looked like Brian May, my curly locks blowing wildly in the now-inevitable wind tunnel of a British racecourse. Ant looked me in the eye and declared that the opening three weeks of my journey had taken a heavy toll. I was not entirely sure that I was enjoying the company of my 'friends' in the opening exchanges of the day.

I would forgive them if they produced winners, I thought. Simon headed off to get drinks and returned with three steaming cups of hot chocolate as we were examining the card for the next race. "Triple Chocolate it is!" said Tammy. Fair enough. It ran an awful race, but that was okay because she has also backed the winner, which she had neglected to mention before the race. This was turning into a farce. I really wasn't sure how a betting system could operate successfully under this amount of chaos and subterfuge, and decided to go my own way.

I was drawn to Lady Dutch in the third race. It had decent form, but more importantly, it was Botti-trained. By that I mean that the trainer was Marco Botti, who'd had several winners already on the all-weather that week. The rest of the crew disappeared to watch the race from the owners and trainers seating area, claiming not to have seen the large sign saying "Owners and Trainers Seating Area", so I watched Lady Dutch win well in splendid isolation. I knew I was better off without these clowns.

I was not the only one looking weary. The racecourse seemed a little tired and lacking in charm. I knew it was not the grandstand's fault, or for that matter the most important quality in a grandstand, but it was unremittingly ugly and I hoped that some of the Jockey Club funds could trickle down to this important venue. I didn't think I would be saying this because of the differences in ownership structures, but the ARC-owned Southwell and Lingfield seemed much nicer settings for a day at the races.

Buoyed from my first winner, I selected an outsider called George Cinq in the fourth race. He scythed through the field down the home straight as I screamed "George! George!! George!!!" more and more desperately, like I was searching for a lost child in a supermarket. You'd think this sort of behaviour would raise eyebrows at a racecourse, but in the usual bedlam of a tight finish it went unnoticed. Somehow George didn't quite make it, and Ant picked up his second winner in a row with Realize at 14/1. He dished out some celebratory Skittles, and I asked whether anybody else got that fizzing Skittle-juice effect in the corner of their jaw, something akin to knocking your funny bone. Everyone looked at me strangely, at which point I got the effect and they then looked at me with horror, like I was having a stroke. Surely somebody out there must know what I'm talking about?

We found a rare empty bench and Tammy put on her serious face, whilst clutching a small child to her as a windbreak.

"So, how do you think it's going, Neil?" She sounded like a psychiatrist, trying to tease out a stunning revelation.

"It's fine," I protested, "really! I'm fine, honestly!"

It sounded a little desperate, like when I was shouting "George!" in the last race, but I managed to distract her for a while by waving the Racing Post at her and asking her what was going to win the next. However, she had that look that I'd seen on a few faces recently, a mixture of sympathetic concern and utter bewilderment at what I was doing, and I got the impression that the inquisition was merely postponed rather than completed.

The truth of course was that I was far from fine, perhaps even as far from fine as I'd ever been. But I don't think I knew it back then, braving the arctic gale on a Kempton bench with an old friend. I was trying to convince myself that if I just kept pushing on with my ludicrous journey maybe, just maybe, it would all be okay. I would reach the end and as I triumphantly crossed the finishing line we would discover that my son was miraculously cured and we would all live happily ever after. My tour of British racecourses ended up being a distraction, perhaps even a useful one in some ways, at a time of enormous stress. But what the journey did, along with all the writing that accompanied it, was suck up all my thinking time so that the stark reality of our predicament came as an even greater shock when it finally arrived. Tammy knew it wasn't fine, and probably the same went for Simon, Paul, Jason, The Wife and everyone else. My jaded eyes weren't just the product of late nights and racecourse beers. It seemed I was the last to admit it to myself, because my protective pigeonholing took over again, but things were definitely not "fine".

The next two races were won by odds-on chances, and after my poor winning bet (if there is such a thing) from Lingfield, I told myself I would not back them at those prices even if they were the probable winners. Tammy secured her seventeenth winner of the afternoon and went off to collect her £3.45, and I realised it was time to go. She excitedly told me later on text that the bookie gave her £3.50 and let her keep the change, and that on the way out she'd encouraged her girls to scour the car park for loose change and secured another 11p. At least I could beat that – I was given £5 for parking my car.

But my all-weather week of unusual betting strategies had been fairly disastrous overall, and the hole in my profit and loss account had reached epic proportions. The spreadsheet starkly recorded a loss on investment running at 33%. It really was the least of my worries that I was only getting back two thirds of what I was staking, but any punter has a limit and I was getting thoroughly pissed off with the constant losses. I dropped Simon at the station and headed off to my mother-in-law's house. I hadn't seen The Wife and Eldest for two days, the Youngest for four, and I felt the need to circle the wagons and hunker down for what the next week was going to bring for our family. We were seeing the consultant on the Wednesday, and deep down I suspected it was not going to be good news. For once, my hunch was right.

# 19) Huntingdon

## Day 25 – Monday 6 April

Huntingdon signposted that I was a third of the way through my quest - 19 racecourses in 25 days. I was sure there were jockeys, trainers and stable staff who had accumulated far more hours and mileage in the same period, so I really had no right to feel jaded at this point, but there was certainly part of me that wanted to stay at home with my family and new trampoline. I ached to spend that warm and sunny Bank Holiday afternoon at home, watching the boys bounce around and enjoying a glass of wine with The Wife on the decking.

When I was getting into horse racing, Huntingdon was my closest track. Well, strictly speaking it was Newmarket, but even by that stage the jumping game was exerting a greater pull on my affections. I'd always wanted to go to the bank holiday meeting but never got around to it. Now was my chance. This was definitely one of those moments in life that wasn't worth the wait. Never go back, ladies and gentlemen, never go back. These things you idolised in your youth may now, with the inevitable march of time, lack the lustre they once appeared to have. This was a point I felt particularly acutely when sitting my boys down to watch the old cartoon version of The Lion, The Witch and The Wardrobe one Christmas Eve not so many years ago.

The car said it was 18.5 degrees when I finally summoned up the will to leave, but as I ventured up the A1 it sank to 11 degrees and was blustery-cold. At least I'd remembered my coat and cap this time. It looked like a Wolverhapton-esque set up as I approached the Holiday Inn, but this time the course was distinct and separate to its partner hotel. Parking was a hassle and took too long, and then a long trek to the entrance was followed by a long trek back to the action. I could not understand the thinking behind putting the entrance on the far side of all the facilities, and it rankled like a poorly loaded dishwasher. When I went to get a drink, a moron jumped the queue and the inept bar staff let him. TVs flickered in and out of fuzziness, and frankly the whole place seemed rather shabby. Children asked "when are we going home?" and whined for sweets, and for once I couldn't really blame them. I know these seemed like minor niggles, but they all melded into the experience of a day at the races. Perhaps the truth was that in my state of mind I too wanted to go home.

The only saving grace was that it was the Tommo Show again in the paddock. It was a similar routine to his wonderful Uttoxeter performance, with the selection of losing betting slips from a bucket allowing the losers, sorry, winners the chance to choose more losers. DT pulled it off with such energy and warmth that you couldn't help but be swept along on his wave of positivity. He is the sort of man in whose company I could enjoy even the dreariest of spectacles, and I even include Riverdance in that sentiment.

"Marcelo Saunders," he intoned as a slip was pulled from the hat, "you don't get many of those do you? Where is she? Marcelo, are you out there? Behind me? Oh no she isn't....."

I'd had a lot of losers recently, and the only way this day trip was going to be deemed a success was if I started making inroads into the betting deficit. In the first race I went for Borguy to upset the favourite Maller Tree, and he would have, had he not fallen at the second last. It was a ghastly, mistimed lunge of a fall. In situations like this I can honestly tell you that the money doesn't matter, it's all about the horse and jockey getting up, and they did. I was happy to lose my money. It was likely that at some point on this journey they would not get up, and I knew then, as I watched Borguy being led back in, that when that moment came I couldn't shirk the issue. I would have to directly address the death of racehorses and possibly even jockeys. But I was so glad that The Injured Jockeys Fund and Racehorse Sanctuary would not be required on this bank holiday Monday, at least not at Huntingdon.

What they take with one hand they give back with the other, and the Gods of Probability awarded me a good winner in the second. I hadn't realised until I'd backed it, and saw it leading over the open ditch in front of the stands on the first circuit, that Arthur's Oak had a big white splash down his nose. I really must listen to The Wife more – she is always telling me this is the key to success (both the big white splash in horse racing terms, and listening to her in general).

The fourth race looked tricky and I managed to secure a small investment on the Jonjo O'Neill trained Clubs Are Trumps at 3/1. By the home turn he and the other joint favourite Cosway Spirit had duelled for too long, and both capitulated to By The Boardwalk. As they jumped the last I started walking to the exit. I was bitterly disappointed by the whole Huntingdon experience and wanted to grab a few last bank holiday hours with my family.

Racing crowds can make an array of unusual noises, and such a deep, yearning boom then came from the grandstand that I had to turn around and see what the commotion was. There is a long run in on the chase course and the leader was tiring. In a thrilling finish, Clubs Are Trumps just got back up to win. I still left straight after collecting my winnings, but in a slightly more positive frame of mind, and the prospect of three days at home further helped my mood. I had perfected the art of winning small and losing big. If I could just add the other two quadrants to the spinner of outcomes, I thought on the drive home, I would be getting somewhere.

# 20) Leicester

## Day 29 – Friday 10 April

The Wife and I left the appointment on the Wednesday like we were suspended on puppet strings. We kind of knew what was coming, so it wasn't exactly a state of shock, more a feeling of numbness and abject sadness. We had left Youngest at a friend's house, and were glad to have done so. The consultant put it in gentle and soothing tones of course, but it was clear from early in the discussion the direction we were heading - a life changing operation for my son. The kidneys were surviving at the moment, but could not stand the pressure for much longer. It would need to be done soon.

When we got back home we all gathered in the kitchen and huddled around him as he cried, struggling to come to terms with the enormity of what was happening. My heart broke that evening, the first of many savage wounds inflicted by the cruelness and unfairness of it all. Any parent would say it, I know, but he was too lovely a kid to have to put up with all that crap. We tried to be positive as we cuddled him - it was for the best, it would help in the long run. Yes, it would be a tough few months, but he was young and could get through it, and we would be with him every step of the way. I didn't know then, of course, just how much worse it was going to get before it got better.

The operation was scheduled for Monday 1 June. This would give Youngest a fighting chance of recovering in time to go back to school in September. It all seemed a bit of a rush, but the other option was to delay until after he had started and our instinct was that he should begin at secondary school with a clean slate.

I looked at the schedule and worked out that my finale

at Fakenham on Sunday 31 May, the day we were due to go into hospital, could be shuffled around. But I also knew that the whole venture was hanging by a thread and was looking an increasingly frivolous and expendable part of our preparations for the operation. In the aftermath of the appointment, I knew that there were more important things than chasing adolescent dreams, but hadn't yet worked out whether or not the two were entirely incompatible.

On the Thursday I spoke to Paul on the phone. I took the call on the driveway and can remember the exact areas of gravel I paced between. Paul is great in these situations. He offered no opinion on whether I should continue with my increasingly insignificant quest, but asked good questions and made astute observations. He noted that whatever happened over the next eight weeks, it was vital that we all felt prepared for what was about to happen, and generously offered help with the boys so that The Wife and I could spend some time together. Then he used the word "grieving". He wanted me to build in time to digest the news and mourn the passing of the old way of life. It seemed an odd way of describing things, but I knew what he meant, and I knew that he was right. Paul sensed that my tendency would be to pigeonhole again and, if I did, I would not be fully ready to support my son.

Again, The Wife was brilliant. She reassured me that we needed to remain positive, for all our sakes, and arranged with her very sympathetic employers to work from home more often, and then take a three-month sabbatical around the time of the operation. I tried to persuade her that it should be me who stopped everything and held the fort, whilst she continued to focus on her job. At the least, I argued, it may have distracted her slightly from everything else, but she was having none of it. She sacrificed her career without hesitation for her son, and for me, and she did so willingly and graciously.

Even so, I was worried. Over the years I had become a

constant for my son, and now I was just constantly away. So I set off for Leicester, not really knowing if this would be my last hurrah before coming to my senses and deciding to stop the whole fiasco. I was staying with Jason that night, who despite his volatile behaviour and ability to do absolutely anything at any particular moment, had somehow adopted the role of my moral compass over the previous 35 years. This was a role he neither wanted nor believed he deserved, but due to some staggeringly important interventions over that timeframe, had fully earned. Then the following day was to be my first ever Grand National, which would be quite a way to go out, if that was to be the case.

Those who know the M1 understand that it can be a cruel mistress. 50 limits abound, often for no particular reason, and traffic that flows suddenly stops, often for no particular reason. In addition, the roads to Leicester were also filled with idiots intent on annoying me, and the anger consumed me until I was swearing and gesturing at anybody who showed moronic tendencies, of which there were many. The Wife was right when she said before I began that one of the biggest challenges I would face would be coping with things beyond my control. Neither of us knew back then how immense those things would be.

So I missed the first race, and things were not looking great with a Huntingdon-esque entrance that worked up an appetite on the long drag from the car park. Perhaps this was the new blueprint for racecourse design, making sure that punters were ravenous as they came through the gates after their extended hike. If so, it was a remarkably clever tactic in ensuring on-site sales, but not an entirely new invention. I'm sure the designers got the idea from the M1, where the service stations always seem to take you on a most convoluted loop before allowing you the chance to fill up – those extra 400 yards of fuel add up when multiplied over millions of cars a year.

Once inside though, all was forgiven. Leicester really

was a lovely course. I was greeted with a wide open vista of a manicured lawn, generously sprinkled with picnic tables to view the horses in the paddock. There was a relaxed ambience and, oh yes, a local food stand selling freshly hand-cut roast beef baps for those who had worked up an appetite. Lucky that I was on a diet and my steely discipline could ignore such temptations (yes, I'd weighed in, weighed in, a few pounds over that week).

When I got trackside I found a quite extraordinary thing. I wasn't sure whether it was a touring museum exhibit or an art installation. Perhaps the best word to describe the creation was 'folly' because it was so incongruent that I had to look around to make sure I wasn't unwittingly part of a hidden camera jape. Someone had parked a truck full of giant lionesses next to the children's playground, presumably to keep the nippers in check. They prowled and growled, in a mute and still way behind their Perspex cage, spying invisible prey on a distant horizon with their strangely beady eyes. They seemed to be made of some sort of fabric, which gave them all the menace of Bagpuss. The only piece of information on offer was a tiny plaque that read "In loving memory of Michael Barry Burbidge". Whoever he was, he must have been a great man for someone to do this on his behalf. In true British fashion, most racegoers simply ignored the elephant in the room sited only yards from the betting ring, and focused on the next race.

Nobody knew who was going to win it, though, and the bookies went 9/2 the field in an eight horse race. Everyone still had a guess, but not many guessed right on the 40/1 outsider. The old guy in front of me said the bookies would be happy, and the lady next to me said "That wasn't in your paper was it?" as I stared confused at the pages of the race just gone. Correct on both counts. The grey filly almost failed to sell in this seller, but then a frenzy of late bidding saw her go for 4,000 guineas. I wondered if the buyer had put £100 on her at 40/1.

168

There was no giant TV screen in the middle of the course, which proved quite refreshing as it somehow made the action more real. I quite liked it, but would have liked it more if I hadn't left my binoculars in the car about three miles away. However, there was a variety of good viewing options around the undulating course, and the lack of TV pictures made for a cosy social vibe as we all eagerly listened in to the intonations of the commentator, like we were huddled around a wartime radio.

I didn't fancy the odds-on favourites in the next two races. Too much could have happened since the previous season and horses progress at different rates as they mature from two to three-year-olds. I was spot on in my analysis as they both ran poor races, but I wasn't clever enough to pick out the winners. It was a small stakes day though, everyone keeping their powder dry for the Grand National the next day. After another loser in the next race I headed for the exit, past the spacious lawn and roast beef stand. As I began the expedition back to the car park, I mused on the litmus-test of any racecourse: if I could walk away without a winner, or a roast beef bap for that matter, and still have enjoyed my afternoon, it must be a good one.

I travelled on to Jason's house in Nottingham and arrived early, waking him up from a nap. He had been struggling for a while with what later turned out to be the small matter of a crushed vertebra, something which two physiotherapists, an osteopath and a chiropractor had all spectacularly failed to diagnose. That he was still off the booze despite his obvious pain was an incredible achievement. As we waited by his local tram stop for the hop into town, I filled him in on the latest developments with Youngest. The anonymity of a crowded tram carriage allowed me to talk honestly about our predicament, and share my doubts about continuing with my tour. Jason listened carefully, clearly troubled by the news and revealing a softer side that others, who usually only noticed his default buffoonery, would be surprised by. He paused for a long time when I asked him what I should do, the gap filled by the rumbling of the tram. Then he fixed me with his clear eyes and said "I think, if I were you mate, I would stop. You can always pick it up next year."

Such was my state of inner turmoil, I didn't know whether I agreed with him, or even whether that was what I wanted to hear. I did know that there was no picking it up again next year, but that was irrelevant compared to the big question of whether my family needed me to stop. Or, for that matter, whether I needed me to stop. I was confused, but whether I decided to followed his advice or not, it was another shining example of why I had given Jason the unofficial role of moral advisor. He said it as he saw it, and that's all I could have asked.

We went to a poker club called Dusk Til Dawn, but they had a big three-day tournament on so we sat down to lose an hour, and a chunk of cash, on the blackjack tables. The dealers, floor manager and (for me at least) lagers made it an enjoyable way to be parted from my money. Big name poker players wandered around, and Marcel Luske, the renowned Dutch master, lingered at the bar, immaculately turned out as usual. The barman complimented me on ordering a Moretti, rather than a Birra Moretti which he felt was the Italian equivalent of saying Lager Carling or Bitter Tribute. I didn't have to work my way through too many Morettis and hands of blackjack before the chips had mysteriously disappeared, so we left to go back for a game of chess. On the way out Jason paused at a roulette table and placed a £10 chip on 11 Black, but his heroics from Southwell were not to be repeated. The luck had run out for all of us.

# 21) Aintree

## Day 30 – Saturday 11 April

I spent an unsettled night in Jason's spare room. I'm not even sure it was the claustrophobic surroundings of his basement, or the narrow and unlit stairway that ushered me downwards. Somehow, the setting was apposite for my state of mind. Youngest still had a temperature almost two weeks after getting over a little bug and I was worried it was another sign that his systems were under pressure. But there was no time to dwell on personal matters the next morning, as I was due to meet Simon in Liverpool for the biggest day of racing in the calendar.

This was my first visit to Aintree and the Grand National, and as I set off I gave myself a little pep talk. If I was to plough on north instead of turning around and going back home, I may as well try to enjoy it. As the miles ticked down my malaise dissipated and by the time I reached Liverpool excitement was high for a race that defined "iconic" in the equine world. I hoped that the real thing would live up to 35 years worth of TV incarnations.

Like most other punters, I would guess, the Grand National was where it all started, before I even knew that the Gold Cup or Derby existed. Drenched in exhilarating fairytale and bursting with outrageous possibilities, it was hard as a nipper not to become beguiled by the event. My Dad used to bring us all back a ticket from his work sweepstake and I can remember crying my eyes out one year when Alverton died.

Somehow, despite the excitement and spectacle, the race has always been stalked by the shadow of death. This difficult and emotive issue is best exemplified by the furore after the 2012 Grand National, when two horses died and horse racing made the front pages for all the wrong reasons.

"He was trying to escape!" was one of the shrill and extraordinarily stupid statements I heard in the emotional aftermath, a comment directed at the scene when Synchronised got rid of Tony McCoy before the start and ran loose for a while. If people are so ignorant of the sport they are watching, it is no wonder that inflammatory headlines make reasoned debate almost impossible. Actually, after Synchronised was retrieved he started fine and was brought down by another horse, before galloping away riderless for several fences and then breaking a leg. He chose to continue. It's what horses do.

Two others died at the three-day festival that year. According To Pete was brought down in the Grand National and Gottany O's broke down on the flat in a hurdles race. The latter received much less coverage – the message from the media seemed to be that horses who died jumping fences were far more newsworthy than horses who died whilst just running.

How many of us remember the name of Great Endeavour? Few, I would think. He was an eight-year-old trained by David Pipe and winner of six of his 17 races, including the Paddy Power Gold Cup at Cheltenham. This fine racehorse died the week after Synchronised, but his accident didn't happen during a race watched by millions. He broke a leg running around his field at home where he had been turned out for the summer, but his sad demise didn't make the News At Ten or the tabloid headlines. The simple truth is that to stop the deaths of horses you would have to stop the existence of horses.

So far you would have me down as a racing fanatic I suspect, cynical about the twisted attempts to portray horse racing as barbaric. And it's certainly true that I find the sensationalist portrayal of this matter both misleading and unhelpful. But now I am about to break ranks with some of my fellow devotees and declare that we should all consider the deaths of horses carefully, and never stop examining our consciences in the light of new evidence. I thought the words of Gavin Grant, the Chief Executive of the RSPCA, to be mostly intelligent and balanced when he spoke the morning after the 2012 Grand National.

"We recognise racing is part and parcel of the fabric of our country but we've all got a responsibility as human beings - after all the horses haven't got a choice, they can't make the decisions - to make racing as safe as it can be."

He was absolutely right to question the size of the field, the construction of the fences and the state of the going, and he did so in a rational way rather than resorting to crass hyperbole and lurid photos. Others were also right to question whether the changes made to the course before the 2012 renewal, where fences were modified to essentially make them easier, actually contributed to some of the problems by increasing the speed of the race. This is not a simple situation, and it will not be solved by knee-jerk reactions to the shrill clamour for change.

When you follow horse racing, as I do, you implicitly accept that its participants may die. It really is as simple as that. The same applies to motor racing, boxing, rugby and football. I'm not trying to be trite here, and fully accept that horse racing is inherently more dangerous than tiddly winks, however many safety measures you put in place. But I have looked at the figures and I am okay with following a sport that has the risk profile of horse racing. The probability of a runner sustaining a fatal injury in a UK race is about 0.002, or one fifth of one percent. I am not blasé to the consequences - the death of any horse is sad and some have reduced me to tears - but I am satisfied that the racehorse is very well looked after, the sport as a whole is well regulated, and that sufficient efforts are made to minimise the risk to both human and equine participants. I wish the death rate was lower, and would welcome suggestions on how to achieve that, but I understand that there are no miracle cures.

The crazed reactions to sad events by lunatics who purport to stand in the name of animal rights should not bully us into sticking our heads in the sand and saying it's all fine. Only with constant and honest appraisal can we truly say our consciences are clear. And it is obvious that both the BHA and the Aintree executive are willing to make those appraisals and changes. Fences have been moderated, landing areas modified, run off areas introduced and watering increased to ensure safer ground. You may not have noticed it, because it was changed without much fanfare in 2013, but the race is now shorter than it was in order to move the start away from the hubbub of the stands and reduce the run to the first fence.

Could more be done? I don't know, is the honest answer, but I would be willing to consider any new evidence or ideas. I'm not sure it's reducing the field size, though, as this has been studied in depth previously and recognised that the average width of fence per runner is no different to most other courses. The Grand National could be made very safe by limiting the field to ten, removing the fences and reducing the distance to 5 furlongs, but then it would no longer be the Grand National in most people's eyes. Even then, significantly, you could not guarantee the absence of fatalities. To me, this is no more sensible a solution than restricting the top speed of every car in the country to 10mph in order to reduce the death-toll on our roads. But, and this really is key, it is absolutely right that we consider it before dismissing it. We have a responsibility to continually question the world around us to see if it can be improved.

I met Simon at the Tarbock Premier Inn on the outskirts of the city, chosen for its reasonable price and proximity to the intersection of the M62 and M57. Our room was not yet ready so he had been shepherded into the adjoining Brewers Fayre to enjoy the spectacle that was 'The Fun Factory!', a padded cell of a soft-play arena where a kiddies party was in raucous spirits. He began proceedings by putting on a comedy Scouse accent in a pub full of Scousers – nice one, mate.

The taxi driver dropped us off near the course where traffic seemed to have ground to a halt. As we began the short pilgrimage to the retail park that is Aintree Racecourse, Simon (who had already managed to lose and find his ticket) discovered he had left his mobile in the cab. As I phoned the taxi firm he added his wallet to the growing list of absentees. The driver kindly returned and then, quite astonishingly, apologised to us for not spotting the items on the back seat as we jumped out. I hoped that we would get him for the return journey later in the afternoon so that he could apologise for failing to stop us from leaving large bundles of cash in the bookies satchels.

And so my crazy tour entered its fifth week with perhaps the most famous race of all, and there was an incredible buzz about the place. The ladies of Liverpool had made an extraordinary effort to wear virtually nothing in the arctic, windswept tundra of Merseyside, and desperately clutched chiffon and vodka-tonics to themselves in order to protect what was left of their goose-pimpled modesty. Following negative publicity in previous years, the management had warned photographers that they would be thrown off the premises if found snapping female racegoers in unflattering poses, explaining "the ladies do express themselves, and that freedom of expression is what the event should be about." Indeed, but whilst there was plenty of posing, drinking, and expressing themselves, none of the media seemed to be taking advantage of the ladies that were all having a damn good time. Over the years I have become increasingly worried about airlifting soused youngsters into racecourses, but it all comes down to the atmosphere engendered, and this was a cracking one.

We discovered three poor, neon-jacketed fellows who had been given the unenviable task of stopping punters

175

from congregating in the icy blast between the Queen Mother and Earl of Derby stands, although it's hard to fathom why anyone would choose to linger there if they weren't filming the latest Attenborough documentary for 'Life In The Chiller'. It really was a stunningly inept deployment of manpower, like strapping cabin crew to the wings of a jumbo jet to make sure no passengers venture out mid-flight, and I could only think that either the stewards had misunderstood their instructions for the day, or the Aintree Health and Safety executive had identified frostbite as the number one risk to the wellbeing of its clientele.

"Is it cold here?" asked Simon to one of them.

The steward kindly refrained from punching my friend square in the face, and replied simply "Yes" with astonishing cheeriness. Simon pulled the same stunt a few races later but I sensed the humour of the situation had drained from the chap, along with his will to live.

A friend called Mike had told me that his grandfather always said number 7 won the first race. Was this the stunningly simple system I had been missing? Not here at Aintree, apparently, as number 7 was a non-runner. Instead, we backed the Ruby Walsh ridden Nichols Canyon who got us off to a flying start. Easy game. We decided to celebrate our success in the Doom Bar Bar, which sounded uncannily like a Beach Boys song. To add to this theme they'd put down some sand and decking, and stuck a reggae number on repeat.

We got chatting to an Irish couple. Jerome liked Sizing Granite in the next. They lived south of Dublin and Liz urged us to do the Punchestown Festival some time. I got particularly animated as I began recounting tales from the quite extraordinary four days Simon, Clive, Jason and I shared at the Galway Festival many years ago, and managed to sweep the remains of my pint off the table and onto my trouser leg. I immediately thought of the technique of applying salt to red wine on a carpet, and smothered the Doomed suit in sand before blithely carrying on my Galway dissertation. Jerome looked slightly askance at my new sand-suit, but was bullied into carrying on the conversation for a while before we had to rush off to get our bets on. We should have listened to his sage advice as Sizing Granite won like a good thing.

I spotted two young lads sporting One Man scarves and cursed myself for not having brought mine, more as a mark of camaraderie than a preventative for hypothermia. We got chatting and I noticed that they were following a big bear of a man who was ambling resolutely towards the paddock.

"That's our grandfather, John Hales!" said one.

We reminisced about the great grey who was owned by the giant barrelling through the throng in front of us, and discussed the chances of one of their newer shades of grey, Unioniste, in the upcoming Grand National. I wished them luck as they headed into the parade ring in the wake of their grandfather, where I was stopped for not having the correct colour badge.

Not to be put off, the Media Centre was next to the parade ring and I attempted to get in there as well by waving my complimentary admission badge, again without success. I explained to the steward that Simon and I had received press accreditation and triumphantly unfolded my letter as proof, but he stood firm. It may not have helped our cause that the Doom Bar Bar visits had made it tricky to pronounce the phrase and I accidentally said "cress appreditation".

Aintree was the only course to respond to my increasingly desperate pleas for free entry under somewhat spurious credentials, and I was extremely grateful to Francesca Bullock for saving the whole project. I had left it late in booking tickets and by the time I looked at the website everything except the Steeplechase Enclosure was sold out. I'm sure we would have had a great day down the side of the Grand National course, but it was not exactly in the heart of the action for investigative journalism as serious as ours, and the other alternative of getting stung by a tout on the day was not appealing.

Francesca was very generous in approving my application, but was initially unclear in what capacity Simon would be joining me. However, once I explained that he'd had a brief spell in the 1990s writing the Ceefax pages, she kindly agreed to accredit him as well. Her positive attitude had resulted in 340 members of the media being accredited for the day, a figure that was alarmingly close to the total number of people who attended Wolverhampton barely a week earlier. In the end, it was not clear whether we had received proper press clearance or just free tickets, but the last two unsuccessful attempts to get 'beyond the ropes' suggested it was the latter. Either way, the tickets kept the schedule intact and gave us access to a magnificent event, and I was hugely grateful to her.

Simon decided that to raise his core temperature above zero we would have to go inside, and we got chatting to two girls from Belfast in one of the many queues for one of the many bars. One was a showjumper and I talked enthusiastically about my visit to the Racehorse Sanctuary and how they helped ex-racehorses into new careers such as showjumping. The other had dreamt about the National the previous night and had backed Night In Milan, but he apparently didn't win. I obviously asked who had won her imaginary version of the big race.

"Mon Parrain," she said, "but for some reason he was called Don Parrain."

This wasn't making any sense at all, which to be fair to her was often the way with dreams, but I decided not to back either of them in the big race, unless Mon Parrain had suddenly changed his name by deed poll to Don Parrain, but I doubted whether a horse could do that. We went to get our bets on and the predicted plunge on the AP McCoy ridden Shutthefrontdoor had failed to materialise. 8/1 was freely available just minutes before the off, and the market seemed robust in the face of the onslaught it was receiving. This made it all the stranger when I later read of the controversy over the starting prices, with the horse apparently going off at 6/1, to widespread criticism that the bookies were exploiting the shop-window of our sport.

We prudently secured a space in the sun on the Earl of Derby (not literally), as I was beginning to worry that Simon would be frozen solid to the steps by the end of the race if he stood in the shade, and drank in the anticipation of the start that was forming horse by horse in front of us. They were away first time, and the crowd gave an enormous cheer that rivalled the first race roar at Cheltenham. The people around us on the steps were all shouting different names, and various groans and hoorays punctuated the commentary over the 30 fences. Almost half the field completed the race, and despite worries at the Canal Turn, all horses came back safe and sound. Everyone was a winner, despite almost everyone being a loser as Many Clouds was relatively unconsidered at 25/1 after his disappointing run in the Gold Cup. Our fistful of bets, representing not only our selections but those of assorted relatives across the country, produced not a single return, but it truly was an awesome spectacle.

The Grand National had met and even exceeded my lofty expectations. Everyone was there to have a great time, win or lose. Despite its grand scale, there were places to go, sights to see and people to meet. Plenty of those people were drunk, some of them roaringly so, but there was not one hint of discord about the place. It was a rampant and joyful party where disparate groups mingled to celebrate the history and tradition of this unique race. The reciprocal relationship smacked me in the face like the hypothermic wind as we left the stands for the last time – we were all there because of the Grand National, but the race existed because of us, and our willingness to embrace the most glorious of spectacles that our sport has to offer.

We found our way back to the Brewers Fayre to thaw out and enjoy a relaxed dinner. At these places I've found that something like scampi and chips is the safest option, but Simon ambitiously opened up his food horizons and could not be dissuaded from an unusual looking "multinational buffet", which to me seemed like a good excuse for the kitchen to use up anything that was going out of date. Fortunately for me, Simon's menu choice seemed to sit uncomfortably with him, and distracted him from what was widely-billed as Scrabble Deathmatch 2 – The Vengeance. I have since framed the napkin scorecard, which chronicled my amazing fight back with a seven-letter word in the penultimate round. The party cranked on late into the Liverpool night, but without the two of us. After a poor sleep the previous night in Nottingham, and a long and eventful day, I became uninterested in proceedings when we got back to the room after dinner. Simon texted The Wife to ask how she stopped me from snoring.

"Easy," came her clever reply, "send him away on an eighty-day tour of the races!"

# 22) Ffos Las

## Day 31 – Sunday 12 April

You may be surprised to learn of Ffos Las's claim to fame, at least in terms of the racecourses of Britain that is. I'm not going to tell you just yet (and no peeking to the end of the chapter) but let's see if you can work it out if I give you a little clue:- it's a very similar claim to fame to that of Perth. Perth, Australia, that is, rather than the Perth I was aiming to visit on 23 April.

Anyhow, back to the morning after the night before. I slept fitfully in the Premier Inn as the man in the bed next to mine kept shouting at me to stop snoring, and yet every time he woke me up with his hollering, I wasn't snoring at all! Simon claimed not to remember the score in the Scrabble the previous evening, so I found the napkin and reminded him frequently. He had a 1pm tee time in Surrey, so scoffed his Full English like a Doberman Pinscher and bolted for the M62 after temporarily misplacing the latest in a long list of personal items, this time discovering his car keys in the zipped pocket inside his holdall, but only after decanting all of its contents on the floor.

He questioned what was happening to him, as though fearing some early-onset Alzheimer's, but I suspected turning 40 and not sleeping for two nights would be a more likely explanation. Either that or the nasty bang to the head he received at Lingfield that left him barely cogent by the end of the day. Simon commented that if you poked a man with a stick for just 72 hours he would die because his body would shut down due to lack of sleep. We then became embroiled in a silly argument over whether the person holding the stick would also die, because he would also presumably not have slept for 72 hours either.

I was also tired, after all of Simon's shouting in the night, and missed the clear jibe that listening to my snoring was akin to being tortured to death. He asked if The Wife had ever tried to suffocate me. I wasn't sure, although I had developed a strange distrust of pillows in later years.

The Satnav insisted that the quickest way from Liverpool to Ffos Las was across the Brecon Beacons. I've been known to put my right foot down at times, but the stupid plastic box failed to comprehend that I couldn't maintain an average speed of 60mph in a Ford Galaxy on a road with more switchbacks than Alpe d'Huez. I made it to the next stop of my tour of British wind tunnels with minutes to spare. As I leapt from the car the door was almost ripped off its hinges by the savage wind, so ferocious that it had blown over metal railings in the car park. This really was getting beyond the pale, I thought, as I struggled to lurch my way to the entrance. It would be nice to go a week without feeling that I was auditioning for the latest Sir Ranulph Fiennes expedition. Was Britain always this windy and I was only now noticing because of my recent fad for standing in fields?

It was a chap called Dai Walters who had a dream to bring a racecourse to West Wales, a place where the population thins as the junction numbers of the M4 reach dizzying heights. The born-and-bred businessman who had made his millions in civil engineering opened the course to great fanfare in the summer of 2009. However, all has not been rosy for the first jumps track to open in Britain since Taunton in 1927 (and no, that's not the claim to fame I was thinking of). Just two years after opening, Walters threatened to close the course after losing 12 days racing through a contraction of the fixture list. Compromise was found and the track remained opened for business.

They had run out of Racing Posts so for the first time in my life I bought a racecard, which I discovered were smaller, thinner and more expensive. Unconvinced, I noted that in the first race, which had already started, it gave only two out of five stars to Driftashore who went on to win at 20/1. Ffos Las had continued the beach theme started by Aintree, and had a big sign up for The Beach Hut, which turned out to be a tarmac-floored barn serving lager. Despite it bearing a passing resemblance to a very large hut, it was hard to work out where the beach theme fitted in, other than people occasionally drinking lager at the beach. I toured the rest of the facilities and discovered a variety of inflatable distractions dotted around for the umpteenth 'Family Fun!' day of my journey. I became obsessed that they might take off in the violent gusts, so much so that I lost track of the time whilst examining their tethers and missed the second race as well.

After the fizzing party of Aintree, Ffos Las seemed a desolate place in comparison, and the irony of being at a family day without my own that I was missing so desperately cut into me like the punishing gale. I decided that I would make Ffos Las my first ever one-bet racecourse, and perused what little form the racecard offered for the third. Surprisingly, I spotted a great betting opportunity in a race of only five horses. Even more surprisingly, it was an odds-on shot. I'd done well recently to avoid some dodgy short-priced favourites, but this one looked like the real deal. Some folk reckon that backing at odds-on is the quick way to the poor house, but you'd back Usain Bolt at any price to win the Dads race at a sports day, and I was convinced this was a similar opportunity.

Tanerko Emery was a high-class hurdler who ran well in some big races for trainer David Pipe in the colours of none other than Dai Walters, including a third place in the 2013 Welsh Champion Hurdle, and two staying-on efforts over a shorter distance in competitive handicaps at Sandown and the Cheltenham Festival a month later. He'd recently produced two modest efforts after being absent for more than a year, but this race was a huge drop in class and he would be running against frankly ordinary

183

opponents. Significantly, he'd always looked like he would appreciate the step up in trip to 3 miles. Less significantly, the racecard also selected him.

I really thought he should be a 1/2 shot or less, and couldn't believe it when I got 5/6. He was backed in to 8/11, which still looked like remarkable value, but I resisted the temptation to dive in again. Jockey Sean Bowen hardly moved a muscle as Tanerko Emery sauntered clear up the home straight. This was as close to printing money as I had found on the quest so far, or perhaps ever for that matter. Strangely, I had no urge to reinvest my winnings in later races and was happy to walk away with a wad of cash for a change. I'd been away for three days and was aching to get home, so completed my seven hours of driving on largely amenable roads. I felt like I'd seen all the colours of the racing spectrum during my extended weekend. The contrast between the glamour and excitement of Aintree and the grassroots fare of Leicester and Ffos Las was stark, but without any of these strands on the spectrum, the light of British horse racing would not shine as brightly, and when the wind blows it can blow hard and cold wherever you are.

And so back to the question that opened the chapter, and well done if you haven't already peeked. Ffos Las is the most isolated of our British racecourses, being the furthest from any other. And they say that Perth, Western Australia, is the most remote city in the world. Luckily, the Perth on my itinerary is only a couple of hours from Heathrow.

# 23) Carlisle

## Day 33 – Tuesday 14 April

My to-do list for the morning remained half finished, and even that half wasn't perfect. The computer had refused to do anything the previous evening, except spin the colourful little beach ball to tell me that it wasn't going to do anything. I shut it down, just to spite it. Before that, the new printer had run out of ink whilst I was trying to print off some information about Youngest's forthcoming operation, stuff I wanted to read on the train to get mentally prepared. Then in the morning the bloody computer refused to start, again spinning the colourful wheel just to taunt me. 28 different applications, most of which I didn't want to open, were all squabbling to start at the same time. Eventually, I managed to hook up the old printer and press 'Print'......out of paper.

The Wife drove me to the station with Youngest sat in the back, quiet again. He was being farmed out to a school club in his Easter holidays that he didn't really want to go to because I was sodding off again. He was being so, so brave, but the enormity of what was about to happen was getting to him and he worried about things, which made him all the braver that he still did them without complaint.

The Wife thought I was stressed because I was swearing at the computer and the printer, but lack of time isn't the same as real stress. Teaching was stressful. Managing a house project was stressful. The situation with Youngest was bloody stressful. The Wife twitters and worries all the time about silly stuff, and yet because I'm normally laid back this shall go down in history as The Time Neil Was Stressed. We were holding it together as a couple and a family, but only just. I asked her to drop me on the far side of the bridge, but she started turning in to the near side car park.

"No, the far side!" I said sharply, "I want to get a paper." Perhaps I was stressed.

"Well how do I know unless you tell me?" she retorted.

I thought that I just had, but some things were best left unsaid. So I left the car thoroughly pissed off. God I hated this shit. A large part of me wanted to ditch the decaying fantasy and start living in the real world again. It would mean Youngest could avoid school clubs, and I would have more time to wrestle with computers. And operations. And the future. But the fantasy was at least a distraction, a purpose, of sorts. So I got on the train. As soon as I did I got a text from The Wife apologising. She is great at that, and so much better than I am. I look at things logically and can't understand why somebody would try and drop me on the near side when I said the far side. What was missing from my ruthless logic was that she was probably more stressed by Youngest's situation than me, and still had to drop him at school club, and pick him up, and cook the supper and do the washing and the bedtimes because I wasn't there. Oh, and do a full day at work in between - proper work that is, none of this swanning around the country going racing. So I am sorry honey, too, and think it pathetic that I can only see that now months after the incident, and couldn't say it back then by text, or when I got home. Men can be idiots sometimes.

The car gets boring after a while and is bad for my back, and Carlisle doesn't have an airport, so I bit the bullet (an expensive bullet it was too) and got a return on the train. The train really does take the strain. I effectively gained ten hours of my life back and to a time-starved man the small fortune I paid seemed well spent. It was not impossible to study form whilst driving, but it was not particularly easy (or legal) either, and boy did I need to study the form and have a good betting day to recoup my expenses.

The train also gave me time to flick through the news stories. The most important article, as far as I was concerned, was that the earlier outbreak of Strangles in Newmarket had proved to be the only case, and the cloud hanging over a possible epidemic had lifted. Again, I thought back to Graham Sharpe of William Hill declaring my trip would be easy, and gave a wry chuckle to myself. The Racing Post also announced a major review of jump racing, addressing in particular the significant decline in the number of horses and owners compared to the flat. However, Carlisle's meeting contradicted the argument that the fixture list was too big for the current racing population. A bumper eight-race card offered opportunities for no less than 84 horses to shine in the Cumbrian sun, and all bar one of the contests offered a decent betting heat with more than eight runners.

Possibly the biggest adrenaline rush of my challenge so far suddenly arrived when I casually checked that I was changing at Birmingham New Street, and not Birmingham International which I had just pulled into. The slow-motion 3G reveal confirmed....shit! Get off! Get off! I stuffed the paraphernalia of a day at the races into my rucksack, remembered my coat in the overhead rack at the last second, and leapt from the train with my laptop power cable slapping wildly against just about everything and everyone on the way out. As the train pulled away I realised I was the only one on a deserted platform. A strange sinking sensation drained through me in an instant – had I misread my phone and the whole thing had unravelled? Carlisle was tricky enough to get to without improvising halfway up. I rechecked – no, phew, this was right, although I later discovered that I could have changed at New Street anyway.

Panic over, and back to the soothing rhythm of a long train journey. The comedy voiceover in the space-age loo made me smile when it urged me not to flush away anything inappropriate such as unpaid bills or goldfish.

And the scenery past Preston became truly stunning as we sped past sun-dappled valleys lined with dry stone walls and fissured rivulets. The driver of the taxi from the station asked me whether I'd been to the course before, and I quickly spilt the beans on my whole ludicrous venture, and the fact that Carlisle had given me the biggest planning headache of all of them, necessitating a 600 mile round trip.

"You're mad!" she said, and I concurred. "You didn't go to Aintree on Saturday did you? You did? Did you have the winner?"

I felt like this was leading somewhere, and I was right. She had backed Many Clouds in the National, £1 at 38/1, which sounded like a betting exchange price to me.

"I just liked the name. I'm quite lucky in the National. That Mon Mome, I ended up getting £300 back, cos me daughter did it online and it were an outsider, weren't it. She opened this Betfair account with £30 and once she got up to £60 she took her original £30 out, so anything in there now has cost her nothing. She went to France with it one year!"

I pondered whether I'd missed a trick so far. Perhaps I should have been looking for different angles – laying off bets on the exchanges for guaranteed profits, or lurking at Tote windows to spot any last-minute glitches in the odds that would, for example, give me more for a place than a win. But that wasn't betting, that was drudgery. That's why I gave up online poker, not that I was ever disciplined enough to make it pay in that way.

The sun was shining as I stepped from the taxi, and the place had a nice open feel to it. Again, the network of the Jockey Club had spread its influence, and cash, far and wide, this time bringing smart new facilities to the North West. If you were asked to imagine what a Cumbrian track would look like, this would be it – you can go up or down, but not sideways. The land of the lakes didn't seem to do horizontal, at least not with racecourses.

However, after a pleasant ten minutes the course turned into another blooming wind tunnel. It was almost like the management realised I had turned up, and phoned the emergency invisible fan contractors sharpish. I retreated inside and got chatting to an old boy with wild white hairs sprouting from his chin, nose and ears. We had a five-minute exchange where I understood about three words that he said, but couldn't fit them into a meaning coherent enough to establish a conversation. I quite enjoyed it though, somehow, and it was not as bad as a bar in Dublin where I spent 40 minutes talking to an old boy and only understood one word: "McCoy". I guessed he meant the jockey rather than the crisps, but for all I knew he may have felt I was shy in getting the snacks in.

In the fourth race I couldn't choose between the two favourites, so went for one of the rank outsiders who ran like its odds of 125/1 suggested. I'd been dabbling so far but, confident from my Ffos Las approach, I fancied a big bet in the fifth race. The favourite was Bearly Legal (that was his name) at 11/4, and he'd improved since being tongue-tied four races ago (and by that I don't mean he had nothing to say for himself when asked to take a long hard look at his previous performances). His form had an obvious reason for improving, and I was hoping it continued. The second favourite Vasco D'ycy was 3/1. I'd backed him at Wetherby and he couldn't go the pace over 2m6f and just stayed on into second. I couldn't see why he should win over 2 furlongs shorter here, and I was right. Bearly Legal travelled beautifully through the race and won easily, helping me to bank the second decent meeting in as many days. Was I getting better as the form lines from earlier in my tour knitted together, or was it just luck? Frankly, I suspected the latter, but as the old phrase goes, I'd rather be lucky than good.

On the way home my brief infatuation with train travel was finally broken due to overexposure with the British public. Two young kids were running amok as what looked like their father and grandmother feebly attempted to scare them into complying.

"Do you want me to take you to the policeman? Right, I'm going to take you to the policeman in a minute," (girl continued jumping on the seat) "do you want to go back in the pushchair?" (boy started hanging from overhead rail) "Policeman's coming, here he comes! I'll tell him to come," (a game of opening and closing the doors began) "quick, he's coming!"

I didn't know whether I was more exasperated with the behaviour of the kids or the woefully inept display from the supposed adults in charge. Surely they realised after the seventeenth warning of the policeman appearing that any infant would have sussed out it was a hollow threat? Kids are great at testing out boundaries, it's what they are meant to do to explore their world, but these kids obviously didn't know what a boundary was. It was the father and grandmother who should have set them, and the brats should have deferred to them rather than some imaginary bogeyman.

Their urgings, of course, had absolutely no effect on the trainee yobs who continued rampaging around the carriage, bouncing off the seats and shutting all the blinds. I opened the blind next to me that had just been shut, and stared at the boy, probably no more than six. He looked back at the blind by my table with a demonic glint in his eye, and then back at me. He paused for a while, suspended in the staring contest, before thinking better of it and going off to terrorise somebody else.

Then on the connecting train there was an older and more contained, but equally delinquent, family unit. Three teenagers hurled insults at each other for two hours across the table, with the mother occasionally shushing them and looking generally embarrassed. She shrugged her shoulders to the lady opposite as if to say she was outnumbered, kids would be kids wouldn't they, and what could she do?

190

So I'd finally discovered a flaw in the otherwise brilliant concept of train travel – other people. Perhaps we just needed a specialist 'Family Fun!' carriage similar to the padded cell in the Liverpool Brewers Fayre where they could run amok without injuring themselves or interfering with others? All my positivity about the social affability of the train crumbled away on that one journey home. I hadn't seen violence or criminal behaviour, just young people being disrespectful, and it made me sad, angry even. My two well-behaved boys were a hundred miles away whilst these brats demonstrated all that was ugly about youth. I couldn't get over the unfairness of it all – those little shits deserved to be going through what my son was, instead of him. And I knew it was wrong to think that, but I thought it anyway.

# 24) Fontwell

## Day 36 – Friday 17 April

Two more days at home helped my mood. I had kept the Easter schedule deliberately light so I could try and be around for the family, but again I felt guilty when I dropped Youngest at school club that morning so that I could go racing.

Eric, a gentle Welsh giant with chunky features and a shock of white hair, picked me up for the ride to the station. He was creaking around the edges a bit, like his ageing taxi (the handle had come off in my hand a couple of months before) but he'd always been there on time and had driven me and my family around for over ten years. He also liked the horses, so I told him about my quest. He listed the courses he'd been to, and there were many. I asked him his favourite

"Ohhh, Sedgefield" he said, "best day of my life that was!"

That was quite a statement. I asked him why, intrigued by the extraordinary happenings of that day to make it the best of his many on this planet.

"Well, you need to go to Sedgefield village first, which isn't so far from the course, and they've got a bakers there. It was the best steak and kidney pie I've ever had! I even took one home for the wife!"

That's why I like Eric - the best day of his life had been shaped by a steak and kidney pie. By the looks of him, he'd had a few of those over the years and must be a very good judge. He'd also won £700 by all accounts, and it was sunny as he remembered it, which both must have contributed as well, but these were clearly afterthoughts compared to the pie.

I'd been to Fontwell twice before, and on both occasions it was connected to a man named Bill. The first was in the early part of 2006, quite by accident. When I say "by accident" I mean that I hadn't planned it that way, not that I was abducted by aliens and forced there against my will (although that might be later what I told The Wife, I can't remember). It was in my early days of teaching at the college, and I'd been sent on a course to Southampton to discover how to tell colleagues that their lesson I'd just observed was only satisfactory, which of course really meant unsatisfactory. Frankly, I'd got bored half way through the day, but I'd already spotted that Fontwell was racing that afternoon which may have clouded my opinion of the morning session.

I arrived unannounced and spotted the diminutive figure of Bill sat at the corner of the bar sipping coffee. For most of his life he had cherished the harder stuff, but had been sober for several years by then. He took a second to eye me up and down, and as recognition spread across his face I knew we would have a great afternoon. Indeed we did, up until I blurted out how lovely it was that his next grandchild would be a girl and he gave me a withering look, one that I'd received many times before, that told me he didn't yet have, or wanted to have, that information. The "fool on the hill", he called me, and I quite liked it.

The second time was in January 2009. Bill had died of cancer a year before and Paul had done remarkably well with the loss of his father. I remember him phoning me on the way back up the A3 on the night Bill died, obviously emotional but somehow also at peace with the situation. The eulogy he gave in Portsmouth's Catholic Cathedral was one of the greatest speeches of all time, and I felt privileged to be one of the fortunate few to be there, both to have known Bill and to have heard those epic words. Paul got it done about as well as I've ever known anybody get something like that done. It was just a shame that Bill wasn't around to see it.

Forward wind a year and we had organised an outing to Bill's favourite racecourse of Fontwell for his family and friends, and Paul and his brother sponsored a race in his honour. They organised a minibus from Portsmouth and adjudged the best turned out in the paddock, and Paul wrote a beautiful piece in the racecard. Unexpectedly, that afternoon it started snowing, and it didn't stop. The Wife got upset with me because I ambitiously attempted to get the train back from Guildford and only got as far as North Camp before the whole thing ground to a halt. I was enormously lucky to find a taxi and to this day I don't know whether the driver perished in a snowdrift on his return journey after dropping me home. So when it came time for my third visit to Fontwell there was nobody I would rather have joined me than my original Passeparone.

The dropping of my new iPhone6 down the loo (long story) had complicated matters logistically, but somehow we met on Platform 4 of Guildford station. I thought back to when I knew this guy at university, in an age before mobile phones, and wondered whether life was harder or easier with the lack of technology back then. We discussed the important issues of the day, such as which party leader had 'won' the televised election debate and how to mix the perfect pint of gin and tonic. We agreed that it should be ice first, then guess the gin from there, and if there was any room left add a dash of tonic. We couldn't agree about the leaders' debate, but this seemed less important than the gin and tonic issue anyway.

Paul is extraordinarily adept at inducing great conversations. He revealed that he had just experienced the weird dead arm thing for the first time in his life at the age of 43. I first had it when I was 15 (if you've had it, you'll know why it's a memorable event) when I awoke in the middle of the night to find my arm had been replaced by a cold and lifeless slab of meat. I sat bolt upright in bed, sweating in shock, with this appendage slapping wildly around and getting caught in the sheets as it did so, and didn't have a clue what to do. Should I scream for my parents? Was it something I'd done wrong? Would it have to be amputated? What would I do for the rest of my life without an arm? After about a minute a faint tingling sensation burnt down through the dead limb, and then I was able to move my fingers, and then my hand, and then after five minutes of petrified agony I had regained my arm, and what a joyous moment that was. Paul and I agreed that it was our responsibility as parents to warn our respective offspring of this potential and not to panic if it occurred, advice as important as "don't speak to strange men" and "if she asks if you like her new haircut, just say yes".

We got the shuttle bus from Barnham and a very fine way to travel it was, especially as it was free and we got a cracking view from the top deck. I love looking in through windows and seeing how other people live, thousands of stories played out every minute through thousands of windows in thousands of homes. Does that make me sound like a pervert? I only do this in passing, you understand, and don't make special journeys to lurk outside houses.

Amazingly, we successfully claimed the first three races between us and celebrated with a late lunch in the very fine facilities. For the record, this was our only lunch of the day, although we did have an early tea later. Paul opted for the fish and chips, which he was very pleased with, and played a game when he'd finished where he tried to flick a pea through a hole in the cardboard tray that was about the same size as a 10p piece. I'd never played this game myself, but it really did seem quite easy. Paul, however, was delighted when he succeeded.

Tracksuit Dave appeared in the food hall and cheered on the winner of the fourth race, which we didn't. Then we really had the fifth race sewn up. It had to be between the top three on the racecard and in the betting. I'd seen

Xaarcet a few times on my travels, and as noble a beast as he was, he couldn't win because he'd been running too consistently to drop in the weights. So it was between the less exposed Follow The Tracks and Exemplary. Paul and I split the bet and we both got 4/1 just before they went 7/2. Paul, in particular, had shown an uncanny knack for getting the markets right and going in at just the right time. Follow The Tracks led but faded to third. Exemplary was cruising behind Xaarcet, but somehow Xaarcet held on. We read the race perfectly, except for the winning bit of course, but a miss is as good as a mile in this game and it became the fifth photo finish out of five to go against me on the tour. There are no prizes for second place in this game, unless of course you are an owner or have backed the horse each way, but neither applied to us.

The afternoon, though, was all about the penultimate race. Morestead, a remarkable chestnut gelding who had run no fewer than 49 times at the West Sussex track, was to be retired after his 50th outing. The Fontwell stalwart recorded the first win of his career at the course in 2008, over hurdles and under the persuasive urgings of none other than AP McCoy, and possessed the unusual distinction of never having fallen in over a hundred races. He set off like a scalded cat, keen to secure his last moment of glory in the south coast sun, but by halfway the writing was on the wall, and he faded to finish fifth. He exited the stage unnoticed, not even receiving a last hurrah in the winners' enclosure because he was unplaced, but perhaps he didn't care.

After I made a few random and, frankly, silly salutations of "Thanks very much!" on the way out, to anybody who would listen (most of whom had no reason to be thanked), I challenged Paul to do five of his own, excluding railway staff, on the way home. He took to his task superbly, rattling them off in sublime fashion and culminated with asking a bunch of guys just outside the station, standing under a large clock, what the time was.

"Thanks very much!" he said triumphantly to their response.

The 17:16 from Barnham had been cancelled because somebody had shat (that's not a spelling mistake) on the seats. Eventually we got back to Guildford, and we allowed ourselves a quick one in the Wetherspoons in recognition of our disciplined timekeeping. Paul, who had been doing rather well up until then, chose that moment to phone home and slur his words terribly, just as his mobile ran out of juice and panic was spread about the home counties concerning his whereabouts. It was almost as though he could hold it together until the pressure was really on, at which point he crumbled in an instant. Predictably, he then fell asleep on his four-minute connecting train home, and then spent an hour rectifying his apnoeic lapse. Somehow, I feel Bill would be proud. Perhaps not of the erratic journey home, but of the truly extraordinary person his son continues to be.

# 25) Ayr

## Day 37 – Saturday 18 April

There was an unexpected breakfast served on the eighty-minute flight to Glasgow. It's not easy to serve a plane-full of people a hot and tasty surprise breakfast on a short flight, as British Airways proved by serving something which was neither hot nor tasty. But it must be tricky, and I had resolved at Kempton to never look a gift horse in the mouth, so gave it my best shot. My mother always says "you never know where your next meal is coming from", which is complete nonsense really as most of the time I have a pretty good idea, but as a young lad I embraced this maternal mantra and have used it throughout my life to justify loading up whenever the opportunity arises.

The train from Paisley to Ayr was as close as I had seen to a Hogarth painting since the streets of Galway nine years ago, but that was past midnight in Galway and this was before midday in Glasgow. Everybody that boarded the train seemed to be carrying their own private brewery in a plastic carrier bag. Anything went, from Buckfast to champagne, as long as it got the holder of the bag steaming drunk before the destination was reached in 45 minutes time.

There were signs on each platform and carriage window that proclaimed no alcohol was allowed on this special service, and that the Police would be in attendance, but the only Police presence was when we arrived, hot and pickled, at Ayr. The assembled menagerie sluiced out of the train, leaving a collage of empty alcohol promises behind them. I consider myself a veteran of drunken racing jollies, but this was staggering even to me. Anything un-drunk was quickly necked by the extremely-drunk before it was confiscated by the real fun-Police.

I joined the soused throng that spilled onto the streets of Ayr, and it became clear that the Hogarthian train was to be followed by a Boschian bus to the course. Being, apparently, the only sober person in Ayrshire, I opted for a taxi. As a mature gent stepped in just ahead of me, I asked him if he was going to the racecourse and whether we might share. Instantly friendly, Robert obliged and shook my hand. The rotund and genial chap, with a Scottish twinkle in his eye, was a professional punter, or "something like that". He'd "done the times" for 20 years, but since retiring from the pub business three years ago he had dedicated himself full time to his form studying – 100 hours a week he said. I felt so lucky to have found this intriguing man in the vastness of the racing world, and was only slightly miffed that he didn't have a tip for me that afternoon.

"The ground's changed now, there's nothing here today for a decent wedge." he sighed.

In the taxi he described how he met a young jockey yesterday and would like to be his agent. This seemed to be quite a departure for a man doing very nicely on Betfair, but Robert explained,

"It's something I've always wanted to do. I just want to see a wee bit of the other side of life."

I knew the feeling. He got the taxi to drop us at what I can only describe as a country club just to the side of the racecourse. The Western Hotel was a haven of tranquillity, so far removed from the bedlam of the train that I wondered whether I was dreaming. Fountains played gently in front of a handsome residence, and a couple of crooners in dinner jackets wafted out some gentle Sinatra numbers to soothe the assembled punters in the glorious sunshine of a perfect Ayr springtime. Famous trainers and owners drifted around and I felt slightly out of place, but Robert assured me that all I needed for membership of this exclusive enclave was a Club badge, and he was right. Inside, we dropped our bags at an amenable reception and, as Robert had refused to share the cost of the taxi, I bought him a beer while he described his punting philosophy.

It was all about the times, for Robert. Therefore, he was very keen on Douvan for the Champion Hurdle next year rather than reigning champ Faugheen, whom he described as a stayer who might not even defend his crown. We agreed that Coneygree's performance was incredible, with so many good horses unable to keep up behind him. Robert instantly recalled the time of his Gold Cup demolition "6:43" and thought he was a good thing next year, if he stayed sound. We then had a minor disagreement about betting strategy. With my record compared to his, who was I to pontificate, but I maintained that very occasionally odds-on can be value in the right circumstances. I used the lovely Tanerko Emery as a case in point.

"No, no, no!" Robert insisted.

He would only bet at 4/1 or more, or perhaps as low as 5/2 if there weren't many runners, and he didn't mind each way. The mathematician in me protested, and I outlined a hypothetical game where Robert could roll a dice and I would offer him even money if he rolled 1 to 5, but still he couldn't be swayed. Whilst I didn't agree with his maths, I couldn't help but admire his discipline.

Robert took me on a tour of the facilities. We crossed the horsewalk to the parade ring area, and he got annoyed with the bookies there for offering poorer odds than the main ring. He championed the common punter, and was upset that the first-time innocents might take 18/1 when there was 25/1 freely available elsewhere. I asked him why he came racing if he only placed bets online and didn't even do that most days. Was it to see them in the paddock, or assess the ground conditions? Or perhaps it was to have a few beers? "You've hit that right on the button!" he said

## Planning

Finding a path through the fixtures maze

## The Racehorse Sanctuary

Anna, Sue and Graham with Repton

## Bloom

Winning the Battle Of The Bands final at the Cavern Club in Exeter

## Chepstow

A stunning creation on the way to the course

## Black Narcissus

My beautiful nemesis strides out at Newton Abbot

## Life On The Road

The Satnav,
the Racing Post,
and of course
the traffic

## Grand National

A fine sculpture
sited near the
Doom Bar Bar
at Aintree

## Full English

It was important
to maintain a
balanced diet
whilst travelling

### Printing Money

Tanerko Emery after winning at Ffos Las

### Country Club

The Western Hotel, a glorious venue for the Ayr Scottish National

### The Bray Royale

Arriving in style at Windsor

to the last suggestion, with a few Scottish expletives thrown in. On that aspect of racing we were in agreement then.

He told me Ayr was his favourite course, and I could see why. It was a sell out, but we could still move around and get a bet on and, with a little patience, a beer as well. Two years ago Robert went to the Cheltenham Festival on Gold Cup day, and walked out an hour later in disgust. And since then, I pointed out, it had got worse with record crowds and reduced capacity. It was hot, very hot, and I realised I'd misjudged the weather forecast and over-dressed. In other words, the forecast got it wrong and it was about 24 and sunny instead of 11 and cloudy. The pressure cooker atmosphere of the train has dissipated and people were having fun in the sun. Robert was adept at talking to anyone and everyone and I got swept along behind him like some apprentice.

I backed The Last Samuri at 5/2 in the first. It had been running very well for a while and I think Robert just about approved. Then we toured the other bookies to prove his earlier point as we could only find 2/1 and 9/4 inside the stand and back at the paddock. Puffin Billy, the Ascot conqueror of my Thomas Crapper, set off in front but his jumping was under pressure on this faster ground, as I'd predicted. What I hadn't predicted was that after my Last Samuri had swept past him at the final fence, he would stoically battle back to get up on the line. That was the second time Puffin Billy had done that to me, but I couldn't help but admire his bravery. Perhaps I just needed to start backing him rather than going against him.

Robert went to the loo and we lost touch in the melee of a busy day at the races. I returned to the idyllic haven of the Western Hotel, thinking he might retrace our steps, but that was the last I saw of him. As he put it in the taxi, you never know what's going to happen during a day at the races – we were flung together by chance, and drifted apart in the hubbub of a large and fluid crowd. Perhaps we would meet up at Perth in just five days time, if I was lucky.

In the Scottish National I fancied both Pricewise horses, as well as three others, but I refused to back five horses. That would be silly. So I stuck with the Pricewise selections of Wayward Prince and Man With Van. I watched the race from the splendid position of the country club lawn. A few others had cottoned on to this marvellous viewpoint just past the winning post, and we shared a strangely muted finale to a thrilling performance from Wayward Prince. It seemed wrong to shout in this peaceful idyll, but inside I was buzzing - he paid 32/1 on the Tote to secure my biggest win of the tour so far. Less than a week later, it was announced that both Wayward Prince and his trainer Hilary Parrott had retired, but what a glorious way to finish!

I became very aware that I had a plane to catch, and so left the serene surroundings of the hotel soon afterwards. The return train was calm before the storm of sloshed Glaswegian humanity smashed in, and I made the plane comfortably. On the flight back I was only a few seats away from Statto, or Angus Loughran as he is sometimes known. But I rued my decision at check in to move to the extra legroom seats of the exit row – if I'd stayed where I was randomly assigned I would have been next to Channel 4 frontman Nick Luck, with commentator Simon Holt not too far away. Again, what the Gods of Probability gave with one hand they took away with the other. The inexorable pull of the balancing scales is never far away where chance is concerned.

# 26) Windsor

## Day 39 – Monday 20 April

Windsor holds a lot of happy memories for me. When the boys were smaller we would go for walks and cycle rides in the Great Park, get as far as the Copper Horse with tremendous views up the straight mile to the castle, and fill carrier bags full to brimming with conkers that rained down on us as we scurried underneath. Later on, I joined Jason, Paul and others on a fun but ultimately exhausting weekend paddle down the Thames in Canadian canoes before finally ending the agony and having a slap up meal to finish in Browns by the riverside. One thing I'd never done, despite several recommendations, was Monday evening racing. Now was the moment.

Browns was again the meeting point, and I was the first to arrive. A smattering of shiny, happy customers drank in the sun on the patio whilst I crouched in the shade and got down to the hard work (in a not-very-hard, non-coal-mining kind of way) that is studying the form. I was to be joined by no less than seven companions for Windsor's first evening meeting of the season, but for half an hour I relished the early meditation - just me and the Racing Post silently swapping thoughts in the seclusion of the form-lines.

The usual suspects arrived and it was time to go. As we crossed the road for the short boat-hop to the racecourse, Clive discovered his car lights were flashing. The chap in the car park, who was 'looking after the car' in exchange for a £10 note ("He was wearing a badge!" protested Clive when we quizzed him on this curious transaction) looked non-plussed. Instead of issuing a proper ticket he had simply put a piece of paper under the windscreen wipers that said 'Jimmy Carr'. This was all very strange. Perhaps Clive's car disapproved of being named after a comedian and was making a scene in protest, but I thought it was just upset about being ineptly slewed across two parking bays – clever, these modern cars.

We boarded the Bray Royale and were enthusiastically told by the ticket staff "There's a bar downstairs!" Perhaps they were on commission? If they were, we did them a favour by attempting the rare feat of ordering, paying, and drinking a round of beers before the boat reached the course ten minutes later. We disembarked and dealt out the complimentary online tickets. Free entry is a growing and welcome trend amongst racecourses, but I was sure they valued highly the database of email addresses, and would probably make it back in beer sales that evening anyway. As we headed through the turnstiles it seemed busy, and the thronging mass was diverse. I suspected a large percentage were new to racing and thought that, despite the slightly crowded environment, it could only be good for Windsor and the sport in general. Someone was singing and playing the guitar (I think they were allowed to) and the buzzing racegoers basked in the warmth of a sun-drenched April evening, drinking lager from pop-up bars to quench their thirst. The fish and chips van had the biggest queue I'd seen at....well, the biggest queue I'd ever seen, really.

My big fancy of the evening, the Godolphin-owned Wild Storm in the third race, was nowhere near the forecasted price and I refused to go in at long odds-on. I'd seen too many good things turn out to not be quite so good this last month. He won of course, but I was quite glad I didn't make the bet, in a perverted sort of way. Clive questioned my ideology, saying that if it was a winning bet then it must have been a good one, but he can't park his car properly and hands £10 notes to strangers in car parks, so I had to take anything he said with a bucket of salt.

After my Lingfield spat with Barry Dennis, I was beginning to really dislike bookmakers, and Windsor only added more fuel to the fire. In the fourth race one of them had a non-runner available right up until the off. I wondered how many newbie punters didn't realise Bushcraft wasn't racing and assumed they had just lost their money? And there was a Russian sounding lady who didn't have a name above her board and issued change with a delayed reaction, possibly hoping that the punter would not realise or forget that it was due and walk off with just the betting slip.

In the fifth race Arc Lighter was backed in from 4/1 to 2/1 favourite, which must have represented quite a weight of money. He was denied by an outsider called Carthage, and a stewards enquiry was called. The replay showed no hint of interference, so the only reason for the delay must have been because one of the stewards had made a hefty investment on the favourite. After ten minutes of deliberation, the placings remain unaltered, as they obviously decided that backing the second horse was not a good enough reason to demote the winner.

The sun waned to a milky horizon and my earlier chiding of Simon for bringing his coat came back to haunt me. I had to buy some fish and chips, purely to keep warm you understand, but at least by then the queue had disappeared. It's all about timing, you know. I found Pete standing motionless in the betting ring, peering at the boards in a mixture of concentration and puzzled alarm, like my ex-students looking at a whiteboard full of second order differential equations. Either that, or he'd frozen to the spot in the gathering chill and required gentle reheating with water bottles before he could free himself.

The trouble with the evening, as Nick described on the way home, was that due to the configuration of the course and the sheer number of punters it was just about impossible to watch the action, other than on the giant screen. None of us even knew where the parade ring was, and the only inkling we had that we were witnessing a live sporting event was a flash of brown on the other side of the running rail every half an hour.

Perhaps we were being too harsh – did the large crowd there really care if they couldn't see the horses in the flesh? Did the lottery winner mind if they hadn't seen the balls come out of the machine? There was a woman sat on the concrete steps of the grandstand scraping a scratchcard, and I pompously sneered at her for gambling on a racecourse! Was her £2 any more ill-spent than my each way on a 40/1 outsider? I didn't know, but I couldn't help but agree with Nick that horses should be somewhat prominent in an evening at the races.

It was a prime example of the paradox that had been shadowing my journey so far. For horse racing to survive it needs to attract new punters with free entry, pop concerts and festivals, but the more successful it is at that, the more the actual horse racing seems to get sidelined. If you'd told me 25 years ago when I began my punting education that I could bet on virtual horse racing from Steepledowns I'd have laughed you out of Ladbrokes, but now it's as much a staple feature of the betting shop day as the fruit machines. Nick no longer takes his son to the 20:20 cricket since its transition from Saturday afternoon sport to Friday night booze-fest.

Again, I know I'm at risk of sounding hypocritical, given that I had a few beers at Windsor and didn't even want to know where the paddock was. And I must point out that there was a good atmosphere and a lot of people would have gone home very happy with their evening. It's a tricky balancing act, the tightrope that our racecourses need to tread in order to evolve and survive without losing their essence, but if any of them is looking for a new chief executive to oversee that evolution, I'd be happy to give it a go.

# 27) Brighton

## Day 40 – Tuesday 21 April

I've always liked Brighton, ever since a football tour at sixth form college. We played well, and then in the pub one night Stevie M bet everyone that he could piss three pints, and he did! Those sort of things were impressive when you were at sixth form. I suppose they still are, really. I liked the place even more when The Wife bought me a print there as a gift for our wedding, and then 15 years later during a family trip I bought her an eternity ring from The Lanes. I could make a joke about our marriage seeming like an eternity but, despite the trying times (reach for the sick bucket), I know our love is eternal.

In between those two events, I had also helped to send two different Stags to their own eternal glories from the East Sussex resort. The first time we stayed at a pub called The Black Horse, an establishment that seemed to cater well for the Stag trade (big dormitories, no locks on the doors to worry about when you stumble in, relaxed serving hours in the bar, and a decent breakfast). Five years after the first, I was invited on another jolly to Brighton.

"Where are we staying?" I enquired.

"Oh it's a little place, you won't have heard of it," I was told "a pub called The Black Horse."

Going to new racecourses was exciting, which was good seeing as I had only previously visited a third of them so far on my tour. I never knew what I was going to find, and there could always be a little gem waiting for me in some unsuspecting corner of the country. The first thing that struck me about Brighton was that I had no idea where the start was. My eyes scanned the distance but it remained hidden from view somewhere to the east, possibly Eastbourne for all I knew. There was an element of Chepstow about the place, but it wasn't as cold or windy. The stands perched tall and resolute, casting a jagged shadow over the course so that in the last furlong it was like watching the finish through an old-fashioned kaleidoscope as they flashed between light and dark.

There was a tremendous view to the distant sea and, to a lesser extent, the housing estate that crouched in the valley in between. Think of three slightly concave sides of a rounded square and you'd not be far off. It was the first course of my journey that was 'incomplete', or not a complete circuit, so there was a limit to the length of the races (which seemed to be about a mile and a quarter if the afternoon races were to be a guide). Until somebody builds a bridge over the housing estate across the fourth seaward side of the square, it would be impossible to 'go around again', but I think that bridge unlikely given current planning constraints, and it would require a feat of engineering that would have Brunel scratching his head. I couldn't see much of the action except for the final half-mile, and I'd not enjoyed that at other courses so far, but it was certainly quirky and for some reason I liked it. It was also one of the most picturesque parade rings I'd encountered, but I wasn't sure the horses really appreciated it.

After the first race I ventured inside to the hall under the grandstand. People started talking to me and it was wonderfully spacious. I got a drink at the aptly named Long Bar and had to wait about 20 seconds to be served. The barman was very smiley and energetic, and for some reason I thought he hailed from Canada, when it was actually Finland. I asked if he liked the horses and he explained he was amazed by the way that some British courses, like this one, are in the middle of towns. In Finland if you wanted to go racing it required a trek into the wilderness.

I supped my pint whilst reading the Post. It's what you do when you go racing on your own. I noticed that the Martin Wills Writing Awards, commemorating the journalist and amateur jockey who died in 1992 at the aged of 39, were inviting entries again. In 1997, during the gap between finishing accountancy and starting training to become a teacher, I was shortlisted for a piece on (rather predictably) the Cheltenham Festival. But my window of journalistic opportunity then evaporated as I passed the age limit for the under-26 award and focused on my new career. It would seem, though, that the writing flame had never really died and was just waiting for an opportunity to burn brightly once more.

There was a competitive betting ring at Brighton. In the third race the five horses were priced at 2/1, 6/1, 7/2, 3/1 and 6/1. I thought that was pretty decent, and later worked out that it was only slightly over-round at 109%. I know that sounds complicated, but anything less than 100% and the bookies are guaranteed to lose money, irrespective of who wins, if you place the right combination of bets. Imagine a race with just two horses both priced at 3/1 (and believe me that would be entirely imaginary!) which would be an under-round market of just 50%. In other words, you could put £10 on both, an outlay of £20, and get a guaranteed return of £40. I also thought it was pretty decent when I managed to secure the 3/1 in the above list at 100/30 and Gannicus won nicely.

A huge barney had developed during the previous few days about the starting prices for the Grand National, played out in the courtroom that was the pages of the Racing Post. At 165%, the market was surely the most profitable of the year for many bookmakers, some of whom had decided to defend themselves by citing free market theories, or arguing that other retailers made their money at Christmas so why couldn't they take advantage of their April bonanza? It was an interesting debate because bigger profits for bookmakers usually means, through a complicated and frequently shifting funding landscape, more money returned to the sport via the levy. But this won't satisfy the common punter who may quite rightly feel somewhat exploited by the odds on offer in the biggest betting race of the year.

I was getting increasingly fed up with bookmakers in general, and whichever way they tried to spin it, a 65% margin was unacceptable. I should point out that it was the powerful off-course firms that were most to blame, as they can manipulate the on course market easily, and clearly had in this case. I was astonished that Shutthefrontdoor went off as 6/1 favourite for the Grand National, given that I saw 8/1 freely and widely available just before the off, but this only demonstrated the depths of their powers. If the favourite had won, hedging their liabilities in this way would have saved them millions, and therefore collectively cost the common punter millions. It also appeared that the big off-course firms knew which individual on-course bookmakers to target. The SP system is not based on an average of all bookmakers in the ring but quite a small sample, and the conspiracy theorists suggested that the list had got into the wrong hands, making it much easier for the big firms to sway the starting prices with less cash.

It may not have possessed the gravitas of the Grand National meeting, but the decent odds on offer made the situation at Brighton all the more laudable. A small but happy crowd enjoyed a competitive market at a seaside holiday venue where you might have expected newbie tourists to be easily exploited. Well done to the ring and management of Brighton – quirky it may be, but a good day out it also undoubtedly was.

# 28) Epsom

## Day 41 – Wednesday 22 April

News reached me from one of my loyal sources that the M25 was up the spout. Closed in fact, which meant that everything was up the spout, in the traffic world of chaos theory. I had originally discounted the train to Epsom Downs due to it taking three times as long as driving, but I then revisited the national rail website and found that Epsom was twice as quick to get to as Epsom Downs, bizarrely.

However, I was up against it and four things needed to happen for me to make the 12:18. Firstly, there could be no hold ups on the three-mile drive to the station – tick. Secondly, there had to be a space in the always crowded car park – amazingly, tick. Thirdly, there could be no queue at the ticket machine – yes, in with a chance! And finally, the train had to be at least two minutes late – ah. The one time I wanted a train to be late and it was bang on time. I contemplated aborting the ticket transaction and sprinting the 100 or so yards across the bridge to the other platform, but the days of jointly holding the school record in the 4x100m relay are long gone, along with my sprinting legs. Discretion, it seems, really is the better part of valour when you're in your 40s.

As I stood on the platform watching the train depart from the other side, I realised that I was beginning to deliberately tempt fate, like an errant schoolboy dwelling on his way to class just to see how his teacher would react. Despite realising I was cutting it very fine, I still decided to put the washing away and grab an apple for the journey. It was almost a subconscious way of stopping my challenge without actually making a decision to stop, so that I could look back and say 'it was out of my hands, you know, fate conspired against me, I missed the train and the M25 was closed, what could I do?' If so, it was a coward's way out of the situation that was enveloping me. Perhaps it was just my way of laying down a marker, my line in the sand – if I was going to carry on with this absurd escapade, it would be on my terms, and with the washing put away. My family might be facing a stressful time without me, but they would do so with clothes in their cupboards! If that was the case, it was at the very least a false economy because losing two hours of writing time on the train would only mean catching up that evening.

Whatever it was, I got back in the car and drove to Epsom. The Satnav thought the M25 had cleared, and guessing that other routes were likely to have been affected by the hold up anyway, I trusted it. We had reached a grudging state of respect, forged in the cauldron of last minute dashes for first races, and it didn't let me down. The clockwise carriageway was backed up for three junctions, but I was going anti-clockwise and got there easily. It was £5 to park, the first parking fee of my tour, but I got a spare ticket from a chap in the entrance hall and I was up already.

I was meeting my campaign manager, Paul 2, who is distinct and separate to my Passepar-one Paul. He was not really my campaign manager, just a friend who I quizzed before I started. He helped me plan out my project in a pub in London, having vast experience of enabling people and companies to do absurd things, and was keen that I considered postponing the venture for a year so that I could get it done properly. But I knew it was now or never, and hoped that the half-arsed nature of the tour lent a little spontaneity and charm to the whole shebang, even if I still didn't know how I was getting from Edinburgh airport to Perth races tomorrow.

He arrived just before the first race and got a quick bet on before joining me in the stand. Paul had backed

Smoothtalkinrascal; somehow I knew he would. There was a great view of the winding, skatepark of a track that finished with a camber that would attract warning signs on any road. It was the second course in as many days that was 'incomplete' and again I kind of liked its eccentricity.

I had been to Epsom once before, on Oaks day in 2012 as a guest of the Household Cavalry, courtesy of a very kind invite from Brian. We were entertained in an enclosure in the middle of the course and spent a fine day enjoying the complimentary buffet. Despite the throng surrounding the nearby funfair, we felt away from the hurly burly of the main enclosures, and because of the distinct camber it felt like the action was specially tilted towards us for our privileged viewing pleasure.

Today I was seeing everything from the other side of the fence, as it were, and it definitely gave a new perspective on the beautiful green setting of the Downs. There were zebras everywhere, and a stray pedestrian would have been forgiven for thinking they were viewing the African plains. There was even one by the finishing post (inanimate, I must clarify) and I became worried that the horses would be confused in the shadow of the post, and pull up sharply to stand rigid with their striped cousins. Paul, who understands these corporate things, explained that the sponsor would have paid some sort of agency a lot of money to come up with this stunningly simple and utterly meaningless image.

I somehow backed an 8/1 winner in the opener and we retired under the stand to celebrate my win. The bar was a study in slow, as young and inept staff operated beer pumps and tills like they were prodding alien life-forms. There was no post-office queuing system here, and the service injustice reeked like nasty aftershave. Paul had demolished his burger and chips by the time I emerged from the scrum with two pints, and he was astounded by the average age in the indoor arena. There were mature people here who would not move from their seats for the entire afternoon, and not get the faintest whiff of a horse, let alone sunshine or fresh air. Paul was confused by the idea of coming to a racecourse and watching the action on a giant indoor TV. I was too, but each to his own.

We discussed the future of racing. Paul did an MBA about 15 years ago that culminated with a three-month stint at Harlequins rugby club. Back then they were struggling with attendances, and the CEO explained to Paul how they weren't competing with football, they were aiming for the families going to the shopping mall on a Saturday afternoon. Forward wind 15 years and they were hugely successful and rugby had clearly demonstrated that a sport could reinvent its way to success. Paul talked about breaking down the barriers to entry for new customers, but I was worried that if you dumbed it down too much, you would just attract dumb racegoers. They tried changing the odds to decimals a few years ago but people didn't like it. Racing is rich with history and tradition, weird and wonderful language and rituals. It's partly what attracted me to the sport all those years ago.

Paul thought there was mileage in a team-based idea, with jockeys' silks in the team colours. This was exactly the sort of blue sky nonsense I wanted from my dear friend, and explained how the Shergar Cup didn't really work, in my opinion, as punters didn't care if they were backing GB&I or the Rest of the World, as long as they had a winner. I'm not sure the two sports are comparable. We both love watching rugby because we have played it and respect the skills and bravery on show. I suspected that only a few people in the crowd at Epsom had ridden competitively – the way the vast majority of us related to our sport was by literally taking a stake in the outcome rather than pinning allegiance to a particular flag. Sure, we had our favourites, but there was always another race half an hour away with different colours to choose from.

I liken Paul to a latter-day da Vinci. Most of his ideas are ridiculous, but at some point he may just stumble upon a helicopter and the whole thing could move forwards - evolution through deconstruction, he called it. Of course, he was utterly right that the demographic under the Investec Stand was alarming, and he was not alone in his thinking – Nick Rust, the new head honcho of the BHA concurred with his assertion that, according to the dramatic headline in the Racing Post, "British Racing Is At A Crossroads!" and "we'll face decline unless we deal with it – the time for action is now!"

Rust's proposals are ambitious, but they need to be. He wants an extra one million racegoers and 1,000 horses by 2020, and is concerned that owners on average get a return of just 26p in the pound. I too want racing to evolve and grow, but not lose sight of what has made it great over the years, and I worry where the extra million people are going to come from. If you replace the old codgers with young trendies who have no understanding or particular interest in horse racing, they will eventually figure out that paying £5 to jostle in a mosh pit for a crap pint of lager is not that much fun, even if Bananarama are playing afterwards. They will return to the pubs and clubs where the lager is just as expensive but served in nicer surroundings, by which time the old codgers will have got fed up with the pop concerts and gone home to watch the racing on TV.

I asked Paul to guess the turnover and profit of as revered a course as Newbury, and he massively overestimated both. He rightly questioned whether the current model was sustainable, and whether a cull of racecourses would be necessary for the future strength of the herd. But I wouldn't know where to start – it's the Fontwells and Market Rasens that give the sparkling variety not found in other homogenised sports. In the harsh light of market forces, natural selection will happen, as Hereford and Folkestone know only too well, but we must cherish our diversity for as long as is possible. If you were building a track now you probably wouldn't choose to build Epsom, but I believe racing would be poorer without it.

The last race we watched featured a hot favourite at 10/11, which I thought was going to win, despite my recent wariness of odds-on shots. Mejazy didn't realise that he was responsible for a minuscule ripple on the timeline of horse racing evolution, but that afternoon he unwittingly shouldered the burden of whether Paul left with a profit or never bet again. He held on, just, and the future of our sport was just a tiny bit safer that night.

# 29) Perth

## Day 42 – Thursday 23 April

Perth was the longest round trip of the journey, but it went smoothly enough. The taxi driver from Edinburgh airport was an interesting guy who gently stitched me up for the fare off the meter. My laissez-faire approach to planning may have been dashingly spontaneous, but it was also expensive. I could have got an earlier flight, or faffed around with trains, but I was fully in the mode of 'buying time', and this seemed like time well bought.

The cabbie, Steve, told me about some of the professional gamblers he'd driven. He'd met a guy who had an incredibly simple system – back the first three in the betting in eight-horse races, as long as the favourite was no less than 2/1. If the favourite won you would at least get your money back, and if the other two won you would definitely be in profit. At the other end of the spectrum was a Swedish punter who knew everything, even down to the softness of the water the horses preferred to drink. This seemed like overkill, but he had apparently won over £50,000 on the trotting that year so the results spoke for themselves.

Then the taxi-talk turned to golf. Steve had got his teaching badge and used to have a simulator that he would travel around schools with, getting kids into the game, but he couldn't make it work so now he just played golf, and bet on it, of course. I have an enormous imaginary filing cabinet full of outrageous hard luck stories with the golf, just next to the enormous imaginary bin full of losing betting slips, so I bored Steve with my first foray into golf punting some 24 years earlier when Christy O'Connor Jnr somehow one-putted the last eight greens at Woburn to snatch the title from Tony Johnstone who I'd backed at 20/1.

After a minor diversion up and down the M90 we found our way to the poorly signed racecourse. As I trudged in past a workshop that the course map described as 'The Workshop' I realised that this was real, proper jump racing. I was immediately drawn to a sign that said 'Hog Roast & Booze!' (I'm a sucker for this sort of thing) and started by examining the offerings from the Strathbraan Brewery. It was a toss-up between the two prophetically named ales Head East and Look West, but I went for the former and a very nice drop it was too. Certainly better than the warm pork and fat roll that was purporting to be hog roast and crackling.

There was a beautifully relaxed mix of people at Perth, entirely diverse in their background and clothing, and I thought back to Paul 2's ideas from the previous day. He liked colours, but I felt they divided people. I remembered a Charity Shield a few years before when, in the close confines of a crowded tube train, red and blue shirts mixed with good-natured banter. Then we all came out onto Wembley Way and the stewards started separating the colours like a giant conveyor belt of washing. Having got a free spare ticket from a mate, and with allegiance to neither team, I strode down the middle as the abuse began to be hurled. It was not the witty teasing of the earlier tube train, but snarling aggression that came from somewhere dark and nasty. I was marooned in a no man's land between the warring factions and so experienced all the venom that both sides had to offer without the comfort of kinship. It was as clear an example as you could hope to see that when you artificially separate people they lose their perspective and inhibitions. No matter that the man on the receiving end of your vitriol was happily sharing a carriage with you five minutes before. Segregation doesn't offer comfort, it breeds distrust and anger, and wearing colours often amplifies the ugliness.

218

Everyone at Perth was looking for a winner, but they didn't care about its colours, and neither did I. The only enemies were the bookmakers, and that was a predominantly well-mannered conflict. I looked for Robert, the "sort of" professional gambler I had met in Ayr. This was his home course, he'd told me, but he was nowhere to be seen. Neither was a Racing Post, and my now regular search for the daily made its Scottish debut. A steward on the gate said they didn't sell them and pointed me towards the racecard shed. The ladies there were packing up, having just sold out, and it looked like I would be bereft of any form guide for the afternoon when a guy tapped me on the arm and offered his.

"Don't you need it?" I called as he marched off, but he just gave a shrug that seemed to indicate that he had given up punting for life after the first race.

In the competitive second race Royal Boru had no right to be up there in the betting. I backed Burnt Sienna, on account of it having decent form, and the fact that I used to paint in oils in my A-level Art class. It ran poorly and Royal Boru won easily. Lesson for the day: if there's no earthly reason why it can win but it is being backed, go with it!

Suddenly, I spotted the gorgeous Tanerko Emery on the card for the third race and rushed to the parade ring to assess his wellbeing. He had a white smudge on his hind pokey-outey bit (I know that's not the right term, horsey people) where he might have scraped himself in the horsebox. Other than that he looked well in the April sunshine, but so did the others, and the drop back in distance to two and a half miles rather than the three that he sauntered home over at Ffos Las translated into a medium wager, rather than the large one I was considering. It was harder work for him than last time, with better opponents, but Paddy Brennan gave him a great ride, keeping him handier over the shorter trip so that his abundant stamina came into play. He won a tad cosily and was quickly becoming a favourite of mine.

It was also proving hard work for the crowd, in a way, and fair Scottish faces went slightly pink in the sunny and relaxed atmosphere. People found space to fall asleep on the lush and welcoming carpet of grass that stretched out over a furlong down the enclosure. I secured a spot against the fence and tried to resist the temptation to nod off, worried about missing my flight home. I listened to the fourth race with a barely cogent mind, and my selection fell at the second last when disputing the lead. Whether he would have won I had no idea – I was drifting into the somnambulant beauty that was a day at Perth Races. I abruptly came-to as I realised that the contest was an eight-horse race with the favourite more than 2/1, and the third favourite had just won at 5/1. Surely it couldn't be as easy as Steve's professional had said?

The fifth race has a prize fund of £25,000, the biggest of the day anywhere in Britain, as the commentator reminded us frequently. I'd seen Creevytennant at Ascot where he won without my support, but I wasn't sure about the ground and the odds of 5/4. There were some decent sorts with excuses for their recent runs at large odds, and I backed two of them accordingly. Witness In Court obliged at a generous 11/1.

I hadn't had a really good day with the punting as yet, but I was getting close, and making inroads into the earlier deficit. The betting really was the least of my worries on this project, but the punter's pride within me wanted to turn around at the end and say I was winner. I wasn't far off, but a little way is a long way in the betting world. It was interesting, though, that this was a day I had drifted through with an almost Zen-like calm – I'd hardly thought about the betting and had walked away with a tidy profit.

I got the train back to Edinburgh and we passed through Kirkcaldy, a significant place name as my Dad used to drive up there and back in a day for his job. It was much easier on the train and plane than in a car, I thought, and was reminded of what a hero he remained to me despite his advancing years. I had struggled desperately with the concept of leaving my boys in their formative and needy times, but the thought that I still loved and revered my father despite his occasional absences, perhaps even more so for the extraordinary feats he achieved behind the wheel, gave me a small crumb of comfort for the preposterous fairytale I was still chasing.

The true turmoil I was going through was still hidden deep below the surface, buried in a box that was labelled 'To be opened in August, perhaps?' but the glimpse of a sign on a Scottish railway station brought the issue into a painful focus. I knew I wasn't a better man for blindly ploughing on, and silently spilling tears onto a laptop keyboard wouldn't make it better. Whatever option my father would have chosen in my situation, he would have made a decision rather than just letting things drift.

# 30) Plumpton

## Day 43 – Friday 24 April

The Wife noted that I was dragging my heels slightly on the way to Trumpton, as she called it. When I eventually climbed into the car The Satnav told me the M25 had gone wrong yet again (if it were a horse it would surely have been retired by now) and it would take over two and a half hours to get to East Sussex. Again, the Gods of Probability seemed to be taunting me, putting obstacles in my path as if to say "do you really want to keep doing this Neil?" But somehow I started the engine and set off cross-country. Six weeks ago I didn't know why I was beginning the improbable mission, and now I didn't know why I wasn't stopping it.

Plumpton heralded that I had started the second half of my shindig, but this landmark just served to magnify the task still remaining rather than promote a renewed vigour for the remaining five weeks. It was also the hardest to locate. The Satnav wanted to take me down a dirt track, but I was still carrying the mental scars from the moment decades earlier when I parked The Wife's car in a soggy Monmouthshire copse after an over-ambitious short cut got disastrously out of control during a treasure hunt for a friend's birthday. To this day I'm not sure how we got it back up the 1 in 3 slippery slope, or whether the two friendly hikers who helped are now suffering from some mud-inhalation related disease. Certainly the clutch was never the same. Or the car, really. So I'd learnt my lesson and ignored the appealing possible short cut.

When I finally found the southern outpost I discovered the racecourse was, how shall I put it, unremarkable. There were a couple of big sheds for stands, and a bar under one of them where a band cranked out some old favourites whilst punters sang along. The one exception to the mundane fare was a big sign with a map of Britain, with little finishing posts marking all the racecourses. For a moment I panicked that I had been usurped by a more organised rival with posters, but then remembered I had read about Richard Farquhar's quest in the Racing Post a month before, along with his entirely noble reasons for attempting it. I recalled that he was adopting a more literal interpretation of the British racecourse pilgrimage by choosing to walk between them, and seeing the route sprawling the length and breadth of Britain, I became even more impressed by his resolve, but also sneakily jealous that he was therefore avoiding the M25.

I spotted a tall and track-suited gentleman and guessed he must be Richard. As I approached I noticed he was replenishing his fluids with Guinness (it's good for you, they used to say before the Health and Safety lot got involved), which immediately drew me to the man. Although his was a far more onerous, not to mention altruistic, task than mine, I felt a vague comradeship with the complete stranger, and was unabashed about introducing myself. It transpired that he was, at that point, just six racecourses into his 13-month journey and had just completed his walk from Brighton. I asked him how it was going, and in particular, how were the legs?

"Ah, it's all about the legs!" he agreed. "They're alright, touch wood. I'm quietly quite relieved at how they feel, because they did 145 miles in eight days this month. I did 62 miles to Taunton and at the end of that I felt surprisingly fresh."

"In a day?" I spluttered in shock.

"No it was three days. 27, 25 and then 10 on the final morning before racing, but it was hard yards, up in the Mendips."

As a 'veteran' of a tiny chunk of the Cotswold Way, I was relieved for him. I was a younger and fitter man when

I did that, but had vastly underestimated the differences between running and walking and felt like I'd broken my feet by the end of just three days. But it was difficult to keep Richard away from his main topic of conversation for long, and he explained the motivation behind his extraordinary undertaking.

"Pancreatic cancer got £700,000 in government funding in 2013, which for a disease that kills 9,000 people a year and has the same survival stats as it had 40 years ago - you've got less than a 1 in 4 chance of living a year - it just seems wrong," he said passionately, "so I want to raise more than the government!"

As he was splitting his fundraising with the Racing Welfare charity, his aim was therefore £1.4 million. This target seemed almost as ambitious as walking nearly 3,000 miles, but a later glance at his website revealed an enormous cast list of horse racing glitterati who were supporting his cause. Publicity had been garnered from such notables as Channel 4 Racing and the Racing Post. Perhaps that was what my campaign manager Paul envisaged when he talked about "doing it properly", and Richard's professional approach contrasted sharply with my own ramshackle affair. Even so, I too had been shown much generosity from good folk who had a lot of other better things to do with their time, including for that matter Richard himself who should surely have been having an energy bar or an ice bath rather than talking to me.

"But people in racing support people who put back into racing," he said, adding "the support I've had has been completely ridiculous."

He looked at my schedule to see if our paths were to cross again on our very different travels, and we made a plan to meet up at Wincanton in mid-May, before wishing each other good luck in our respective travels. So I'd met John at Taunton when he was finishing his quest, and now Richard in Plumpton who was just beginning his own.

Mine was a little past halfway and I was feeling increasingly weary, but really had no right to given what others were attempting. The next day was to be the end of the road for a certain champion jockey, and his unbridled commitment over 20 years really did put my jaded approach after just seven weeks into context. If AP could ride over 4,000 winners, and Richard could walk almost 3,000 miles, surely I could visit 58 racecourses without moaning about it too much?

# 31) Sandown

## Day 44 – Saturday 25 April

There was only one story to be followed at Sandown and, strangely, it didn't concern my amazing achievement of passing the halfway point of my racecourse quest. AP McCoy was to ride his final race in a glittering career spanning a quarter of a century. For the last twenty of those years, he had been Champion Jumps Jockey.

It is hard to compare achievements in different sports. Was Tiger Woods a better golfer than Phil Taylor a darts player? Did Muhammad Ali dominate boxing more than Michael Schumacher did motor racing? By whichever criteria you attempt to rank them, it would be hard not to have near the top of the list a man so famous in his particular world that he is known simply by his initials, AP. It is as near a certainty as you are likely to get in horse racing that we shall never again see anyone dominate in the way he has, and in a sport where the randomness of injury takes a regular and inevitable toll, it is an astonishing achievement to remain undefeated in a professional career spanning two decades.

Of course, by that I don't mean that McCoy won every race, but there were factors beyond his control that the other sporting immortals on the list never had to contend with. A golf ball will not have an off day, and darts do not care what type of ground they are flying over. With AP you felt as though he was good enough to win even if his mount wasn't, and he often made them do just that. Nobody except the man himself, and perhaps those closest to him, will ever know what possessed him to plough on through the immense pain of so many hidden injuries, the gnawing and constant drudgery of semi-starvation, and the endless hard graft of a day job which embodies 'commitment' more than most professional sportspeople will ever know.

And yet (and you can remove my name from the New Years Honours List now, as well as the McCoy Christmas card list) I never particularly liked the bloke. In fairness, he probably doesn't care much for me either, especially now I've said that, but for much of his early career AP seemed remote and almost blind to his adoring public. Perhaps it was just his stubborn refusal to play the PR game that made him seem aloof. In later years emotions crept onto the once imperceptible face, and during his extended farewell tour he did remarkably well in the limelight of the media circus that surrounded his retirement, a position he had previously seemed so uncomfortable in.

However, there is a sense that to be truly great in your chosen sporting field, you have to remain detached from the minutiae of life and focus on only one thing – winning. Schumacher and Woods had it, McCoy also, but what made him different was that he never became arrogant or conceited. At times it was difficult to warm to him, but you could never doubt his humility. The weighing room is not the place for self-importance, but even in a peer group full of hard men McCoy carried a certain aura about himself, not forged by clever words or a knowing swagger, but by his relentless deeds at tracks up and down the country. He was simply the best at making horses win races, and not just for a while, but for twenty years!

So the management of Sandown must have been delighted that he chose them for his last hurrah, not least because of the publicity generated and the chance to charge punters an exorbitant £5 for a racecard. There was certainly a buzz around the place that was more than just the annual celebration of the finale of the jumps season, and it was clear that many were present specifically to pay homage to the passing of a career that, as the eloquent wordsmith Alistair Down put it, "redefined the art of the possible".

It was a sell out well in advance, and that brought its own challenges to a day at the races. Most bars were four or five deep, and staffed with the usual brand of inept youngsters. At one point the Sports Bar had only one out of five lager taps functioning, and the staff squabbled and jostled to pour a pint in a bizarre mirror image of the usual bedlam the other side of the counter. Later, I felt the need for a hog roast, purely in the interests of investigative journalism, and after paying my not insubstantial sum, I was told it would be a ten minute wait. I could have objected but I was hungry so said I would switch to the roast beef bap, which was perhaps the worst choice of my entire adventure, certainly in a culinary sense. It was so dry and stringy as to be inedible, but I couldn't face another queue to complain.

Unlike Cheltenham, however, we just about found spaces to settle throughout the afternoon, and the expectation of a rousing finale for the outgoing champ wafted the feel-good factor around the crowded terraces. I was joined by Clive, Simon and Murray, and the afternoon started well as three of us backed Lil Rockerfeller in the first at 6/1. Simon gleefully explained that it was an even sweeter victory because Clive's horse was second. We'd seen Lil Rockerfeller win well at Ascot earlier in the tour, and it was no surprise that the longer this jaunt went on the more insight I gained into the nuances behind the bare form facts. The winner wore cheekpieces last time and retained them today. Again, there was a reason for him to improve.

Simon thought I was winding him up when I explained my cheekpiece theory, as he'd never heard of the fluffy attachments. I was full of pride for my disciple when he announced that he'd bought the Racing Post for the first time in his life that morning, but my pride quickly turned to despair when it became apparent that he had 'read' only the Gee Bradburne piece and hadn't even turned to the racecards or form pages. After the second race, however, I really did manage to wind him up. I'd lingered by the parade ring to see the beginnings of the hoopla for AP coming out to ride Mr Mole in the third, and later joined the guys in the grandstand.

"Did you see all of that in the paddock?" I started.

"No. What was going on?" asked Simon.

"Well the other jockeys all came out and presented AP with a retirement gift, some of those long thin balloons for making animals, cos it's apparently a real hobby of his, just to while away the time in between races, except nobody's known before because he's such a private person....." Simon was actually falling for it, and I went in for the kill, "and so he starts making all these amazing balloon animals, horses and stuff, and starts handing them out to kids in the crowd....." Realisation swept across his face and the game was up, but I had him for a while!

In sharp contrast to the sentimental vibe of the day, I wasn't feeling the emotion for dear old Sprinter Sacre, and as much as I would have loved to have seen him return to his majestic best, I let my head rule my heart and opted for the younger legs of Special Tiara. I was right, as was Simon who had been getting a little dejected with the constant losing at Lingfield et al. He had somehow managed to back the first three winners and was in a chipper mood. AP finished third, but still had one ride left to write the fairytale ending that the public craved.

I suggested that we should watch his final performance on the giant screen by the parade ring so that we could soak up the atmosphere as they came back in after AP's final ride. I was chuffed with myself that we'd secured front row spaces to the denouement of an extraordinary career, and was amazed that others hadn't had the same idea. The record books will show that AP McCoy's final mount, the aptly named Box Office, running in the colours of AP's boss JP McManus and trained by Jonjo O'Neill, finished a creditable third in a hot handicap hurdle. He may not have won, but as a placed horse he would at least allow his rider a final moment of glory in the crucible of the winners' enclosure.

What happened next was a bit of a blur. I'm not sure if it was a dawning realisation, or the sudden jolt of a cutting remark from one of my friends, but it became clear that at Sandown, unlike a lot of other courses, the parade ring and the winners' enclosure were very different entities. I made a mad dash to where the more knowledgeable crowd had already assembled, cursing my stupidity, and wondering whether I had missed the defining moment of a remarkable career.

Luckily, the horses had not yet entered the arena, and all of a sudden I found myself somehow inside the winner's enclosure itself, carried there by the wave of emotion, a generous interpretation of the Club badge on my jacket from the security guard at the entrance, and not an insignificant amount of momentum following my sprint from the parade ring. It really is amazing where you can get in life if you don't mind giving it a go. I was to be one of a select few who would bear witness to this extraordinary moment of both celebration and succession on a very close up and personal level.

There was Jonjo, JP, AP's wife Chanelle who was overcome with relief, and assorted journalists who I had admired over the years, including my literary hero Alistair Down, who through the gift of his writing had helped me come to terms with the death of One Man. Oh, and a tall and borderline-obese goon who was wafting about the place, not quite knowing what to do next. This was where my lack of training, not to mention killer instinct, let me down and I bumbled around aimlessly, soaking up the calm before the AP storm came in, and taking photos like some random tourist whilst occasionally waving at Clive and Simon in the cheap seats. The winner and possible successor to the crown, Richard Johnson aboard Brother

Tedd, arrived and disappeared almost unnoticed, but I sensed that he too was caught up in the emotion of the moment.

Suddenly the green and gold colours were upon us, and photographers swarmed around a steaming horse to get the shot of the champ jumping off for the last time. I found myself very close in as the last photos and interview were concluded. Channel 4 anchor Nick Luck, as assured an interviewer as racing could wish for to conduct this important moment, stood a yard from me and didn't flinch one bit as I thrust my Dictaphone at his chest whilst he gently guided the slightly dumbfounded jockey through the concluding media circus. But even the broadcast veteran seemed to appreciate the significance of the moment, and up close it was just possible to notice Luck's hands trembling as he ping-ponged the microphone between the two of them. To his final question AP offered no response - emotion had overcome him too, and possibly the greatest career in the history of the sport was over. It was strange to see jockeys, forever the fearless and granite-like creatures from my Saturday afternoons, on the verge of tears, but I suppose that when the façade is removed we are all just human beings underneath.

AP went off to weigh in, Luck performed his closing words to camera, and then a strange atmosphere fell upon the winners' enclosure, warm but somehow muted, like a wedding when the bride and groom have just left. I said well done to Jonjo and shook his hand, perhaps the first time in racing history a top trainer had been congratulated for coming third in a handicap hurdle, but he took it well and was all smiles. I was standing by Chanelle, surrounded by a gaggle of children and family, and could easily have asked for a quick interview – what was it like to get him back in one piece? But her face said it all, and she seemed almost as lost as her husband had been at the end of the interview. She reminded me of John when he was finishing his quest in Taunton, basking in the glory of something momentous passing through but not quite knowing what to do next. I began to feel that I was intruding on a personal moment, and left the winners' enclosure past the same bouncer who had so generously allowed me access to the party.

So at the end of an afternoon of high emotion, the main feeling I was left with was admiration. There was no fairytale ending, but I don't think one was needed. That was not AP's style anyway – his success was incredibly hard fought over 20 years, mostly at the unglamorous tracks with unwilling horses, and in years to come if a new racegoer wants to know about AP McCoy you may as well show them winner number 3794 from the selling hurdle at Fakenham as his Grand National win or last ride at Sandown; they all count. That was the true mark of the man – he rode every horse as though it were his last, which in this unpredictable game it could well have been.

Simon and I walked back to the station across the course before the final race. We pondered briefly a rerun of the infamous Galway Final Furlong Dash, but that moment seemed to belong to the past. Like AP McCoy, our racing days were over.

# 32) Nottingham

## Day 47 – Tuesday 28 April

The 'Curious Incident of the iPhone in the Loo' was finally resolved two weeks later. The insurance company had prudently taken my second month payment a week early, I discovered as I attempted to cancel it after the first free month, so I was unexpectedly covered for one of the apparently 600,000 phone-down-loo mishaps every year. Not quite instant karma, but pretty close to it. However, they weren't going to make it easy for me, and one of the hoops I was required to jump through was a visit to the nearest Apple Genius Bar to obtain a piece of paper that said "This man has dropped his new iPhone down the loo". Despite having an appointment, I was spiralled into a convoluted queuing system and set off for Nottingham an hour late. This was an hour late from my already optimistic timings, and an accident en route meant that I arrived at the course just after the third race.

On the way I had a sudden déjà vu panic. I was worried that the schedule has spasmed itself into a duplication, and the whole thing was ruined. Then I remembered it was Leicester that I visited earlier on the same roads, and relief swept over my fatigued brain. I was beginning to get a little weary now, and still had the big trips ahead of me, but if I was searching for sympathy none was forthcoming, and rightly so.

A nice man in the smart entrance foyer let me in on a concession ticket as way of compensation for missing the first half of the afternoon's card. Even inside, Nottingham was quite reminiscent of its close cousin Leicester. The entrance gave way to sweeping manicured lawns big enough to host polo matches, I suspected, even though I knew nothing about polo (note to Nottingham management – you can have that brilliant idea for free, further consultancy shall be invoiced). It was quiet, and the sprinkled racegoers sauntered in the sun between grandstands and parade ring.

The first race I watched was the fourth, although I later discovered that I was looking at the form for the fifth. That is why number 4 was available at an absurdly generous 10/1 and ran a shocker. In the next race the real number 4, who was also known as Steve Rogers (that's the horse, not the jockey who was known as Frederik Tylicki) stayed on late to beat a wall of horses that had formed at the furlong marker, and I got a nice winner. It was a significant one as well, as it put me within touching distance of the Holy Grail that I had been chasing for weeks – being ahead! I simply love playing games, and this was a very real and expensive one spread over eighty days, with probably in the region of 300 different roles of the dice. I was meticulously keeping score, and was now agonisingly close to winning.

So it was heads down for the final race, a five furlong handicap, in an effort to find that elusive winner. There were seven to choose from, six of whom were making their seasonal debuts and could have progressed to an unknown degree. It was a bit of a guessing game, and I guessed wrong. My finishing line would have to wait for another day, although I recognised it was a constantly shifting finishing line as I severely doubted I would stop if and when I reached profit. As The Wife was increasingly concerned about the slippage in my diet, I paid a stranger, who we shall call Neil, to sample the fish and chips – really delicious, he declared.

I left to meet Jason and we again tried our luck at the Dusk Til Dawn poker club. This time they had a suitable opportunity for a couple of jokers like us, and we entered a tournament with the toughest players I had played against anywhere in the world. I kid you not, the standard of play in Nottingham put Galway and Edinburgh, London and

Vegas to shame. It soon became apparent that I was woefully out of practice and at the wrong end of the old adage "if you can't spot the fish at the table in the first five minutes, then you are the fish." Most hands were followed by an open and honest analysis, like it was a university tutorial and everyone was studying for a degree in poker. I realised that my previous playing venues were skewed towards the drunks or tourists (or if you were lucky, both) but everyone here was sober and knowledgeable, a dangerous combination in an opponent over the green baize. If at any point in the future I get serious about the game and improving my play, I could do a lot worse than buy my education the hard way at Dusk Til Dawn for a few weeks.

That I managed to eek it out for four hours, even briefly holding the chip lead at my table with some moves that bemused the experienced locals, only proved that the Monkeys And Shakespeare Principle could also be applied to poker, at least in the short term. Jason had also built an enormous chip stack at his table, with some chaotic and audacious moves that raised many eyebrows, before crashing out soon after I had when it became apparent he hadn't got the faintest clue what he was doing.

We then broke rule number one for the evening by playing some blackjack to wind down from the intensity of battle at the poker tables. It was chalk and cheese, with punters bonding over the unequal struggle to beat the common foe that was the casino, rather than fighting each other. It reminded me of my comrades at the racecourse, unknown allies that I stood shoulder to shoulder with almost every day. In less than 24 hours I was due to rejoin the fray at Pontefract, where I would be searching for just one more minor victory to tip the scales in the ongoing war against the bookies.

# 33) Pontefract

## Day 48 – Wednesday 29 April

Jason offered me a different bed and I slept a lot more soundly than the night in the basement. We blew the cobwebs away by taking Oscar for a walk across the recreation ground, and stopped in a delightful café for breakfast. They had good coffee, a tempting range of homemade cakes and a great mix tape on the speakers. We had a good chat and even managed to avoid resorting to a Connect 4 tournament until our Full English breakfasts arrived. Delicious, but too much even for my appetite, and the patient Oscar was well rewarded. But it was time to hit the road again, with a two-day excursion north beckoning.

The welcome at the Premier Inn Castleford was about as good as it gets. Everyone smiled at me when I entered, and the check-in was efficient. They explained an enormous amount of things I didn't know about the Premier Inn, and if I didn't sleep well they would refund my accommodation costs. I was surprised the hotel wasn't permanently booked out by the Insomniac Association. They ordered me a taxi and a chap turned up who had started yesterday. When I clarified this, the mature gentleman assured me he hadn't passed his test yesterday, but was working in Wakefield before then. He asked me where we were going and I said "The races, please." He mumbled something I didn't quite catch, and seemed generally uncertain about things. "Horses, the horse racing, Pontefract horse racing!" I reiterated.

I must have been speaking a different language as the confused cabbie then asked for a postcode. Luckily the car park of the Premier Inn had 4G and eventually we set off, but his satnav seemed to have reversed everything, like it was set up for the continent. It took us off the obvious main road and then asked us to turn right onto a left only carriageway. The driver ignored my sane suggestion to turn left and do a u-turn, and instead obediently followed the urgings of the errant box into oncoming traffic. After narrowly avoiding death, we discovered that the racecourse was really not very far from the hotel, but the driver wanted to drop me at the starting stalls next to the A639. When he said he had "started yesterday" I was beginning to wonder whether he meant his time on planet Earth? Perhaps he thought it was I who was racing, although in horse terminology I would be 'carrying a bit of condition'. Eventually we found our way to the main entrance, and I felt a pang of anxiety watching him stutter away, wondering whether he would survive the hazardous journey to his next pick up. At least his satnav didn't try and take him across the racecourse.

No ticket was issued on the gate, which I was slightly miffed about. I'm not a trainspotter or anything, but I was keen to collect all my entry tickets on the tour, which I'd managed to do so far except for Warwick where I'd got in with my Festival badge. So I approached the Raceday Office and a lovely lady gave me a badge saying 'Guest'.

Pontefract was a course of two halves. On entry I stepped into a serene oasis of sunny reflection, with studious onlookers ruminating around the sloping parade ring. There was a lovely view of the historic buildings and the food outlets were dotted around in a slightly secretive fashion, encouraging punters to embark on a foraging treasure hunt when it was time to eat. Benches lined the nooks and crannies, and there was a lovely relaxed vibe to the place. Out the front, on the action side of proceedings, was a different matter though. There was a decent view, but it was mostly of football pitches and the M62. Pontefract is considered the longest racecourse circuit in the world at a little over two miles in length. In the distance I could see the hotel I was staying in, and resolved

237

to walk back there after racing, which would be a lot safer than getting another taxi. It was windy and cold trackside, and a number of comments from Yorkshire locals assured me I was not being a wimp in the matter.

So after not quite reaching a positive position in the betting account at Nottingham, I resolved that this would be the day of my journey when I finally became a winner. I started with a tiny dabble on Bracken Brae at 80/1 who ran much better than his odds suggested, perhaps around 73/1. This prompted me to have a similar tickle on Swilken for the same trainer-owner combo in the next at 25/1, who ran like a 100/1 shot. Anyhow, the next two races were where it was at, and would decide my fate for the day and possibly the entire charade. They were both four-runner affairs with favourites around Evens, and it came down to whether I thought they would win more than 50% of those races if run in perpetuity. I did, and I know that if Scottish Robert were reading this now he'd be shaking his head and firmly decreeing "No, no, no!"

Pleasant Valley won very easily under an intelligent ride from Adam Kirby, and then Sparring in the next, who I'd seen win impressively at Windsor nine days previously, completed the double after looking in a spot of bother some way out. He stayed on up the rising ground of the home straight, under a very different but equally skilled ride from Kirby, and I had done it.

A weight was lifted from my shoulders and replaced with an unusually full feeling in my wallet. It had taken 48 days but I was finally winning! Suddenly I was talking to anyone and everyone like I'd developed some form of racing Tourettes. When Bill and Arthur sat next to me on a bench to sup their coffee they were subjected to a lengthy speech on how cold it was out of the sun and how the taxi driver had nearly killed me and how Sparring needed more than a mile and a half now. I floated down the drive to begin the brisk ten minute walk back to the hotel, which was actually about three-quarters of an hour away.

The Premier Inn was on a trading estate containing a variety of tempting fast food options, but after the warm welcome that morning I was happy to sign up to the meal deal, which gave me a three course dinner and full breakfast the next morning for not very much at all. The lure of a two-for-one happy hour eased me into the evening, and I sat at the bar and watched amused as more and more eyes lit up at the news of the unexpected bonus. Such was my elation at finally being in the black that I was still babbling away merrily to anyone unfortunate enough to stray within a few yards of my bar stool. This may have prompted the staff to seat me at an isolated table for one in the dining room, so that I couldn't harass any more guests, but I didn't mind as I had my Racing Post with me and pored over the day's racing, reliving my modest glories. The extent of my success wouldn't even pay for the hotel, let alone the entirety of the voyage, but somehow it meant a lot, and reminded me that despite a laid-back exterior I am really quite competitive.

You wouldn't think it to look at me, but I quite like salads and chose the prawn cocktail to start, which came in a retro glass and was lovely. The triumph, though, was the trio of curries, beautifully presented and exquisitely flavoured, and sufficient enough for me to only make a half-hearted stab at my crumble pudding. I was quite astounded at the standard of food at what was, after all, a fairly humble hotel chain, and it completely put to shame all the ordinary offerings at inflated prices I had sampled at racecourses around the country thus far.

For some reason as I entered the lift my mood quickly darkened and when I returned to my room I opened up the iPad and feasted on the self-pity of some old home videos showing smiling, laughing, happy times. The sudden switch from elation to sadness surprised me, but could well have been due to the glaring gap in importance between winning a few quid and taking my son to hospital for his operation, then just a month away. Perhaps I was taking Paul's advice about finding time to mourn a little too literally. It was almost like I was scheduling my tears for the dark seclusion of lonely hotel rooms, but it was the best I could manage, and probably better than nothing. Like most emotionally inept males, I had an unshakeable notion that I had to be strong when with my family and keep my own anguish private and discrete. I had to set the tone for our march towards a brave new world. The Premier Inn guarantee was not required that night; the outpouring of grief meant that I slept like a baby.

# 34) Sedgefield

## Day 49 – Thursday 30 April

I was enormously excited at the prospect of visiting Sedgefield as they were promising to take visitors 'Around The World In One Raceday!' What better for a man going around the British racecourses in eighty days than to also go around the entire globe in just one? On closer inspection of the website, I discovered that Sedgefield had not decided to branch out into supersonic air travel, but the theme was food related. There were just two options: The American Hot Dog Package and the extraordinarily named Around The World In A Jacket Potato package. Immediately my mind wandered to visions of sailing the seven seas in a coracle made by scooping out a giant potato, being washed up on distant shores and sampling the local delicacies. My daydreaming was stopped in its tracks when I scrolled down to see a photo of a jacket potato with cheese on top. Really, I cannot begin to tell you of the stark inanity of this image that left me laughing hysterically, like I was back on the Norfolk Broads that Sunday morning.

As I turned off for the racecourse before entering Sedgefield itself, I remembered the words of my taxi driver Eric. Briefly, I considered turning around and finding the steak and kidney pie that made his visit to the town the best day of his life, but reasoned that I had got a cosmopolitan feast waiting for me at the races, and I really needed to stop the double-lunch protocol that I had somehow slipped into.

It was cold and windy as I stepped from the car, but there was a warm welcome in a Teesside field. The Racing Post seller told me that all the winners were in the paper, and all I had to do was find them. There was some indistinct music crackling over the PA system as I entered. I couldn't quite locate its origins, but it could have been continental, or Caribbean, or even a strange fusion of the two. I wasn't sure but, either way, it hinted of untold riches to come, if only I could discover them. The barman called me "my friend", in a warm and genuine way, and I asked about the Around The World theme that must have had the staff abuzz.

"No, I don't follow the horses myself, really, although I did have three bets at Punchestown yesterday and they all won!"

Clearly he had not been briefed on the food side of things, and thought I was talking about a horse. I made a mental note to look out for any such themed horse that afternoon. Then I approached a steward and quizzed her about the vaunted global delights, but she was similarly baffled and suggested the 'Chips & Things' van might have a burger. Tommo was in the paddock, and if anyone could warm up a frozen crowd it was him, doing his now familiar routine with losing betting slips. It occurred to me that I'd like him as impresario at my funeral, just to lighten the mood. He could collect Orders of Service and choose some at random to get a bottle of champagne or something.

In the first race there were two hot favourites that I didn't fancy, so opted for the third favourite, who finished third to the two hot favourites. The winner, Prince Khurram, was given a great ride out in front by conditional jockey James Cowley, and Tommo joked that he was now leading the new jockeys championship. After a break of just four days since the end of season spectacular at Sandown, the jumps season was beginning afresh at the Teesside venue. It would be an intriguing contest this year, for once, and perennial prince Richard Johnson was slight favourite to finally claim the crown, despite fervent opposition from a variety of comparative whippersnappers. His agent, Dave Roberts, had also worked for AP McCoy for many years and would presumably be keen to see a smooth transition of power to his new number one.

I was hungry, and slightly perturbed by the lack of colourful and diverse food stalls, so set off on a mission to hunt out my lunch from a hidden corner of the globe. There was a Collins Seafood stand with no seafood (or any food at all, for that matter), and the Hoops Restaurant did have a variety of offerings at exorbitant prices but no hot dogs or jacket potatoes. Frankly, I was beginning to think it was a theoretical campaign that never received management approval, created by some marketing trainee whose idea of haute cuisine was a trip to Spud-u-like. I stormed into the Racecourse Office, demanding to know if I'd been brought there under false pretences. The calm and pleasant lady directed me to the tiny Durham Edition Bar, which I had missed in my earlier wanderings, and eventually I secured my prize.

The promised exotic fillings such as Chicken Tikka and Bolognese had not materialised and it was a choice of Tuna Mayo, Beans or Cheese. So in a way, I thought, I was indeed being transported to the Southern Seas via a can of John West's tuna. It was served by a mardy teenager who had to be shown how to open up the potato rather than just dumping the topping on.

"Masterchef, is it?" she moaned to her patient supervisor.

Not quite, but to add to the multinational street-market vibe, it was served in a cardboard box with a plastic fork. It was nice enough, although slightly stingy on the topping.

The second race featured Bertie Moon who I had seen win at Perth, but I wouldn't back him at 7/4 as his form before Perth was patchy. Jebulani had won over course and distance last time, and after watching the first race I realised that this undulating and unbalancing track with tight bends was a unique test that may not suit some horses. In particular, the camber on the back straight made Epsom look like Holland, and I was surprised that no horses slipped off into the adjacent field as the afternoon progressed. Jebulani was only five years old and could have some improvement in him to defy the ten pounds hike in the weights. Incredibly, he was 10/1 and I backed him each way as I was slightly worried about Bertie Moon but couldn't see him finishing outside the first three. Bertie Moon did indeed follow up his Perth win nicely, and Jebulani finished fourth, beaten a short head in the sixth photo finish out of six on this tour to go against me.

I felt that after the jubilation of finally getting ahead at Pontefract yesterday, the Gods of Probability were exacting their revenge and it was not going to be my day. I went to the paddock because I couldn't decide between the two favourites in the third race. Classinaglass was a fine looking individual who nonchalantly defecated all over his hind legs as he sauntered around – not very classy, and not in a glass either for that matter. I'm no equine expert, but it was definitely a big one, stretching out for about 20 yards of previously pristine rubber matting. I estimated that he must be carrying at least five pounds less now, which could make all the difference over two and a half miles, and that swayed my decision. I think you can work out how he ran.

Bob Champion was being interviewed in the paddock by Tommo and managed to use the phrase "let's be honest" an astonishing four times in three minutes. Although it was nice that the former Grand National winner was not going to be dishonest with us, his stock phrase seemed to be a pre-cursor to a diatribe of stunning mediocrity, the sentences devoid of meaning or value, a bit like the broken promises of the website's advertising campaign. After all the recent news about various attempts to reinvigorate the sport and attract new racegoers, I'm afraid that the Sedgefield theme was exactly the sort of marketing absurdity that does nothing for horse racing. If any of the locals were there to sample world cuisine they would have been sorely disappointed, but luckily nobody (including the staff) had taken a blind bit of notice of the awfully executed attempt at promoting the course.

People were there on a cold Thursday because they liked watching horse racing in a relaxed and friendly ambiance. Let's concentrate our efforts on improving the sport and the facilities rather than this PR nonsense which is neither believed nor delivered. The assembled crowd would much rather buy a decent sandwich, or failing that, they'd have had the good sense to get a steak and kidney pie from the town before they came, which is of course what I should have done. I headed for the exit before being tempted to buy a jacket potato with beans and cheese to continue the crazy culinary tour of this strange land called Britain. The drive south took five hours, without a pie in sight, but I was glad to be heading home.

# 35) Newmarket

## Day 51 – Saturday 2 May

On the drive up to Newmarket there was a feeling of going back to the beginning. I passed within 400 yards of the house where I was born and grew up, the garden where I learnt to ride a bike and the fields and woods where I used to play manhunt. A little later, I saw signposts to my old schools, and the pitches where I played my club football. I was transported back to the time-rich summer of 1990 when I called that place home and the extent of my world was the drive into town on a Friday evening. It was the last summer before everything changed forever, as my cohort was flung to the four corners of this island and I would begin the lifelong process of calling other places home.

I was 18 and had decided I was going to find the perfect horse racing system. I analysed for weeks the selection boxes of the Sporting Life, searching for significant results when various combinations of tipsters concurred. I then tested the new system by placing £1 bets on all the qualifying horses (and there were many) for a week. Needless to say the method, which if I remember correctly involved backing any horse selected by all three of the Daily Express, Daily Mirror and Form tipsters, didn't pre-empt my requirement to go to university in the autumn and study for a proper career.

That was the year Timeless Times won an astonishing 15 races, mostly over five and six furlongs and occasionally on consecutive days. He was as close as I have ever seen to printing money in the equine world. I think that was the same summer that my Uncle Tom took me to my first meeting at Newmarket. As I remember, we didn't have a winner between us, but the flame was fully alight by then and could not be extinguished by one fruitless evening.

Back to 2015, and I detoured to pick up Luke en route, an old friend recently returned to the area. I could write an entire book on the silly japes we got up to at school, but my favourite has to be a routine we performed every time a supply teacher was unfortunate enough to be assigned to our French class. Luke would pretend to faint, and three of us would manhandle him outside as he lay limp in our arms, textbooks and pencil cases sluicing to the floor as his lifeless limbs drooled over shiny school desks. As we shuffled out, crab-like between dishevelled chairs, we would cheerily reassure everyone that it was all totally normal and he just needed some fresh air to revive himself, and once outside we would all sit giggling on a bench for five minutes before returning to the classroom to dream up some other nonsense. Luke deserved an Oscar for his performances, or at least greater recognition than he received from the often indifferent supply teachers.

Those shenanigans were unlikely to be reproduced on the occasion of the 207th running of the 2,000 Guineas and, even if Luke did faint, I wasn't sure I could carry him on my own anyway, not with my bad back. Time catches up with everyone eventually, as indeed it did by the end of 1990 for dear old Timeless Times – the cashpoint machine ran out of money and he never won again.

Yellow signs directed us around three sides of an unnecessary square to the racecourse entrance. It was a convoluted route, but it did at least take in a vast array of different stables and stud farms, and it was easy to grasp a sense of the domination this industry holds over the Suffolk town – it isn't called Headquarters for nothing. When we finally arrived the place was busy, but not oppressively so, and there were a vast number of different food stalls where racegoers were offered a decent variety of options. Perhaps the Around The World street market theme was transferred at the last minute from Sedgefield to Newmarket? We chose the burrito, which was fairly good, and a welcome diversion from the standard fare of the last two months.

We got chatting and the conversation catch-up soon turned towards Youngest. Luke, not a stranger to health adversity himself, was quietly positive and said that the new post-operative routine would just become a part of life after a while. It was comforting to get the views of an old friend who knew what the term 'resilience' meant. We lost track of time and realised we were too late to bet as the next race was off. Somehow though, Luke found a bookmaker who would still accept his bet, as well as allowing him to change his mind to Second Step half way through the transaction. I too would have been on at 7/1 in a four-horse race, had I found as accommodating a bookmaker, but those were the swings and roundabouts of racing, and I cheered him on as he overhauled yet another disappointing odds-on favourite in the dying strides. When Luke went to collect his winnings (and this is the bit I really can't fathom) the bookie deliberately paid him out more than he should have, saying "get yourself a drink!" I suspect he was pleased to see the favourite beaten, but it was still remarkable generosity.

Getting that celebratory drink was less easy than the food, and the usual scrum formed around a bar under the main stand. I really don't know why racecourses can't sort out this astonishingly prevalent problem, as it is surely in their financial interests to process punters quickly so they can move on to other ways of spending money at the course, and everyone would be happier. A big bunch of guys had donned denim shorts and stilettos in a bizarre re-enactment of the slightly disturbing 'You're So Money Supermarket' advert, but they mingled easily with the assorted clientele of a day at the races.

There was a buzzing atmosphere surrounding the feature race and opening Classic of the flat season, and we

248

watched them as they circled the paddock. Luke liked Glenalmond because he was looking feisty, like a boxer wanting to start a punch-up at the pre-fight weigh-in. I thought Celestial Path and Kool Kompany both looked very well, but this was trying to short cut the form studying which I hadn't managed to fit in. Luke said that I must be an expert by now, but I explained that bizarrely I had done less analysis per race for the last couple of months than I normally did. It transpired that going around the races in eighty days and writing about it didn't leave much time for the form studying. Only near the end of the parade did Gleneagles, the uneasy favourite appear, sweating heavily and arsing around like a drunken older cousin at a family wedding disco.

We got our bets on and secured a spot in the stands as a computer generated fantasy version of the 2,000 Guineas played out on the big screen, bringing together old favourites from over the years. This confused some in the crowd who thought the actual race was off and feverishly scanned their racecards because they hadn't realised that Frankel was running again this year. Then the real race was off and it made a better spectacle than the virtual one. In hindsight, the easy-to-back favourite Gleneagles was the best horse in the race and proved it, but unfortunately the Racing Post didn't have a 100% successful tipster called Hindsight.

On the journey home I caught a glimpse of my uncle's house, which again prompted the fond boyhood memories to come flooding back. I was going home to The Wife and my boys, but somehow that neck of the woods will always seem a bit like home, irrespective of where I choose to live my life.

# 36) Salisbury

## Day 52 – Sunday 3 May

Another day, another racecourse. Sunday was Salisbury, and it was sunny. Friends had spotted a slightly jaded attitude in recent weeks, which had prompted encouraging noises such as "you're in the last month now" and "it's the home stretch!", to which I usually retorted that it was a marathon, not a five furlong sprint, and I felt as though I'd just shambled past the Cutty Sark and had been overtaken by a pantomime horse who was being interviewed by Bob Wilson. As if to confirm my declining mental state, I'd spent the previous week looking for the charger for my now lifeless new dictaphone, before remembering just before I set off that it was battery powered.

I drove past Stonehenge on the way down and wondered what it was all about. If my tour of the racecourses could be described as a folly, it was a significantly lesser one than the enormous stone circle in a Wiltshire field. There surely must be a message in there, I pondered, a meaningful if yet undiscovered reason for the preposterous thing to exist. I was thinking about Stonehenge by the way, rather than my ridiculous undertaking, although both fitted the same mould of 'as yet, not fully explained'.

When I got to Salisbury I was kept waiting for a full 20 minutes before I could enter because I had parked the other side of the track when a race was due off. This struck me as poor customer service – why direct people to park on the far side and not give them an alternative route for crossing? I hadn't left my family on a sunny Sunday to stand on the edge of a car park! I was also utterly confused by the sight of what I was pretty sure were flat horses approaching a tape rather than entering stalls, and wondered whether I had got it wrong and Salisbury was actually a jumps venue. I later figured out that this was because the 1 mile 6 furlong contest both started and finished in the same spot, albeit in opposite directions after navigating a loop, and if there was a problem moving the stalls the race would have to be stopped.

Starting stalls were first introduced to British racecourses at Newmarket in 1965, although they had been in operation in other countries for many years. The five furlong Chesterfield Stakes was the first race to see them used, and was won by Track Spare ridden by Lester Piggott. They were swiftly away from stall one, and both benefitted from previous experience in the stalls that some called "those damned contraptions", highlighting the wariness with which this new technology was viewed. In some ways, their introduction perfectly highlighted the issue with which horse racing has had to wrestle over the years – how does the sport change for the better without losing the faith of its stakeholders?

My Racing Post hide and seek championship entered its southern series, and if there was somebody selling the paper they had long gone by the time us stragglers were allowed into the facilities. In the end, a nice man on the turnstiles gave me his own copy, and I settled into the form. I was beginning to get a feel for prices that were wrong, and I was getting strong feelings at Salisbury that afternoon. Great Page was backed into 1/3 after winning nicely on his debut at Windsor a couple of weeks ago, which I had watched first hand, but they were silly odds when so little was known about the opposition. I was right, but again I chose the wrong vanquisher, and Illuminate showed his rivals the way home.

There was a great view from the top of the grandstand and the vibrant crowd formed the usual herbaceous border of humanity on both sides of the course. There was a good atmosphere and plenty of different areas to explore. Some hadn't even bothered paying the entrance fee – caravanners got the deckchairs out and watched the giant screen from the other side of a chain-link fence, whilst tweeded folk laid out picnics in the car park. Racing doesn't necessarily bring these diverse groups of society together, as such, but it allows them to mingle easily and get what they want out of their afternoon, and Salisbury racecourse facilitated that coming together rather well. There was an enticing Chinese catering van, but the noodles were disappointing compared to the sublime Plumpton version (I heard someone nearby mention).

By the time I left I had yet to find a winner, discover the hidden meaning of the stone circle a few miles away, or gain a shining insight into why I was still continuing with my ludicrous odyssey despite all the obvious reasons to stop. I suppose, like Stonehenge, whatever the justifications they would both stand as a monument to stubbornness – when you've decided to start something, you may as well finish it.

I charged back up the A303 to get back home as soon as possible. It was Paul's birthday and I had been standing in a Wiltshire field rather than spending time with my old mate. When I dreamt of my journey for all those years it all seemed so idyllic – smiling, positive interactions at sunny racecourses around the lush green corners of Britain. There would be champagne and winners flowing like nectar, and amusing anecdotes with which to entertain the family when the intrepid hero returned. As it was, when I got home with the best of the day gone, thoroughly cheesed off that I had missed a Sunday afternoon on the deck drinking beer with Paul and watching our children rampaging around the garden, I was asked how it had gone and simply said "another day, another racecourse".

# 37) Beverley

## Day 53 – Monday 4 May

The family and I had been watching the latest Bear Grylls diet programme 'The Island', where mostly slim young things got even slimmer (if not younger) on a desert island which appeared really nice from a distance but actually resembled 1980s Beirut at close quarters. I'd bought a prawn sandwich after dropping Eldest and his mates at the latest rowing competition that I'd be missing, and in deference to the bravery in the face of food adversity that The Islanders displayed, I decided that I wouldn't touch it until 11am. As the minutes ticked down this became more and more painful, until a Pavlovian response as the clock digits flashed over meant I inhaled the poor thing without it even touching the sides. But it must be easier for them on the Grylls programme – they don't have to stare at prawn sandwiches for over an hour!

I feel I can cope with things better when I have a Racing Post with me, and I know that makes me sound a little bit weird. I'm sure when Armageddon erupts I'll be nipping to the nearest newsagents to make sure I can face the end of the world with some statistics to peruse. The mini-apocalypse that had me diving into Smiths on the four-hour journey to Humberside was the usual and totally inexplicable hold up just past the Tibshelf Services on the M1. Traffic jams are just about doable, but only if there is form to study.

I faced a total of eight hours behind the wheel, and I'd been wondering for a while about the differences of opinion between my speedo and The Satnav. Which of those two took precedence would make an interesting case in a court of law. I was favouring The Satnav to be the more reliable (how quickly you have devolved power to it, Neil, in less than two months), not just because it allowed me to drive a bit quicker, but the GPS aspect must surely make it more accurate than a guy at Ford's putting a plastic dial into a plastic dashboard? I hoped so, or pretty soon I would start getting letters from the DVLA telling me to surrender my license. I didn't often listen to the radio, or even a CD, when driving on my tour. Perhaps this was the way of an ex-teacher who craved silence, or even solitude? Instead, I wallowed in the luxury of allowing my mind to wander where it would, unhindered by the pressures of the modern world. Part of me, however, saw this as a monumental waste of time and felt I should be learning Spanish, or fighting with Siri over the content of the next blog.

After driving through the pretty villages of East Yorkshire, festooned with blue and yellow bunting in deference to the Tour De Yorkshire, I eventually reached my destination, and Beverley was just gorgeous. For the avoidance of doubt, and because The Wife could be reading, I mean the racecourse at Beverley was one of the finest examples I had yet discovered of what a day at the races should be like. The Racing Post informed me that chief executive Sally Iggulden was worried about the 12:30 start, a trial by the BHA race planning team to spread out the action on a busy bank holiday Monday, but people had certainly arrived early and in their droves, and everything seemed just dandy under a clear east coast light.

Despite the big crowd, bars and food outlets were efficiently run by experienced staff and it was easy to get a pretty decent drink or a bite to eat. I thought back to the hopeless service offered by cheap teenage labour at so many of my previous stops, and got annoyed at those false economies. Yes, it may cost a little more to employ adults who know what they are doing, but they are friendly and efficient and provide a smooth canvas on which to paint your day. As I wandered through the enclosures I noted several little touches that gave the racegoers a better experience. Beverley must win the award for the highest number of benches per head, and the plethora of grandstands meant it was easy to find a spot to watch the action over the undulating circuit. And, of course, an early winner always helped to sweeten my view of proceedings.

At this point I was drawn to a bizarre scene playing out just yards away from me as a nine foot tall flower tottered carefully past the betting ring. I pondered briefly whether I'd finally cracked, the pressure of the travel, writing and homesickness finally catching up with me, but it appeared that others were also seeing what I was seeing. Many punters gave it a wide berth (it didn't look all that steady on its roots, after all) and a toddler in a pushchair screamed in horror, but my investigative reporter inclinations decided that I had to confront the benevolent Triffid.

"Dare I ask why you're dressed like that?" I said to the mutant daisy.

"Why are you dressed like that?" the flower fired back, in a strangely Scottish and dreamy lilt, before adding "I started small....and I just kept growing!"

This last sentence was accompanied by a scene straight out of the 'Playschool' locker, as the flower bent low and then reached for the sky. Was she on drugs? And if so, could I have some please, because I was unsure how to continue the interaction otherwise.

"Genetically-modified?" I asked. Ah ha - have some of that, you stupid giant loon, if you think I'm the odd one out in this surreal duet!

However, the daisy appeared not to have heard my witty comeback and continued gurning at the sun, babbling incoherently in a way reminiscent of the programmes you get on Radio 4 in the early hours of the morning. It appeared that I really was getting the worse of the bizarre exchange as I was the one standing listening to a demented flower, so I made one last effort at bringing it back to some sort of normality with the staple of any racecourse conversation.

"Had any winners today?"

"No, I don't have any money, you see – I'm a flower!"

Right, that was it. I couldn't stand any more of the nonsense and bailed out of a 'conversation' I should never have allowed myself to be drawn into. I drifted away bemused and defeated, back to where I felt secure, and started studying the form for the fifth race. At last I found a favourite that I liked (it had taken days) and astutely waited for 2/1 to appear just before the off. Rousayan led all the way and just held on in a driving finish. It was the first photo finish I'd won in seven attempts on the journey.

On the hefty drive back down to Fakenham, I couldn't stand to be alone with my thoughts any longer. I was feeling slightly bruised after being outwitted in a debate with a tall talking flower, and so turned on the radio for some comfort and company. The studio had just cut to an on-the-scene roving reporter, and occasional 'royal expert', who was explaining that the new Princess Charlotte had been given the middle names of Elizabeth Diana in deference to Her Majesty The Queen and the late mother of Prince William respectively. Really? Thanks for that. Time for a CD.

I reached The Bull in Fakenham by the time evening was drawing in. It was another last minute grab for accommodation and I hadn't realised that the town centre venue was without parking. It was definitely a local pub with a few rooms rather than an expensive boutique hotel with gastropub attached, but the welcome was warm. The friendly barman directed me to a pay-and-display across the street, and I had soon parked up and dropped my bag in my room. There were three single beds to choose from, and I queried that I had booked a single, but was reassured that they were not full that night and the room was all mine. The three beds and the room didn't seem to quite fit together coherently, but I chose the bed with the best view of the TV and flicked on the final of the snooker whilst I unpacked. There is something rather hypnotic about watching snooker, I've always found, seeing the order of the green baize restored as the chaotic balls disappeared one by one. But I snapped myself out of the trance and was soon back down in the bar enjoying a Bitburger which I was pleased to find on draught.

It was strange, though, how most pleasing moments soon morphed back to my internal sadness if I wasn't fully occupied. As I drank my Bitburger I thought of a lovely holiday with The Wife in Germany, back in the pre-kids era. We went to a traditional village hostelry with big, doughy pretzels on the table, and when I finished my half-stein of lager a message was revealed on the bottom of the glass that read "Bitte ein Bit!" to encourage me to order the next one. But thinking of the holiday made me think of my family, and I became a little maudlin again. I distracted myself in the way I knew best.

"So what are the food options around here?" I enquired of the barman.

The Bull didn't do car parking or food, it appeared, but I let it off because I was still enjoying the Bitburger. It had cleared out by now and the two of us and the one remaining regular discussed the many delights that Fakenham had to offer. For a small market town it seemed replete with a wide range of take-aways, and I was drawn to the unusually named Hot And Cold, which apparently served Chinese food. When I returned to the pub, still with just the one other customer, the barman kindly offered me an Alan Partridge sized plate (you'll know what I mean if you've seen the episode set in the Linton Travel Tavern) to eat my supper and said I could have it in the bar if I wanted. But it had been a long day and the hypnotic coloured balls were calling, so I went up to my room to eat alone in front of the last few frames of the snooker.

# 38) Fakenham

## Day 54 – Tuesday 54 May

I slept fitfully in my triple bed suite at The Bull, possibly due to an MSG overload from my Chinese feast, but more likely because of the noises from the street, which had been transformed into a motocross circuit for the youngsters of the town to enjoy until the wee small hours. I went down to the bar for breakfast and the cleaner cooked me a solitary Full English.

I had to scoff it, lovely though it was, because the Galaxy needed a ticket for the car park. I arrived to find that I had a puncture - my car that was (I hadn't yet burst from eating too much take away). It could just have been the Fakenham Yoof having their fun, or even my tyres themselves having a laugh at my expense. Just like the engine, if I didn't pay them enough attention they started playing tricks like that, and a few sweet words usually sorted them out. That, or a threat that if they didn't pull themselves together they would be going to join the tyre wall at Thruxton just after the bend that everybody gets wrong. Anyway, I had a clever box in the boot that started engines and inflated tyres when they were throwing tantrums, which thus far had demonstrated none of the attention seeking behaviour itself.

As the box chugged away noisily, I surveyed the town in daylight hours, when the dirt bikes no longer used the centre as a racetrack. There was an extraordinary number of hairdressers, including Alan who "pleases people every day" and had posters saying "OH! OH! OH! OH!" to prove his point. I fancied a coffee whilst I caught up with stuff, and searched for a Starbucks or Costa. I'm not sure why really, because I get confused in them when staring at the multitude of options, but when I am far from home I suppose I grasp at normality. And wifi. Instead I found Gallery Bistro on Market Place and was glad that I did. When I asked the efficient and friendly owner for a coffee he immediately understood that I just wanted a coffee, and very good it was too.

I returned to the car and checked the pressure of the troublesome tyre – all quiet on the Goodyear front, for the moment at least. To go with its hairdressers and takeaways, Fakenham had two tyre places almost next to each other on the way to the racecourse. I pulled in to both of them in turn, but discovered that, despite an apparent absence of any other work, I would have to fill out a form and it would take several hours before anyone could muster up the interest to look at it, so I carried on gingerly towards the races. I parked in the centre and got a great view of the facilities as I walked across the course. I've made a lot of my wind problem so far on the journey, but this really was a proper gale, and after getting the lie of the land I returned to the car to shelter, enter the fifth hour of 'Tyrewatch', and study the form for half an hour.

Just before the first a sudden gust was strong enough to blow over Wigmore Racing's coin tray, which brought cheers from the stands and a sour face from the bookie. In the second, I again detected that the prices were all wrong and favoured Alright Benny at 5/1 over Waddington Hero at 5/4, and this time I was right. I celebrated with a Cromer crab sandwich from Weston's of Blakeney, which brought back memories of family holidays on the beach and the little racing cars that looked like cut down daleks and went about half a mile an hour but seemed so thrilling. I also quickly remembered that I don't particularly like crab, but eating only half a lunch helped the diet, I suppose.

However, the afternoon was all about Hunt Ball. The handsome bay gelding caused quite a stir a few seasons ago as he racked up a sequence of seven wins from eight races and rattled up the ratings accordingly, rising an astonishing 93 pounds in the handicap. His eccentric owner, Anthony Knott, attracted almost as much publicity as he enthusiastically rode the exponential bandwagon to its crescendo, reputedly winning and losing millions on massive bets struck on his horse. Cattle farmer Knott was a breath of fresh air in the sometimes stuffy world of racehorse ownership, infamously incurring the wrath of the stewards after one win when he got so excited that he jumped on the back of the horse behind the jockey and started punching the air, like Pele scoring in the World Cup. But the fairytale began to fade. Following a Cheltenham Festival win in 2012 Hunt Ball continued to run with credit but generally found life a lot tougher in the upper echelons of steeplechasing. Knott put him up for sale and he was bought to race in America, but a year later he returned to Blighty and the care of Nicky Henderson, and again put up some decent performances in defeat.

Which brings us back to the third race on the card, where he faced just three rivals when switched back to hurdles. The heart of the matter was whether Hunt Ball's unquestionable class over the bigger obstacles could translate to a first win over the smaller ones. It was really never in doubt, and the old favourite secured his first win for over two years.

So it seemed that switching things around really could pay dividends. I mulled this thought over as I drove back from the Norfolk venue, hoping that Around The Races In Seventy-Eight Days would be equally as, if not more, impressive than Eighty, although perhaps not quite as catchy when shortened to ATRISED. At the very least, I mused, it would scupper the plans of anybody planning a 79 day campaign to beat my potential world record. Stratford now had the dubious honour of being my last port of call on Friday 29 May, a little over three weeks away, and for the first time there was just a glimmer of light at the end of the tunnel.

# 39) Worcester

## Day 56 – Thursday 7 May

You may have been aware of a general election in the first half of 2015, although with all the media interest surrounding my heroic attempt to visit all the racecourses in eighty days, it was quite possible you may have missed it. It was a fiendishly difficult outcome to call, with even the most renowned of pundits seemingly clueless in the face of an extraordinarily fluid situation, and I'm not talking about whether I'd complete my challenge, by the way. It was dubbed the most unpredictable general election in generations and the odds on the next government just a day before the electorate voted were extraordinarily open, with a Labour minority the uneasy 2/1 favourite and a Conservative majority freely available at 8/1. If any handicapper had produced a small-field race as closely contested as that they would have been justifiably proud of their efforts.

So in a world of change and uncertainty, and with the nation in a state of flux, I found it comforting to begin the day at a tranquil oasis that I knew would be constant – Oaksey House in Lambourn. The chief executive of the Injured Jockeys Fund, Lisa Hancock, had been extremely generous with her time in a phone interview a few weeks before I began my journey, and as we concluded our chat she said I should visit and tour the facilities with John and Jackie Porter who had run the place since its grand opening in 2009. How could I refuse such a kind offer? Lisa had been clear during our interview that she did not want to get involved in the politics of racing because it could disrupt the independent stance of her organisation. Whatever else happened in the big bad world, when ill fate befell the brave men and women who rode horses for our entertainment the IJF would be there to pick up the pieces.

I voted and then headed for Lambourn, just up from Junction 14 of the M4. As I swept down Hungerford Hill a sign proclaimed that I was entering The Valley Of The Racehorse. I must admit to a few goosebumps, thinking about the big names sent out from there over the decades to secure their own small piece of horse racing glory: Mill House, See You Then, Mr Frisk, Party Politics and, more recently, Cole Harden and Many Clouds. I wondered why I hadn't been before – there is an Open Day every Easter.

The village is blessed with no less than 30 training yards, from smaller operations with fewer than ten boxes to the giants such as Henderson and Sherwood, but it is not blessed with wide thoroughfares. Two lorries passing on the narrow Oxford Street caused a traffic jam, in a rural Berkshire sense anyway. Perhaps it just added to the homely feel and sense of community. This is a racing village through and through, from the shop to the pub to the residential streets. The blockage cleared and soon I was over the River Lambourn, turning right through an impressive entrance, and shaking hands with John in the foyer. Oaksey House still seemed fresh and had an aura of calm about it. His wife Jackie was there, as was Lisa who was overseeing some training for the Almoners and volunteers.

John ushered me into his Land Rover for a tour of the village. He was clearly a racing man to his core with a background in point-to-points, first as a jockey and then a trainer. He had lived in Lambourn with Jackie for over 30 years and took me past all the yards, talking through the trainers past and present. I asked whether, with all the competition confined to such a small area, there was still a sense of community?

"Oh yes" he enthused, "Many Clouds was fantastic the other day! Equally, when Rough Quest and Party Politics won, they were all great parties."

"You must know an awful lot of people round here," I enquired, my punters instinct kicking in, "do you get the nod then, when one's got a good chance?"

"No, no, a little knowledge is dangerous. You can be at the races and get four different tips in the same race!" laughed John. So no insider information for me at Worcester that afternoon, sadly.

We headed to the gallops and climbed Fishers Hill, used for interval training. The horses go up the steep incline three times at a steady pace - the 'Martin Pipe method' as John called it. This extensive area of land is maintained to a high standard by Jockey Club Estates, and the trainers pay a monthly fee for each horse that uses the gallops. I asked about the history of the place, and why Lambourn became a big training centre.

"Oh the gallops have been here for hundreds of years," explained John as we left the Land Rover, "it's the chalk downlands, they drain well. Nowadays you can train anywhere by putting in drainage and an all-weather surface, but this turf has been down for centuries. Feel how good it is?"

We walked over to the all-weather schooling area where two horses were popping away, rhythmic and nimble over the fences. Barry Fenton, assistant trainer at Emma Lavelle's yard near Andover, had brought them up this morning and was keeping a keen eye over the youngsters learning their trade.

"We haven't got an all-weather schooling ground, but it's no harm to bring them away, you know. You see that big horse there, he's in a bit of a wash, but a bit of travelling does them good."

The big one in front turned out to be Bit Of Bob, ridden by Aiden Coleman, who was an unraced five-year-old brother to See The World, the horse that famously won his bumper in January after hanging so badly left off the home bend that he was virtually pulled up, before regaining momentum and the lead. Set List, who had already had several outings over hurdles, followed under Richie McLernon. To my untrained eye, both jumped well and looked like they would take to chasing.

Barry discussed the season, the ins and outs of stable form, how they had got through a virus and changed the forage, and all the other things a racing yard has to cope with.

"We had a nightmare at the start of the year, lost two lovely horses. Timesremembered, promise you he was going to make a serious chaser, never jumped a hurdle great, but the first time we schooled him over fences Gavin Sheehan came back in and we both just said fucking hell! Went to Liverpool, winging the first 3 fences, then a horse fell in front of him....."

No stranger to injury himself in a distinguished career over the jumps, including wins in a Welsh National and a Whitbread Gold Cup, Barry's voice then briefly trailed away. He'd seen it all before, but I could tell that the loss of a horse still affected him. Suddenly it started hosing it down and John and I scurried back to the safety of the Land Rover, leaving the hard men of National Hunt racing to carry on their business in the downpour.

Back in the sanctuary of Oaksey House, we dried off and then John led me around the facilities. All the rooms were named after famous horses, and evocative photos adorned the walls, charting the history of the sport. The gym had an anti-gravity treadmill, developed by NASA, which could adjust the amount of weight you ran with. I could do with one of those, I thought. We crossed the garden to see the twelve units that accommodated those in need of respite and rehabilitation, as well as members of the racing community requiring longer-term care. Along the way we passed the statue of Lord Oaksey, the inspiring founder and tireless fundraiser of the IJF who passed away in 2012.

We met Emma, one of the in-house physiotherapists who worked not just with injured jockeys, but eventers, showjumpers, stable staff and retired jockeys, as well as other sportsmen and locals. The centre is not an exclusive club but instead cascades benefit throughout the community and industry. Emma was also shortly heading off to Worcester as one of a team of fifteen physios nationwide who cover all the jumps and a majority of the flat fixtures. She said that the jockeys would often head straight past the doctor, who had the power to stand them down from racing, and she would pick them up in the changing room when they were looking very pale. Then I chatted to Michael, the strength and conditioning coach who also ran the young jockeys academy, helping the stars of the future learn about diet and psychology as well as the physical side of the job. He had worked with football and rugby players before, and I was intrigued to know the differences.

"A lot of equine people have just done equine stuff and are not used to tumbling or rolling. Sometimes I'm teaching a 20-year-old jockey what a ten-year-old rugby player would know naturally," he explained, adding "these guys didn't used to think they were athletes, but AP McCoy has changed all that."

On the way out I paused to sign the visitors book and asked John one last question: "It must give you a buzz coming to work every day?"

"It's very satisfying, you know," he said as a smile crept across his face, "we've been here since Day 1 and the Chief Executive said we've just spent £5m on this place so make it fucking work, and luckily we have!"

I didn't think it was luck, just the hard work of good people and the generosity of the racing public, and I headed to Worcester safe in the knowledge that if the worst were to happen that afternoon, IJF support would be immediately available.

I parked at the house of some friends and got a taxi to the course. The cabbie remembered a horse called Kendal Cavalier, and I was amazed that two complete strangers could be connected by a horse that hadn't run for over 15 years and was probably unknown to 99% of the British population even then. He had a mate who'd had a runner in the Grand National a few weeks before. Ely Brown had fallen at the first fence, but it was his mate's childhood dream to have a runner in the race and he'd achieved it. Perhaps there was something about following your dreams, I thought, even if it didn't all end perfectly.

I met Ivan in the Wetherspoons near Worcester Foregate station to enjoy a decent and unusual pint before heading to the racecourse. As soon as I sat down he started off into one about the election, and I sensed that his forthright views were about to light the touch-paper in a hotly contested Worcester marginal so tried to calm him down. Ivan muttered "oh but I'm not going to talk about politics and all that", which was code for "I will be wittering on about this exact same subject at frequent intervals throughout the entire afternoon".

I distracted him by switching the conversation to one of his other favourite topics – beer. Ivan talked about the guy who had created the chain of pubs that we were sitting in. Tim Martin had worked in the city, but when he left work and could not find a nice pint and something to eat, he apparently thought bugger it, I'll set up my own place. When he was at school his teacher said "you'll never make anything of your life" and that teacher was called Mr Wetherspoon. Ivan said he was keeping an eye out for his first surname-inspired business founded by a disaffected ex-pupil. Then he got back on his Doom Bar bandwagon.

"What annoys me is when a pub calls itself a real ale pub and you walk in and all it's got is Doom Bar and Tribute. I just walk out."

We met another old teaching acquaintance at the course, also called Ivan, which could get confusing for you, so I shall call him Ivan H whereas the Ivan you already sort of know shall remain simply Ivan. Glad we've got that cleared up. I taught and ran the chess club with Ivan H at a school in Cheltenham for several years before random quirks of fate took us in different directions. The three of us pondered the combinatorial problem of the probability of two Ivans meeting in a group of three, but these were always fiendishly tricky questions that were soon dropped from most maths syllabi, so we talked about the horses instead. I told Ivan H that there was quite a story to be told about the happenings on this course almost two decades ago, but it was one that couldn't be rushed and we needed to wait for the correct moment to give it due ceremony.

We went for a drink, and Ivan demanded that his Guinness come in a non-Guinness glass because he didn't like the shape. At times it felt like I was acting as care in the community for a more mobile and less deaf version of my own father, and decided it was just easier to placate his foibles rather than try and fight them. The barman also went along with that theory and carefully poured the pint in a John Smiths glass, which Ivan claimed made the black stuff taste like nectar. We assembled near the finishing post to watch the fourth race and it seemed like it was the right time for The Story.

Once upon a time, when I was a young man training to be a teacher, I was assigned to a school in South Gloucestershire. I was given a mentor, an experienced chap with a reputation for taming even the most unruly of classes. As a wide-eyed innocent, searching for my persona in the classroom, I admired Ivan for his no-nonsense style and fearsome approach. It wasn't until I realised he was a horse racing fan that my admiration turned to friendship.

Ivan also wrote the timetable, which as luck would have it often resulted in some gaps in his timetable on Tuesday, Wednesday or Thursday afternoons (remember, the Cheltenham Festival was only three days back then). So it was, in the March of 1998, that I was told I would be having an extra class that Wednesday afternoon – Ivan's Year 8s, who were otherwise messing up his free afternoon. Whilst I tried (and failed) to stop them

267

throwing Pritt Sticks at each other, he watched my beloved One Man win the Queen Mother Champion Chase, and in all honesty, I didn't begrudge him one bit. I smiled as he later recalled the scenes after the grey's momentous victory, the cheers ringing in his ears as he watched from the overpass when our hero returned to the stable block.

And so we forged a strong bond through the joyous highs of Festival justice and the savage lows of Aintree despair, as well as through the imperceptible complexity and extreme privilege that was teaching. He was the perfect mentor for me, despite me not realising for another six years that I couldn't be him in the classroom. I had to be myself, because at some point the mask would slip and there would be nowhere left to go. But that's another story.

Anyway, in the long summer of 1998, in the gap between me finishing my training and starting my career, we toured the tracks of the region. Ivan wanted to become a professional gambler, a period he now refers to as his mid-life crisis, but over that summer he won a substantial sum and came pretty damn close to finally giving up the day job. He was on a good run, and we went to Worcester one sunny afternoon to back an old favourite called Zaitoon, trained by the late and mostly-great David Nicholson. I think the money we both had on this grand old chaser differed by a multiple of 1,000, I kid you not. Somehow it didn't matter though. The 11/4 favourite jumped fluently under top weight, galloped his rivals into submission, and from a long way out there was only one winner. Coming to the last some 30 lengths clear we held our breath - things happen in jump racing – but the brave old stalwart didn't let us down, clearing the fence cleanly and cantering towards the line.

Ivan and I both started walking down the concrete steps to collect - him to literally start a new life, me to be part of the moment, and us both to celebrate like never before. Suddenly we became aware of a hush in the crowd, and we looked up from our footings on the steps. The horse still looked fine as it approached the line, and the jockey Richard Johnson sat motionless on top. But people in the crowd were pointing back down the track, to where somebody standing just after the last fence was holding something up in the air, like a small rug or perhaps some sort of bag.

Zaitoon was disqualified because his weight cloth slipped off just after the last fence, within sight of the post. Of course, running the last 100 yards without the extra weight hadn't made a blind bit of difference to the result, but rules are rules, and Nicholson took full responsibility for the incident. I suggested that Ivan should send the betting ticket to The Duke to see if he wished to be held financially responsible as well. We saw out the evening in Worcester as best we could in the circumstances – getting blind drunk and lamenting what could, what should, have been. They somehow let us in to a snooker club and I've no idea how the cloth survived unscathed.

So Ivan never became a professional gambler, and I realised there was no such thing as a dead cert, even if your horse jumped the last 30 lengths up and cruising. The betting exchanges now record in great and stark detail the regular occurrences of the unimaginable occurring, but they can never show the whole picture. Behind every massive fluctuation of the in-running odds there are winners and losers, a hidden human cost that cannot be properly quantified in purely monetary terms. It is interesting that in all my years of punting I have never let my passion become a problem. Whilst my stakes have undoubtedly increased over time, I have never bet more than I could afford to lose. I don't say this because I feel morally superior to those with a gambling problem. I have enough problems of my own to realise how fallible we all are, but luckily none of them are gambling related. And I suppose that's it, really. In the end I may have been incredibly lucky to watch Zaitoon be incredibly unlucky.

And although I've never admitted it to myself, I may even have something to thank David Nicholson for. I'm not sure Ivan would say the same though.

The End. And back to the current version of Worcester, with two Ivans rather than one. The horse we had all backed in the fourth race, Vif Argent, was leading over the last and fortunately there was no Zaitoon ending. Ivan H left to get home and Ivan decided it was time to go to The Dragon, a proper real ale pub that didn't serve Doom Bar or Tribute. He led me on a clever short cut into somebody's back garden before realising it was the gate next door that we should have gone through, but the ale was worth the detour. His eyes lit up when we discovered that we were both at Haydock in two days time, and that he could lead me on a tour around the region he knew so well.

After a quick pint I headed back to where I had left the car to catch up with Frew, Rob, Katy and Fraser. They were providing a bed for the night and I was providing supper from The Bell in Eckington, which turned out to be a lovely pub that successfully combined the two strands of 'gastro' and 'local'. There was an entire blackboard dedicated to the local asparagus, which I partnered with the lamb rump. This may have been a slightly touristy mistake as the rest of the table, who were in the know, ordered the Bell Burger. The food was great, but what the place didn't have was many cushions, so I instituted a game where the person with the most at the end of the evening would be declared the winner of the cushion crown. The competition was going well until a party with an average age at least double our own sat down at a nearby table that has been looted of soft furnishings. Fraser and I shared a sudden pang of guilt and returned the cushions swiftly.

# 40) Chester

## Day 57 – Friday 8 May

I slept well and awoke to the startling news from the general election. The opinion polls had been more wayward than my recent tipping, and various pundits were required to eat various items of clothing. It wasn't quite as incredible a victory as the 1985 council election in Cork, when independent Bernard Murphy pulled off a 33/1 shock after encouraging voters to back him both politically and financially at the local bookies, but it wasn't far off. The most extraordinary part, to a statistician such as myself, was the huge disparity between the national percentage of the vote and the number of seats. Depending on which side of the electoral fence you sit, you could argue that this was a ringing endorsement of the political system, but the idea of proportional representation was to rumble around all day, as I was to later discover.

I could have driven to Chester, but the train from Cheltenham was quicker and nicer. My new theory on buying time had by now been attached to a wider strategy of buying nice things, which included two nights at the swanky Best Western Queens Hotel that was literally yards from the station entrance. With the finishing line now definitely in sight, I had become a little extravagant, the extent of which revealed itself when I got to my room and found a sumptuous double with stunning elevated views over the Chester cityscape.

After settling in, and watching some of the parliamentary post mortem on TV, I retraced my steps to the station's taxi rank. I shared a cab to the course with three lads from Liverpool University. I was pretty sure they hadn't been racing much before because they carried a plastic bag chinking with lager and vodka, which I was pretty sure would not be waved through the turnstiles. They were finance and business students in their last year of studies, about to find their way in the world. One was intent on trading in London, following in the footsteps of his uncle who'd retired at the age of 39. Another had a job lined up with the accountancy firm Baker Tilly and was interested in my previous life as an auditor in London. I told him how I couldn't think of a more worthless thing to do, before realising my lack of tact and mumbling something about how much fun he'd have in London. He was slightly taken aback, but was young and would shrug it off, I was sure.

It was a bit of a mess at the course with various poorly signed entrances all bedecked in a slick of wet Cheshire rain, and I joined a queue that trudged forwards slowly. When I'd watched televised action from the track over the years, the sun always seemed to be beaming down on the lush green turf that contrasted so beautifully with the dappled brown of the city walls and the bright outfits of the ladies of the region. The ladies were present, but the walls looked hard and drab, and the sun was nowhere to be seen. Umbrellas seemed to be the new must have fashion accessory and managed to temporarily save some of the painstakingly planned summer outfits.

Suddenly out of nowhere there was a TV camera in my face. In the shock, my first thought was that the hitherto uninterested media had finally latched on to my amazing journey around all the British racecourses, but that fanciful notion was quickly dispelled.

"Do you have a moment to talk to BBC North West? Great!" said the enthusiastic reporter before I could claim that I was far too busy standing in a queue to talk to her. "What do you think about the first past the post system in the election?"

In my travel-weary state I entirely missed the clever 'first past the post' link, and I wasn't entirely sure why the good people of the North West would give a toss about the views of a southern softie huddling under an umbrella, but I really had nothing else to do so gave it a go. For once I was lucid and cogent, giving a reasoned soliloquy on how it was unfair to have 80% of votes across the country being utterly wasted in constituencies where there was only one possible winner.

"Great!" enthused the reporter, before turning to the cameraman and saying "Steve, do we need to do that again because of the woman in the background?"

Woah, hold on lady, I thought, that was a one off! I was not some sort of performing seal put there for her entertainment. But Steve seemed to have had enough of traipsing around in the rain with a heavy camera and shrugged that it was fine, so we were all spared a repeat performance. The 'woman in the background' then admitted that she was making silly faces and mouthing "Hello Mum" to the camera over my shoulder, which would hopefully make it less likely that the footage would ever be used, and if it were, would hopefully distract the audience from my beer chin.

It was £35 to get into Tattersalls, and to be honest the facilities really didn't merit the entrance fee. An already crowded enclosure resembled an episode of 'Runaround', the Mike Reid vehicle of the 1980s, as huge clusters of racegoers congregated under sporadic shelters like refugees clinging to a raft. Perhaps it was unfair to judge Chester when it was hosing it down, but this was an outdoor event in England and the management really didn't seem to have any contingency plan in place. You could argue that the course, which had reputedly been racing for almost 500 years, had limited space to play with, but in that case it was back to the Cheltenham scenario and numbers needed to be similarly limited.

I arrived just before the first race, but the bottleneck after the turnstiles resembled a herd of wildebeest reluctant to tackle the river crossing, so it was impossible to make progress and get a bet on. The one success in amongst all the drenched chaos seemed to be a smattering of 'bottle bars' where, without the hassle of pouring a pint, the turnaround was almost instant and therefore surprisingly queue-less on a feature day. Or was it, perhaps, that at £4.50 for a small bottle of Stella (yes, really) nobody could afford to buy one?

The adverse conditions prompted a weird Dunkirk spirit and despite the weather there was a pleasant atmosphere. The queue for the gents stretched to preposterous lengths and meant that I was also fractionally late to fight my way back out to the ring and get a bet on for the second race. Packs of young men were respectful and almost sympathetic to the reams of young women whose outfits were getting slowly ruined. It was like the final of Miss Chester was being played out on the set of It's A Knockout, with pantomime chefs throwing buckets of water over the unfortunate contestants below.

As the going on the famous Roodee turned very soft, the form turned upside down, and most of the races were won by outsiders. It was a course which was always turning sharply left, normally favouring those drawn on the inside rail who showed a liking for running anti-clockwise around telephone boxes, but in the downpour it was a case of whichever horse coped best with the mud. I decided it was time to get up high in one of the covered stands, but thousands of others had the same idea. As the inevitable outbreak of non-runners gathered pace, I was left stood by a chilly brick wall with no view of the track, trying to study form from a wet newspaper and with no idea of which horses were still proposing to run through the quagmire.

Then something really very strange happened. I left. This was quite a sudden, almost subconscious decision, with a violent exit reminiscent of David Cameron marching out of shot at one of his recent soundbite-to-camera interviews. As I searched for a taxi I began to consider what I'd done and attempted to find reasons to turn back and see it out, but there were none. The cabbie joked that the jockeys would soon be wearing wetsuits.

After Ffos Las became my first ever one-bet racecourse, Chester broke new ground and became a no-bet racecourse. I had spent over £50 to stand in the rain for an hour, interrupted briefly only by a reassuringly expensive small lager and a long trip to the loo. Nobody, it seems, predicted the election result, but surely somebody should have guessed it might rain in May and planned accordingly? People deserved more for the money they were spending and the effort they were making. I thought about asking the cabbie to drop me at a good pub to watch the rest of the races on TV, but the comfort of my hotel bedroom was calling and I needed to dry out. So I settled into the warm and luxurious surroundings and took the opportunity to catch up with some writing and the last bits of planning. Then I ordered room service and enjoyed a pretty decent attempt at a rump steak with a nice glass of red wine. I had just flicked on the BBC News at Ten and was relaxing on the bed when I heard a sound that I somehow knew well but couldn't quite place.

They say that listening to your own voice is one of the most embarrassing things a human can do. What they forget to mention is that when your voice is on national TV, and accompanied by the image of a fat, bedraggled man huddling under an umbrella, the embarrassment is multiplied by a million. My beer-chin hit the proverbial floor as I stared in disbelief at the screen. I wondered briefly whether I had drifted off and imagined it all, but then the texts started coming through and I knew it was real. Many of the messages asked where I had got the figure that 80% of all votes were wasted, to which I replied that in the spirit of all good statistics, it was entirely made up.

At that point I was FaceTimed by The Wife who was having dinner around at Andrew and Maura's with the usual suspects. She appeared both devastatingly pretty and entirely unattainable, and I felt instantly buoyed to see her but slightly morose that I wasn't there. She passed the phone around the table and everyone seemed in raucously good spirits, most of them unable to decline the golden opportunity to rip the piss out of my television debut. Again, it rammed home the point that I was choosing, by my very act of every moment of every day not choosing otherwise, to continue with the increasingly ludicrous charade when there were a thousand other things I could be doing instead.

I remembered my harsh words to the young lad in the taxi that morning, and wondered whether I could truly describe my current employment as "worthwhile".

# 41) Haydock

## Day 58 – Saturday 9 May

The breakfast hall of the Queens Hotel in Chester was creaking just a little under the weight of hungry racegoers recovering from the three-day meeting, but a complimentary glass of bucks fizz always smoothes things over at 9am. They had forgotten to deliver my Racing Post but quickly sorted it out, and I sat and ate whilst perusing the day's races. I had been to Haydock Park once before as part a friend's Stag weekend a long time ago. We watched a punch up in the car park at the end of the day, between friends it appeared, the brouhaha apparently starting over who would get on the minibus first. A feisty lot, up here in Cheshire. Later, we managed to lose the Stag in a Liverpool nightclub under slightly dubious circumstances before he reappeared the next morning, but that's another story.

I was meeting Ivan at the course, even though he was going via Chester, as we'd had a minor disagreement about the best way to get to Haydock. I was going to Newton Le Willows, which was 38 minutes on the train followed by a short taxi. He was going via Liverpool and St Helens, and then getting the bus, which was an awful lot longer. He rightly pointed out that my route was just a means of getting from A to B, whereas his was a journey that would take in a good pub he knew in Liverpool. Ivan's journeys usually involved a good pub he knew. As it was, my train was delayed by six minutes, which meant I arrived as the first race was underway and he claimed victory in his route selection.

There was a decent crowd and they clearly liked a drink. This was the only mixed card of both flat and jump racing in my eighty-day window, after Sandown decided a few years ago to split its end of season action between two separate days of the different codes. I couldn't work out the ground. It was clearly soft enough to turn the flat form upside down, like it had at Chester, but didn't seem that soft for the jumpers. Like Pontefract, no ticket was issued on entry so again I found the racecourse office and explained my predicament. The lady offered to give me any uncollected ticket at the end of the day and as I thanked her I already knew it was a 100/1 shot that I would remember. Food options were again severely limited, except if you wanted a burger, in which case you could have it single or double, with or without cheese.

The punting progressed in frustrating fashion with seconds and thirds. My only winner was a silly bet on an outsider in a flat race that I hadn't studied and only selected because the flat races were giving weird results.

So the last race became the 'getting out of a bit of a hole' handicap. After the betting bank went into the black a week earlier at Pontefract, it had now, with the usual combination of bad luck and poor judgement, swung back into the red, and I needed a good result to turn things around. It was a good betting opportunity because I didn't like the favourite and was sure it was between Bincombe and Glen Countess. The former had won well at Chepstow last time, while the latter had been off the course for almost 500 days, over which time she'd been transferred to the Sue Smith stable which had won a race earlier in the afternoon. It was a real struggle to choose. I waited to see if there was any smart money for Glen Countess that would indicate she was ready to run well after her long absence, but if anything she drifted out in the betting and I decided to secure 7/2 on Bincombe. Just before the off I popped back to the ring to torture myself with the news that late support for Glen Countess had finally come, and I knew even before halfway that I had chosen wrong.

We went back Ivan's way, and on the bus to St Helens I realised that I had secured the final loser of my long afternoon as I had completely forgotten to go back to the office for a spare ticket. When we reached Liverpool, Ivan led me to his pub past a big building wrapped in blue plastic, explaining that it was previously an eyesore.

"So they're rebuilding?" I assumed.

"No, it just looks better covered up."

If encasing a building in blue plastic improved its appearance goodness knows what ghastly monstrosity lurked beneath the wrappers. It must have caused crashes and had people vomiting at the sight of it. After a few more minutes we reached The Ship & Mitre which was an unassuming prospect from the unattractive street, but once inside offered such an enormous range of beers that I couldn't help but love it. Sections of the busy pub were in raucous spirits, clearly out to enjoy their Saturday night to the full, but there was a decent atmosphere and a wide range of clientele. Ivan stuck with his hoppy stuff but I couldn't resist a Belgian beer called Kwak, which sadly didn't come in its trademark test-tube glass but tasted lovely all the same. The food looked good too, but it was time to move on to Chester.

Ivan had planned a little pub crawl near the station and we started at Old Harkers, which was a little pretentious, but the Thirsty Moon bitter was lovely. We moved on to a Camra award-winning watering hole and I sampled an extraordinary dark and fruity concoction. I wasn't sure it entirely worked, but I love the incredible wealth of brewing riches we are treated to in this country, surely better than anywhere else in the world. Perhaps that is a thought for my next ludicrous adventure?

I was still smarting from my wrong bet in the last when we reviewed the afternoon's racing. Ivan explained that his bet in the penultimate race was because he had been "kicked in the goolies" too many times when not backing a horse trained by Nigel Twiston-Davies. I took this to mean metaphorically, rather than getting too close in the parade ring, but the pain of this was obviously raw enough for him to steam in on a horse he hadn't really considered or fancied. I likened it to insurance, and gave Ivan the benefit of a full exposition on how buying insurance when you are not legally required to do so made no sense – the five year extended warranty on your TV is where they make their profit.

Ivan listened patiently, before declaring "Yeah, but I don't do the logic like that, I'm just more emotional than you", and he was probably right. "Why didn't you back Glens Melody in the last?" he insisted.

I explained that I didn't like backing horses when I'd missed the better price, and he came out with the old 'winner is a winner' line, which I vehemently disagreed with on the grounds of the punters holy grail of 'value'. I had also run out of cash by that point, but I could have borrowed some from Ivan, and perhaps should have in hindsight. We come at betting from slightly different angles but are both true gamblers because the pain of situations such as these burns deep and long. Somehow it's not the money, it's the getting it wrong. But if it doesn't hurt, I suppose it doesn't matter, and the honest and heartfelt conversations of later in the evening reminded me that, in the overall scheme of things, backing the wrong horse really wasn't such a big deal.

# 42) Ludlow

## Day 59 – Sunday 10 May

The breakfast hall of the Queens Hotel was a little more relaxed now that the dust had fully settled from the Chester May Festival. As if to signify the new vibe, a girl sat down and played the guitar, quite nicely, and at the hot buffet they had proper sautéed potatoes rather than those weird triangular hash brown creations. I got the train back to Cheltenham where Frew kindly picked me up. She was blissfully unaware of my new celebrity status from my political punditry debut, and didn't think there had been any paparazzi lurking near my car on their driveway that morning. Even so, I didn't stay long as I didn't want to tempt fate, and quickly crossed the M5 towards Shropshire.

I was really looking forward to Ludlow. Not only was it nominated by Chesterfield John as his favourite course, when I quizzed him after his Taunton finale, but Ivan informed me that it served a wonderful prawn curry from an outlet in the middle of the track. When I arrived I found it was indeed lovely. The Edwardian stands gave the place a sense of history and the punters seemed at ease in their varied and comfortable surroundings. I climbed the stairs to the roof and surveyed the glorious scene from a stunning position. The tiered viewing angles gave a feeling of watching gladiators from an amphitheatre, although the runners in the first race fought out a mostly civilized battle with a 14/1 outsider winning – that probably wouldn't have happened in Roman times.

After the race there was a steady stream of people heading towards the centre of the course. Either they were going to the curiously-sited paddock, or they too had heard rumours of a sublime prawn curry, so I put a little more spring in my step, worried that they would sell out. I found…..a burger van. My search became more frantic, like Anneka Rice in the closing minutes of Treasure Hunt, and reached its nadir when I somehow thought a prawn curry stall might be lurking behind a bouncy castle in the Course Enclosure. Of course it wasn't Neil! Why would they hide a food outlet behind a bouncy castle, and even if they wanted to, the Health and Safety executive would have been worried that a child would launch themselves into a hot wok and vetoed the idea.

I pondered for a second what extraordinary twists and turns of fate had led me to be standing in a Shropshire field peering behind a giant inflatable for a mystical curry. Luckily, I managed to snap out of it quickly because thinking like that can mess you up. It's a bit like the concept of infinity – we've lost too many good mathematicians to that cruel mistress over the years. In any case, I hadn't given up the search that easily and I tracked down a couple of neon-vested stewards, who had apparently never heard of a prawn curry and repeated the words like I'd just asked them where I might obtain a Chinook helicopter.

"Prawn curry? Prawn curry?? No, no I don't think so." They looked confused, like I was talking in riddles, and quickly referred the matter on. "This man here will know."

A senior neon-vest then ambled over and confirmed the worst.

"Yeah, the guy packed up a couple of years ago, sold the business and retired. Loads of people still ask about the prawn curry."

I was left deflated and meekly thanked them before moving on. Possibly the lowest ebb of my journey so far had not been derived from an unlucky loser or a pang of homesickness, but from a missing Indian dish. It seemed an overreaction, but once you've got a curry in your mind it's hard to let it go.

In the second, I fancied Greenlaw to improve from his previous race. I had seen him win at Wetherby, with Big Casino (a winner at Haydock yesterday) back in third. More importantly, he'd hung to his right that day and finished wide on the course, and I thought he'd be better off going clockwise with the inside rail to help straighten him out. This was just one of the many imponderables to attempt to factor into the rocket science that was form studying. Betting on athletics, for example, must be a lot simpler as the tracks are a standard size and configuration, and with fairly similar surfaces I would guess. Furthermore, the athletes are always running in the same direction, left-handed in horse racing parlance. I wonder if there have been athletes over the years who would have been better going right-handed and never got the chance to shine, a thousand unknown Olympic champions defeated by a convention.

Greenlaw didn't realise, though, that he was meant to improve for going right-handed. Perhaps it had got nothing to do with my theory, and it was instead the ground, or the opposition, or he just didn't fancy it today because he was promised a certain type of food in Ludlow that had failed to materialise. The Twiston-Davies team sent out Belmount to win well on his debut over fences. Ivan would have insurance-backed it if he were here to avoid another "kick in the goolies".

For the drive home Frew had lent me a Dick Francis audiobook. I loved the way the narrator's voice changed halfway through a line when he realised he was doing the wrong accent, and how all the female characters ended up sounding like Dick Emery. It was arrant tosh, but at least it stopped me moping about the prawn curry.

# 43) Towcester

## Day 60 – Monday 11 May

Before I began my journey I gathered my closest friends to tell them what I was doing. It took on the guise of an informal planning meeting as I wanted their strategic input and inspired ideas – I wanted them, but of course never got them, and as the evening wore on their contributions grew more and more silly as each beer went down. Some of the suggestions were so inappropriate that they cannot be aired in this book before the watershed, and the pinnacle of their collective achievements came when one of the assembled clowns (luckily, I forgot who it was by that point) came up with the genius suggestion of taking a toaster to Towcester. This idea was so well received that we tried to extend it into a countrywide theme of taking an appropriately named household appliance to all the racecourses. We got as far as taking a boiler to Worcester and a bath to Bath, before running out of inspiration and getting tired of our joke. The whole line of thought may have been inspired by Tony Hawks taking a fridge around Ireland, but he only took a small fridge, and a bath is a whole different ball game, although better for sleeping in. And bathing in, for that matter.

Anyhow, when I arrived at the Northamptonshire venue I found a large and toaster-less crowd relaxing in the evening sun. I had forgotten that it was free entry and therefore began the usual wild goose chase of trying to secure a small piece of cardboard that said "I was here!" I was beginning to wish I hadn't started collecting my tickets and badges in the first place because I had spent 20 minutes on the phone to the similarly ticketless Haydock that morning discussing audit trails. However, the staff at

Towcester were enthusiastic and found me a hospitality badge. "But it's not valid for today!" they added, before I got any clever ideas.

Towcester really was a Jekyll and Hyde character. The positives included that there was plenty of space available, even on a sunny May evening offering free entry. The grandstands were roomy and there were nice touches throughout – a tent had been erected out the back and filled with tables, chairs, TVs and old people. Off to the side, there was a grassy area where two small football goals had been placed on mown grass for the Dads to take the kids to in between races. However (and I know I'm beginning to sound like a cracked record here), unless I was missing something, there was one bar and one burger van to service the entire main enclosure. It didn't seem particularly like a 'drinking crowd', but the sheer numbers resulted in a six-deep melee at the understaffed bar. Surely Towcester had implemented free entry in order to try and increase attendance – why would they not want to sell more food and drink?

If I had to give one piece of advice to racecourses, from my lofty position of having gone racing a lot, it would be to sort out this very sortable issue right away - it is surely much easier to rectify than all the other more complex financial and industry-wide matters our sport has to tackle. Management need to realise that queues at tills don't mean more money, it means the venue is managed inefficiently and more staff and tills are needed in order to produce more money. So I humbly present my blueprint for a rapid transformation of the racing experience, and Nick Rust can contact me at any time to discuss consultancy terms:-

Food:- follow the lead of Newton Abbot and Doncaster by producing good in-house food at reasonable prices; if this isn't possible for whatever reason then invite more and better quality outside caterers; invite Chinese and Indian vans to provide respite from burger overload; sell pies and sausages with mash and gravy; ask artisan companies to exhibit; and serve decent sandwiches (people like them at lunchtime, and they speed things up because they require no cooking, yet I found it virtually impossible to buy one on a racecourse).

Drink:- employ more and better trained staff in the bars; if there is not enough space then build temporary stands for racedays; have quick-turnaround bottle bars sprinkled about (but charge less than Chester!); ask local breweries to stage mini beer-festivals; and adopt post office queuing systems to avoid the service injustice.

Ambiance:- buy more outside benches; buy more indoor tables and chairs; get the chippy to build shelves around spare walls and pillars, with hooks underneath for coats; and if people are buying a proper meal give them proper plates and cutlery rather than plastic.

I believe all of these solutions would cost little to implement but would reap huge rewards, not just in the short term increased turnover of food and drink sales, but in the longer term overall product of an enjoyable day at the races, which is the only way to build sustainable growth in attendances. This is not rocket science. If you asked ten random punters at your nearest racecourse I am sure they would say the same. Perhaps the situation is different in hospitality, and the service is skewed towards the people with bigger £ signs above their heads. I wouldn't know, because I don't do hospitality (even when I've just been given a free hospitality badge!), but if this is the case then I would also argue that being nicer to customers in hospitality was a false economy. In the next recession companies will stop doing hospitality, by which time your average punter will have got fed up, eaten at home before they arrived and smuggled in a few drinks because they've become so disillusioned with the racecourse offerings.

Of course this rant is not at all directed solely at Towcester, which only bears the brunt of my ire because they happen to have a name that suggests nice simple food, quickly served. This is endemic throughout the land, and it's simply not acceptable to park a burger van by the paddock and say it's job done.

The other problem with Towcester in particular was the course itself, a large loop with a stiff uphill finish. I wanted to really like it as another fine example of the individuality of British racecourses in a beautiful setting, but they'd gone and built a greyhound track slap bang in the middle, on a raised mound just the other side of the finishing post. The issue wasn't so much that you therefore lost sight of the horses on the far side (plenty of tracks suffered a similar issue), but the dog track just seemed so incongruous and overbearing. To me, greyhound racing suggested the bright lights and clamour of the city, not a Northamptonshire country estate.

Owner Lord Hesketh, boss of the 1970s Formula 1 team and a colourful character by all accounts, added the greyhound track in 2014 in an effort to secure the future of the operation, saying "If this place is going to survive and prosper, it's going to have to operate for more than 17 days a year." His vision was not only a boost for the local economy (creating 80 new jobs) but for greyhound racing as a whole, which had suffered some big-name closures over the last decade. It was certainly a welcome alternative to a pop concert or car boot sale, and I like going to the dogs. My only problem with the otherwise eminently sensible business proposition was the siting of the track. I understand it needed to be in front of the main stand, but couldn't it have been just a little lower, so as to be slightly less obtrusive? It somehow sent the subliminal message that the horse racing you were watching was not enough on its own. In my opinion, it distracted the attention and drained the atmosphere, like watching a football match in the middle of an athletics track.

Returning to the equine from the canine, the lessons to be learnt from the horses that evening were that the

Henderson ones seemed to be in better form than the Pipe ones. I thought I'd backed a Pipe winner in the second when the unusually named Susie Sheep nipped ahead of the labouring Henderson-trained What A Jewel, who then rallied to see it out. The Henderson dominance was confirmed in the last race when his Divine Spear upset the Pipe favourite. They were finishing tired up the fearsome climb to the line, as indeed I was with a little over two weeks to go until I completed my venture, but with a little encouragement the summit could be reached.

I didn't eat or drink at the course, and on the way home I stopped for a KFC. It may not have been fine dining, but I did have a choice at the service station and I didn't have to queue for that long.

# 44) Wincanton

## Day 61 – Tuesday 12 May

I arrived more than two hours early for Wincanton, which was virtually unheard of in those time-pressured months. The reason was that I was meeting Richard, the brave and slightly bonkers chap I met at Plumpton who was visiting all the British racecourses on foot over a period of 13 months, to walk the course.

He greeted me warmly and recounted his journey from Newton Abbot. Walking from South Devon to the eastern tip of Somerset, a journey he described as breathtakingly pretty, seemed an enormous undertaking to someone such as myself who can lap Tescos car park for hours to get a space near the entrance, but to Richard doing less than 20 miles per day was just a stroll in the park. This wasn't always the case, though, as he revealed that before his venture started his wife would say that the furthest he would walk would be to the corner shop to get a Racing Post. He introduced his daughter and campaign manager Minty who had planned the whole adventure.

"I talk and walk," he said modestly, "and she does everything else. She's the real brains – she's done all the PR and marketing stuff, all the organisation and liaising with the racecourses."

I chatted to Minty about the nuances of the fixture list and how the race planners, unbelievably, didn't seem to have people like Richard and me in mind when writing their schedules. We swapped notes on the logistics of touring the courses and she revealed that she was worried about the winter meetings at Uttoxeter, Sandown and Ludlow. I told her that Ffos Las went wrong for me on Day 3, but where there was a will, there was a way.

As we set off on the lush turf we were suddenly joined by a large group of supporters. Most of them seemed to know Richard very well and I felt slightly guilty about gatecrashing a personal party, but he was extremely generous with his time as we lapped the chase course (it being marginally shorter than the hurdles course - clever guy, this) and when he introduced me to everyone I got gently teased for not walking my eighty day tour.

I described him as bonkers because he surely must have been to contemplate a walk of almost 3,000 miles, but when we got chatting I found a man who was at once intelligent and warm, eloquent and positive. He fondly remembered going racing with his father on the occasion of his 21st birthday.

"The only definite when planning the route was that I wanted to start and finish at Newmarket. Part of my birthday present from my father was a day out to the Craven meeting. We started at 5.30 in the morning, drove to Newmarket, went to Warren Hill for first lot, followed by the Rutland Hotel for breakfast, then visited three different yards....."

The itinerary for the day was rattled off like it was yesterday, and they enjoyed it so much that they repeated the trip every year for the next quarter of a century. He now walks in honour of his father and to raise funds for the charity that fights the miserable disease, pancreatic cancer, that claimed him three years ago.

"I haven't been back to the Craven meeting since my father died. I have this pipe dream to try to get everybody who walked any part of any leg throughout the entire 13 months to come to Newmarket that day, and we will all walk up the July course to the intersection and down the Rowley Mile."

I was impressed by Richard's ambition – I was planning on a carvery at Stratford with the usual suspects to mark the end of my journey. The other half of his immense fundraising efforts was to be directed towards

Racing Welfare, a charity that looks after the unsung heroes of the industry. The racing community had taken him to their heart and Richard cited their incredible support as the most pleasing aspect of his journey so far. That was in stark contrast to his worst moment, which came only the day before when a Jack Russell bit him and its owner told him to bugger off.

Richard said he had a horse with Oliver Sherwood a while back who was "absolutely useless" but they'd stayed in touch. He made Many Clouds his informal project mascot before the Hennessy but the wonderful chaser quickly became a full-on equine ambassador for the charity and they had a special rug made for him. Richard and Minty were invited to the Grand National, where Jonjo and Jackie O'Neill asked if they could walk the course with them (yes, really, that way around!). Minty was in tears at the top of grandstand even before Many Clouds rounded the home turn, and apparently there was quite a party afterwards.

"There are many, many really good people in racing," he continued "but there are none better than Oliver and Tarnya – they've had more than their fair share of ups and downs, and they've just helped out without being asked. Nobody suggested that they sell cups of tea and pass round the bucket for Walking The Courses when they had Kauto Star up at Rhonehurst, they just did it."

I asked Richard what happened next, at the end of the thirteen months when the music stopped. It's a question I asked Chesterfield John on Day 4 of my quest in Taunton, and one that I would have to ask myself fairly soon. Did he have any grand designs on a new project?

"No, no, back to the day job," which had been very understanding by all accounts "I'm not planning on walking the courses in Ireland or France, although if anyone wants to take the brand on, I'd be happy."

I quickly ruled myself out. That was a conversation I really didn't want to have with The Wife, at least not yet.

We would soon go our separate ways, Richard heading off to Salisbury and myself to Bath, but our paths were due to cross again in Ripon at the weekend.

Wincanton's sales and marketing co-ordinator, Katherine Dalgety, was taking photos of the spectacle and we got talking about my own quest, which seemed a little banal alongside Richard's. She asked me how it all came about, and I had to admit that I was still searching for an answer to the big question of "Why?" Perhaps there just wasn't one. Ian Barlow, Chairman of the Racecourse Association came up to join in the chat. He had recently completed his own "full house" and was pretty chuffed with his achievement until a friend pointed out that he hadn't seen both flat and jump racing at the dual-code courses, but I thought that was getting picky, like saying you hadn't been to Chelmsford if you had visited Great Leighs. I enthused about the wonderful variety his racecourses offered, and I mentioned as a prime example Ludlow and how it seemed to bring the community together, even if it wasn't over a prawn curry. Ian concurred and said that inclusivity was a big selling point in his discussions with the government.

As if to prove the point, I met a lovely couple over lunch in the Grazers restaurant and we started chatting whilst attempting unsuccessfully to cut our roast beef with flimsy plastic cutlery. Bob and Margaret were originally from Essex but now spent a lot of time touring with their caravan. They weren't exactly devotees, but were staying just down the road and thought they would give it a go, and I think they would have enjoyed their day, especially if they later found a way to cut up their food. There was also a bunch of guys causing a bit of a stir in the Premier Enclosure who did not look entirely normal, depending on your definition of normality. It transpired that they were on a stag from Devon, and their off-the-shoulder numbers were merely to make the most of Ladies Day. The paddock commentator leading the Best Turned Out Lady competition recognised that they had certainly made an eye-catching effort, but they narrowly failed to win the prize. I'm not sure they were that upset as they seemed to be having a whale of a time in the winners' enclosure entertaining the galleries.

Wincanton was just fantastic, with an abundance of places to sit, eat, drink and settle. You could get a freshly made sandwich or a pint of real ale, both of which had proved astonishingly hard to find in the previous nine weeks, and the whole place was tidy and friendly, with a good view of the action. I backed a brave winner in the first by the name of Karl Marx, who led all the way and stayed on gamely, philosophically sharing the funds from the bookmakers around the racecourse community. As I walked back from the ring with my winnings I passed Richard going the other way, happily grasping his own winning ticket and adding slightly to his already extensive mileage with a trip to the payout queue, although I'm sure he didn't mind. I racked my increasingly feeble brain to find a course I'd liked more. They were all so different that it was difficult, and perhaps even unfair, to compare them on such unlevel playing fields, but I felt this unassuming local track must be near the top of most lists. Generous facilities, a sunny day, and the feel-good factor of the Walking The Courses bandwagon had undoubtedly combined to make it a great start to the afternoon. Perhaps I just felt more at home with the place because it was the only course I had walked in my life?

I chose I'm In Charge in the second race, who just failed to get up close home in the handicap chase during a rousing, grandstand-shaking finish. And then, all of a sudden, the bubble burst on my beautiful afternoon. A hush spread through the crowd as it became apparent that an ambulance and horsebox were attending an incident on the far side of the course. The commentator said that Allerford Jack had been pulled up after jumping the eighth fence. It was a long way in the distance, but I grew more anxious as time ticked by because I couldn't see a horse. The guy next to me was also watching matters closely through his binoculars, and we stood there mutely for ten minutes as the stands emptied, comrades in expectant grief. Eventually the vehicles seemed to be moving and I looked at his expression.

"Any positive signs?" I said with empty hope, because I already knew the answer.

He just shook his head and walked down the steps in silence. I stood there a while longer, watching the horsebox drive along the back straight to the stable area. The words of Graham from the Racehorse Sanctuary came back to me, when he had said at the end of my visit that I should give him a call if I thought he could help - he would jump in the lorry in an instant, and drive anywhere in the country if needs be. Again, it was hard to see what was going on, but when the horsebox stopped I couldn't see any horse emerging. I too left the deserted stand and headed to the car park. Allerford Jack was dead.

# 45) Bath

## Day 62 – Wednesday 13 May

It had taken 61 days of my quest before I was present at the death of a horse, and it cut me to the bone. I had several fanciful ideals when I started out – I wanted to be ahead with the betting, I wanted the project to be a success, I wanted to discover a new direction in my post-teaching tundra, and I really wanted them to all come home safe and sound. My odyssey had been challenging and difficult in so many ways, but now the shadow of a horse dying would forever taint its tapestry. The only thing I could be thankful for was that I hadn't witnessed the tragedy close-up, but I knew that was a vain straw at which to grasp and was certainly no consolation to Allerford Jack or his connections.

I'm not going to tell you that I considered stopping my tour, because I didn't. I had seen horses dying whilst watching the sport I loved before, and whilst it had always been a terrible and sickening thing, I had managed to move on. However, I'm also not going to tell you that my views were, or are, set in stone either. If I saw a fatality at Bath later, would that change my mind? Two? Five? If 17 horses died in the remaining 17 days of my quest, would that change my mind? I didn't know back then, just as I can't tell you now, exactly where that line lies. But there is a line, in there somewhere in the midst of those numbers, and I shall know when it has been crossed. For me to tell you otherwise would be terribly conceited and inhumane, not to mention entirely untrue.

When friends have asked about the matter, I have never really come up with a perfect response. Yes, I watch horse racing and some of them die, but I still watch horse racing. At the moment, I am okay with the numbers involved. In the future, there may come a time when I am not. That is the stark truth of the matter, and any clever words about "well looked after", "risks are minimised" and "could die running around a field at home" will not change that. My son was about to have a major operation, and general anaesthetics carry risks. Every year people die as a direct result of the procedure. But the numbers are low and I was okay with the very small risk involved. I hoped he would be well looked after in hospital, and that risks would be minimised, and knew that there were many and various other dangers in life, including possibly greater ones driving him to the hospital than during his stay, but all of these hopes were secondary to the main issue – I desperately wanted him to come through the operation and have a better life because of it.

So the day after Allerford Jack died, despite the loose and vague sadness that I felt, as well as the savage and heart-wrenching grief that others more closely connected must have felt, life carried on for the rest of us, as did my journey.

I was relieved to finally be free of the big stretches of time behind the wheel, but as if to rain on my post-driving parade, the Gods of Probability did a right royal job of screwing up the trains. Two cancellations and some random guesswork later, via both Bristols (so to speak) and with the first race long gone, I arrived in Bath having picked up Al along the way (intentionally, and a mate, in case you were wondering). There were no taxis, though, and the second race also disappeared to the results pages without my involvement.

Eventually we found a taxi, and the cabbie told us that the golf club were buying the racecourse and that soon Bath Races would be no more. The geezer, bedecked in shell suit and mullet, also said he owned half of the valley and his son had horses in training with Paul Nicholls, so I resolved to keep a waiting brief on the imminent closure.

Liam was waiting for us at the entrance, kitted out in his country squire attire with an added straw boater, which he claimed made his outfit more racing-ified. This affable chap will talk to anyone, and Al described him as "fly-paper for freaks". I couldn't miss another race so we rushed in and I panic-backed an outsider because I didn't like the odds-on favourite, and yet again I was right but wrong. Lead A Merry Dance did as his name implied to beat Glastonberry easily.

After almost four hours of train travel for what would have been a one and a half hour drive, I was in need of a beer, and we retired to the Bath Ales bar. The barmaid poured the wrong pint and when I corrected her she let me have the other one for free. This proved to be my only winner of the evening. The racecourse had developed an array of clever ideas for efficiently using space. They had apparently tackled the problem of being inactive most of the year in a different way to Towcester – instead of building a greyhound track, they had put an office block next to the grandstand. Suited gentlemen multitasked by working and watching, and in another ingenious initiative, a mobile phone mast doubled up as the furlong marker. Clever, that.

If you wanted a main meal it was the usual racecourse Model T menu - anything you like, as long as it's a burger and chips. However, I was ecstatic to later find a stall selling fresh fruit. To a racecourse-hardened cynic, this was an oasis in a desert of mediocrity and I opted for a bowl of mixed berries. I was intrigued by the sign on the table that offered "Chesse and Pineapple" in a modern twist on a 1970s classic, combining board games and exotic fruit, but despite the abundance of horses there were no bishops or castles to be seen. I wasn't sure it would catch on.

After an enjoyable if mostly losing evening, we headed for the taxis and secured a Ford Galaxy with a spitting image of ex-England rugby prop Phil Vickery behind the wheel. I had to ask, and he confirmed that he was indeed the younger and better-looking version without the cauliflower ears. Liam and Al called him "Drive" in their weird Bristolian ways, like you might call a hairdresser "Cut" or a racehorse "Run". He dropped us outside a bar and, sheep-like, we headed straight inside. Perhaps Drive got commission for dropping gormless punters outside?

We had a big discussion on whether racing was crooked, and I produced a couple of prime examples from the evening's racing where I felt the jockeys made some odd choices in their quest for victory. Without naming names, in the fourth race one drove his mount right handed into the scrimmage when a left handed smack, or even hands and heels to keep it straight may have produced a 33/1 winner. Yes, I was talking out of my pocket. Later, an apprentice successfully manoeuvred his mount from a promising position on the home bend to a hopeless one by the furlong pole. Neither incident was investigated by the stewards, and nor would I have expected them to have been. Disgruntled jockeys could rightly question whether I have ever tried to steer an animal at 40mph in a constantly shifting sea of others, but I feel that would be missing the point. It is not prevalent, but it does happen, and the Disciplinary Notices on the BHA website make for interesting reading.

Let me deal with this directly:- I do not believe all British racing to be 'straight'. In other words, I do not think all horses are put in the best position to win races all the time. But, and this is the surprising thing, it doesn't bother me that much. Part of the initiative test for me is to spot the potentially dubious races. If I back a favourite that isn't run on its merits, I think that will be counterbalanced in the long run by 'accidentally' winning on the horses that are. I understand that two wrongs don't make a right, and that it may sound an ugly proposition to the uninitiated, but I would argue it's not that far removed from any other area of life. In my early auditing career I got very disillusioned that none of the numbers in a set of accounts were correct, and yet plenty of people play the stock market based on financial data that is, if I'm being blunt, almost entirely wrong. I put it to you that most of our decisions in life are made with incomplete knowledge, and the game is to beat the system without even necessarily knowing the various injustices that we are fighting against.

Perhaps that sounds defeatist, but I believe it is also a realistic stance. Most people gamble enormous sums on property or pensions with very incomplete and biased information, yet would run a mile from putting a fiver on a horse race where it is vaguely possible that some might be trying more than others. Can anybody truly say they found a situation where they had perfect information? Surely that is a luxury only afforded to professional 'chesse' players. I just try to do the best I can with imperfect information. And that evening at Bath, I hadn't done very well.

A mini pub crawl ensued, passing Clinton Cards which surely had no right to still exist in the harsh reality of the modern trading environment, a bit like Bath racecourse perhaps, but both clung on stubbornly in the face of mounting pressure. We finished up in the Be At One Bar which was packed with young ladies and, frankly, not very many young men. Perhaps that was because blokes were reticent to pay £9 for a swanky cocktail twirled by a tattooed barman? We were confused by the choice, intimidated by the gender bias, deafened by the music, and were also doing nothing to raise the number of young men in the joint I might add, so shuffled outside to the terrace to drink our creations and be harassed by beggars. However, if you are a trendy young thing out for the evening in Bath and have a spare £300 to get a round in, you could certainly choose a worse venue. I bade Al and Liam farewell and headed for the station hoping that the trains would be kinder on the way home, and they were.

# 46) York

## Day 64 – Friday 15 May

To say I cut it fine for the 10:30 from Kings Cross would be putting it mildly. In fact, I would hazard a guess that I cut it just about as fine as anyone has ever cut it, in these modern times of train doors not opening whilst the train is moving.

It all started off well enough, Eric arriving on time to take me to the local station, but unfortunately not my case which sat mutely in the hallway at home. He whipped the car round and we set off back home, the suspension groaning as we flew over the speedbumps. Eric is normally a steady driver, but he drove as if the fragile future of my project rested in his ageing taxi. Case retrieved, we set off again through increasingly congested roads. I made the connection in Reading by about 23 seconds, and kept quiet and involved with my laptop as the train conductor fined people around me for having off-peak tickets. In the taxi at Paddington the cabbie gave me an unwanted pep talk.

"You'll get there, mate, even if you miss the 10:30 and catch a later one. As long as nobody dies, that's the main thing."

I refrained from telling him that he would die if he came out with any more of that crap, as I wasn't sure it would help my cause. Instead, I simply mentioned that it would be really nice to make the 10:30 as we had Advance tickets for that service only. The traffic was shocking. It was like that scene in The Truman Show where Jim Carrey is trying to leave the city and all the choreographed stooges rush to block his path. I phoned Simon to explain that it was touch and go, and that he may have to accidentally faint whilst boarding the train and loll halfway out of the doors. He told me he would do his best and I was to head for platform 1 on the right hand side. The cabbie dropped me at 10:26 and I rushed inside, shouting at strangers "Where's platform 1?" but nobody seemed to know, or if they did they weren't telling a wide-eyed lunatic with flailing limbs and baggage. I saw a sign and sprinted past a phalanx of tourists just before a bottleneck, but there was still a long way to go and I wasn't sure my burning lungs could cope with any more sprinting.

I found what I thought was the last platform as whistles were blowing sharply, but I hesitated as all I could see were signs for platform 0? What station in its right mind would invent a platform 0? As I paused, I felt the whole escapade drifting away from me (or was it the blood draining from my head?) and momentarily wanted nothing more than to lie down on platform 0 and sleep for a very long time. Then I saw Simon at the train door, frantically waving, and managed to summon up one last Herculean effort with my legs and lungs screaming their objections. He was getting short shrift in his attempt to delay the train, the guard barking "Get clear of the door lad!" as Simon boarded like a Thunderbirds puppet having a stroke, all exaggerated and interminably slow pantomime movements as if participating in a bizarre game of blind man's buff. I was losing sound and vision as my oxygen-deprived body shut down superfluous systems, but had just enough strength to croak "never in doubt" as I flopped through the door literally a second before it closed.

We then began a march up the train to find our pre-booked seats, through never-ending carriages that seemed to get narrower and longer, like some nightmarish Escher drawing. Eventually we were seated and celebrated that the whole shebang was still on track (on track, geddit?) with some of his clever little M&S alcopops. The lady sharing our table looked askance at our early opening hours whilst she sipped at a green concoction of spinach and goodness knows what else, but couldn't help secretly smiling as we recounted the events of the last hour from our differing perspectives.

"Why on earth did you stop when you were just yards from the train?" Simon demanded.

I explained my 'rabbit in the headlights' act by saying that all I could see was zeros, like an internal fuel gauge telling me that the project had finally run out of gas.

Then Simon took a work call and attempted to set up a meeting, but explained to the guy that he couldn't access his diary because he'd already lost his phone, looking around and padding aimlessly at the table before realising that he was speaking into

it. There is something about a long train journey that I just love. I think if I ever won the lottery (which would be highly unlikely, seeing as I don't play it) I would just take mates on day trips to faraway places, chatting and playing poker around the train tables. Simon was soon to join Clive on their annual cultural tour of Las Vegas and said they were staying in the luxurious Aria this time.

"The Steve Wynn one?" I enquired, and a silly exchange started about winning one in the Wynn one.

At Peterborough the spinach-drinking lady at our table seemed to have had enough of the nonsense, pretended that it was her stop, and left the carriage (probably to re-board the train further back). There was a bit of a hoo-ha over the seats with the new cohort, as various people sat in slightly the wrong place. We were joined by three mature ladies who were celebrating a 50 year school reunion in York and were visibly shaken when I disclosed that we may be staying in the same hotel, before working out that Judges Lodgings and Judges Court were separate entities. As the Scrabble dictionary didn't make the cut in the packing list, the ladies kindly agreed to be arbiters in the very likely event of a word-related dispute in our game. Almost immediately Simon placed the word 'Frig' in a taunting manner, knowing that I would not ask the ladies for their opinion. The astonishing thing is that this guy sees these sly gamesmanship tactics as an entirely acceptable part of any match he contests. He invented, for example (and seems very proud of it too), the ripping of the Velcro on a golf glove during his opponent's downswing.

We were met by a variety of 'straight bat' responses from the good people of York. The taxi driver to the hotel simply pretended not to hear Simon's repeated questions concerning the loud groaning noise coming from underneath the car, and a young man that stood in the street holding a large sign for a watch shop missed the irony when I asked him if he'd got the time on him, and simply said "12:48". The hotel was so well hidden away that we had to phone for directions despite being 20 yards from the entrance. The receptionist was Polish and explained in a weird cocktail of accents that to get in and out of the gate we needed to press the "green booten".

"There is a chill wind coming." Simon decreed at 1:27 like some bible quotation. He used this assertion to justify bringing his coat on a day of sauna-like heat. I made sure to comment how wise this was about eleven times in the first ten minutes as we staved off heatstroke by keeping up our fluids in York's hostelries. We had a really rather nice lunch in the Pitcher and Piano, and I realised that this was the way to get decent food when going racing – eat nowhere near the course! We arrived at the course just before the first race and found an empty bar, ordering a lager for myself and a Pimms for the lady (that cost more than the lager). Simon's request of "You haven't got any cut fruit for that, have you?" was met by another Yorkshire straight bat "No."

York racecourse was a revelation. The grandstand had immaculate facilities to rival any Premier enclosure in the country. Space abounded, service was quick and efficient, and there were a full four floors to explore, with a relaxed balcony out the back overlooking a piazza where a band played. The sun was shining, the views were great, and the winners were flowing. I can tell you that for £19 this is an absolute must for any racing fan. After panic-betting and winning on Delizia in the first race, we only realised that the Mark Johnston and Silvestre De Sousa combination were literally on fire, sort of, when not backing them in the second race. We soon decided that we were not going to miss out again and secured two more winners, one of them at 25/1 before it plunged into 12/1, called Indescribable – it is hard to explain how I felt after that. The betting P&L had dipped negative again since Pontefract, and York went a long way to restoring parity once more.

We went back to the hotel via a quick stop in Pound World. This was my first trip to the chain and I was utterly taken with the experience. I snapped up a five-pack of Brannigans ham and pickle crisps for a pound! I suppose I shouldn't have been surprised by the price, given where I was, but somehow I thought that it was the best thing ever. I celebrated my success by also investing in a Party Prize Trophy Set – I wasn't entirely sure what I was going to do with the three (yes, three for a pound!) finely crafted plastic mini trophies, but I just knew that I couldn't leave the store without them. Back at the hotel Simon made short work of his five-pack of McCoys as we watched some It'll Be Alright On The Night clips on YouTube (as you do), before hitting the town and exploring York. There was a slight essence of Galway about the place as tired and emotional racegoers lurched about the Shambles. It was a fine city but we couldn't seem to find our niche in it, so after a few bars where Simon claimed he was too "waterlogged" to drink any more, we returned to the Judges Court to face the sentence of sleep. We played out the finale to our earlier Scrabble game, one so thrilling that it was regularly punctuated by one or both of us nodding off. It had been a long day, but a good one.

# 47) Thirsk

## Day 65 – Saturday 16 May

Dawn heralded the last fortnight of the tour. It didn't sound that long, but when those fourteen days were filled with twelve racecourses spread around Great Britain, it was still a little daunting. The morning also marked Lynsey's 40th birthday, and instead of attending that evening's lavish celebration of a remarkable woman (not least for her enduring marriage, or should that be enduring her marriage, to Paul), I would be tucked away in a small market town in North Yorkshire. Add one more event to the list of missing moments from my decision to continue with the absurd undertaking.

Simon mooched around the city whilst I did some writing in the room, and kindly sent me a photo of the street sign to the Shambles with the message "That's you, that is." Nice.

As we left the Judges Court in York we awarded Asia (the Polish receptionist, not the continent) a small plastic trophy for best hotel so far in our Yorkshire swing. She appeared slightly baffled by the presentation ceremony but accepted the tat graciously before no doubt chucking it straight in the bin after we went. We had brunch in Bills which was stuffed full of smiley, friendly front of house staff. They seemed, though, to have forgotten to employ anybody in the kitchen and when our meal finally arrived it was a curious mix of raw bacon and savagely overcooked eggs. We dashed for our taxi but it was late, and over the next ten minutes when I phoned the firm at least four times I got the same automated message that it was "two minutes away". Hmmm. We gave up and rushed to the station on foot, recreating the last minute sprint at

Kings Cross to step onto the train steaming and breathless for the second time in two days.

When we arrived at the B&B, Barry was waiting for us at the door as the taxi pulled up. I felt like I already knew him well after the short matter of booking the room had seeped into a half hour conversation. He looked like a cross between Tony Hart, the old art presenter on kids TV, and Mr Burns off The Simpsons. Simon instantly decided there were Royston Vasey undertones about the whole set up, but I hadn't seen that programme, and was quite relieved that I hadn't. Barry seemed excessively interested in how tall we both were, as though he was measuring us up for something macabre. Then there were some convoluted goings on about keys. Barry eventually consented to give us a key to our bedroom, but wanted us to leave that key on the table in the front room, just in case. He did not give us a key to the front door because he said he would be ready to open it whenever we returned. I believed him.

It was then that Simon, who had been examining the place like a forensic scientist would view a crime scene, spotted a display cabinet of truncheons. I think I can honestly say that I'd never stayed anywhere before that had truncheons on display. Barry explained they had different uses. I was afraid to ask, but the direct inquisitor that was Simon discovered that the smallest was used to hit fish over the head. "A fish cosh?" he suggested, but Barry simply responded "Pish cosh". I'm not sure why. I tried to move things on by asking about wifi, but Barry explained that the walls were so thick that you couldn't get a signal from the bedroom. Or hear the screams?

Anyhow, we couldn't talk about wifi and truncheons all day, we'd got a race meeting to attend, so after only another 20 minutes or so we managed to extricate ourselves and headed into town for a loosener. There was quite a selection of hostelries in the main square, but most of them sounded like there was a Mexican prison riot in progress inside, so we opted for The Royal, which was far from regal, we discovered after entering. Over the years I've developed a rule that once I've gone into a pub I must have a drink before leaving, however many alarm bells start ringing. This is not only to prevent a wasted journey, but also to avoid attracting attention as some sort of namby-pamby. The only time I broke that rule was with Paul in Portsmouth on match day about ten years ago, and the visions from those brief, ghastly moments in the Pompey fans enclave still haunt me to this day. So Simon and I decided to butch it out and ordered a couple of drinks. The only female in the pub then started singing Bohemian Rhapsody very loudly, and far too closely for comfort. For the second time in ten minutes I felt my flight or fight reflex kick in and, as she built to a crescendo, inhaled my pint of lager before marching Simon out the door.

The atmosphere at the races seemed better, but only in the way that if you give a box of fireworks more space to go off you get a less concentrated but larger scale show. The James Herriot Bar was a holding pen for myriad creatures of all sizes, and may indeed have been the inspiration for some of Hieronymus Bosch's later works. The people of Thirsk were very loud, but perhaps it wasn't their fault – in a town of loud people you have to shout to get heard, and they were certainly not shy of shouting.

The punting was not going so well. Mark Johnston was on fire yesterday, but today someone seemed to have hosed him down, so to speak. One of the two-year-olds we backed was given another suspicious ride that turned an obvious winning chance into a distant third. We selected a few more losers and decided that it just wasn't happening. It was not the worst course I'd been to, but it was not far from it and suffered dreadfully from the comparison with its neighbour York. We headed back early, this time via Lidl, but somehow even that didn't seem to have the vibrancy of Pound World.

Barry was waiting for us when we arrived back at the B&B and dragged us into an extended dissertation on his life. He started off being a draughtsman, before joining the RAF for five years. With an early interest in politics, he discovered that you could leave the air force without having to buy yourself out if you were applying to be an MP, which he did. He wasn't elected, of course, and went into the antiques trade.

"I was one of the many exporting at the time, and I think we just saturated the American market. At one time, there might have been 100 containers a week going in. Norfolk in Virginia, Wilson in North Carolina, Charleston in South Carolina....."

Then he was onto China, and benefits, and how the house used to be a brewery and they made the barrels in the back yard, and how he had planted the trees out the front in 1976 and now they were bigger than the house. Actually, he was a warm and intelligent man who seemed a bit lonely, and not a little eccentric. His wife had died quite a while back and he'd carried on the B&B business. After only 45 minutes or so, Barry paused for breath and we made our getaway. Later, we crept out for a curry. Thirsk seemed to have quietened down a bit and there was only the occasional animal noise emanating from the main square. On the walk back we realised it wasn't clear how we were going to get back in without a key, but rest assured, when we returned Barry was swiftly at the door to let us in.

# 48) Ripon

## Day 66 – Sunday 17 May

Barry held court over the assembled guests sprinkled around the dining room for breakfast. His clearing of the plates turned into an elucidation on Europe, via some strange balloons in the second world war and his time on the town council. It was a bit like when I used to sit at my grandmother's kitchen table – if I drifted off for just a few minutes suddenly it had changed from Marjorie marrying the wrong chap to who had given her the sherry glasses and I'd be unable to piece the segue back together. Barry revealed that he was a regular on various talk radio stations, and we were not surprised in the least.

In the taxi to Ripon, Simon began what proved to be a series of lengthy phone calls to national rail enquiries in a brave attempt to book a ticket to take him home after racing. The lady in India asked him to jump through an extraordinary array of hoops before apparently securing his prize. Simon was so exasperated by the whole fiasco that he developed TCB, also known as Temporary Cathedral Blindness, and asked the cabbie if Ripon had a cathedral as we swept past an enormous old building with an abundance of stained-glass windows and pointy bits.

It had been a festival of stairs recently and as we trudged wearily up to the top floor of our hotel room I considered requesting easy access rooms for the few remaining stops on my tour. However, we were rewarded with a stunning view of the big pointy building with colourful windows, and Simon was so impressed by the lodgings that he decided he would change his train booking until the next morning. It was comforting that, despite my sparkling company not being enough to keep the man in Yorkshire another day, my choice of accommodation was. Simon sat on the bed, which immediately collapsed, as did I in giggles. Then the fire alarm went off and we were told that it was only the dust from some work going on in the room next door, and not to panic if it went off again. I wondered how we would know if it was a genuine fire alarm next time, and visions of another Fawlty Towers scene came to mind.

The Old Deanery had a relaxed and friendly vibe, and as we settled in the lounge I felt as though I could spend the whole afternoon in the comfy sofas bantering with my old mate. We ordered some drinks and I flicked through the papers while Simon tried to change his train booking.

"No I booked it on the phone." (Simon gave his postcode and surname to the representative) "I went through to national rail enquiries and they referred me to Grand Central. The reference? Again? 5K..... hello? 5K7..... yes..... you can't find any record of it?" (gave postcode and surname again) "What? Say again? You're now going to give me my postcode?.....(then he was on hold, listening to inane musak and my frequent giggles) "There's no record of any transaction?....Hello?"

On hold again, he confided in me that it wasn't going well, and we agreed that it was probably their policy to make it really awkward to cancel so that half the people would eventually give up. They obviously hadn't reckoned on Simon's stubborn persistence, though. For some reason we started talking about the Duckworth-Lewis method, the myth-shrouded formulation designed to calculate target scores in rain-affected cricket matches. It had always seemed a fiendishly tricky thing to understand, but I was beginning to think it was slightly easier to comprehend than the national rail booking system. Simon recalled a recent game which was halted, and when it stopped raining the batting side came out to discover that they needed 12 off the last ball. Then Simon was put through to Virgin, who he had apparently booked with.

"Hello, I'd like to book a ticket, sorry, cancel a ticket. Yes, 5K7....." (postcode and surname again) "I seem to be speaking to the dark side of the moon. Where are you?..... Booked my tickets with who? First Great Western? So you've got my booking but it's not booked with you? So who do I cancel with? What number? 08457....." (Simon called said number)..... "No longer in use!"

I started chatting to the manageress who was interested in my tour, and said that the owners of St Saviour, who was running in the last race, were also staying that night. She said that they often had guests who were doing the cathedral tour, but there were only 26 cathedrals, and as far as she knew I was the first racecourse tourist. Simon was still going strong.

"Do I have a what? Why do you want my email address, I didn't give you my email address....." (postcode and surname again) "....uh huh....yes....right..... Why would I give you an incorrect reference number?..... I've given it to you twice, but let's go for it again shall we..... I've just told you my name!"

During the next 'on hold' interlude the cricket theme continued as we reminisced about the famous commentator John Arlott, and Simon told the story of him trudging up to the commentary booth at the top of Lords one morning with two heavy cases, which his new colleague assumed were notes and Wisden annuals, only to discover at the top that they contained four bottles of claret, which Arlott opened with the famous line "This should see us through to lunch". Then, for some reason I cannot now recall, we had difficulty saying the phrase 'the cast of the Last of the Summer Wine'.

40 minutes after the call started, and finally Simon discovered that he was unable to cancel his ticket because he had apparently never booked one. "Oh ok, so if I end up with something on my credit card bill I can quote you on that? What's your name? How do you spell that? And this call is being recorded?"

We were told that the racecourse was a 15 minute walk, or 10 for us guys, as though being tall somehow increased your walking speed by 50%. Half an hour later we reached the track and immediately bumped into Richard again. Minty didn't recognise me in my authentic flat cap (Simon looked embarrassed when I put it on, but he goaded me into buying it a couple of years ago anyway, so deserved all he got). Richard said he loved the first day of his walk over the Moors, but the second day was interrupted by the A1 which he didn't fancy negotiating so involved a two mile detour. I asked him whether he thought there would come a time when he just didn't want to go walking again, but he seemed pretty resolute at the moment. Then he dashed off to talk to Jack Berry – ex-trainer, IJF vice patron, and famous wearer of red shirts – when he spotted him in the paddock, and Simon and I dashed off to the bar, underlining the differing approaches to our respective quests.

Ripon was lovely. Only a small section of the zoo enclosure had made the short hop from Thirsk, and they kept themselves to themselves, hollering from a distant corner of the terraces and leaving the rest of us to enjoy the brass band that was churning out the favourites. Bars and eateries offered a swift service and variety of options, and it felt like the venue lived up to its self-appointed title of Yorkshire's Garden Racecourse. Simon wondered if Minty was short for anything, and persuaded me briefly that a previous girlfriend of his, Molly, was actually named Molleithia. Touché – it had taken him several weeks to get me back for my AP McCoy balloon animals routine at Sandown, but he'd finally got there.

For reasons I couldn't really explain I thought it was time for a big one in the sixth race and selected a four-year-old filly called Rozene. She was making her seasonal debut and would be the latest to test my 'could have improved from three to four' theory. I managed to secure 9/2 before she was backed into 7/2. She flew out of the stalls and was never headed, awarding me the biggest payout of the trip so far. On the way back to the hotel, Simon and I started singing her name to the tune of the Toto track 'Rosanna', which prompted us to YouTube the song and question why the American band used English comedian Bob Carolgees as their lead singer.

We headed into town for some food and ended up in Prezzo where I waited 20 minutes to be told that my chosen dish had run out. By this stage we were attempting to drink an awful bottle of wine but had to concede defeat, and when we asked them to change it they got really arsey and our replacement bottle and the food took an age to turn up. This couldn't dampen our spirits, though, and we celebrated my win late into the night. "Ro-ze-ee-ee-ee-ene!"

# 49) Redcar

## Day 67 – Monday 18 May

I awoke in the fine surroundings of The Old Deanery to the soundtrack of our reworking of 'Rosanna' on a constant loop in my head, vying for attention alongside a hangover. Simon had spent the night on the floor after another bed collapse, but seemed in chirpy enough spirits – it appeared that obtaining some earplugs in York had kept our friendship intact for three days.

We were told downstairs that we were nearly two hours late for breakfast, but they were still accommodating and seated us overlooking the pretty garden. We couldn't have the Eggs Benedict, though, because it would have involved Chef boiling some water. Remarkably, Simon's persistence on the phone to his various pals at the train operators had somehow resulted in a ticket back to Kings Cross, so we man-hugged a goodbye back at Thirsk station, and my faithful Passepartwo headed south towards home, whilst I went north, further away from home.

It was sheeting it down when I got to the course, and a security man frowned at my luggage. Admittedly, it was unusual to see a man wheeling a small suitcase at a racecourse, and he was unimpressed by my tale of heroically touring all the British racecourses, so wanted to check inside. I opened the case and my dirty washing from the previous three days smacked him in the face like the salty North Sea rain, just reward for him doubting my intentions. In the cosy bar I sipped gingerly at a diet coke whilst examining the Racing Post and myself. My Yorkshire Swing with Simon had been hilarious, but I was feeling distinctly jaded. However, after today I would have only nine courses left to complete, and counting down to single digits really did make it feel like I was in the home stretch. Redcar was a nice enough local track, but there was no left luggage facility, so I had to cart my case and rucksack out to the betting ring and, in my dilapidated state, looked a little like a vagrant.

Jockey Daniel Tudhope had a great record at the course so I fancied the debutant he was riding in the first at 17/2. Mon Beau Visage had never raced in public, but cost 41,000 guineas as a yearling and was well connected. I also liked the favourite, Risk Adjusted, who had more experience and form than the rest of them and could have been value at 11/4. Feeling flush from Rozene, I backed them both and they were only split by a photo, the former just getting there. It was weird waiting for the outcome of the photo finish knowing that I'd won either way. Finally the Gods of Probability appeared to be on my side, and things that were fractionally against me earlier on the journey now seemed to be swinging my way. I could cruise to an overall profit (for the betting that is, rather than the venture as a whole), if I was disciplined enough.

It was another eight-race card and I pondered the pros and cons of these elongated meetings. If, as the BHA says, there are not enough horses and owners in the sport, turning six or seven races into eight seems an odd way of doing things, although for racecourses struggling with attendances it does at least keep the tills ticking over for another hour. But it is the punters perspective that I am most interested in, and whether two extra opportunities to bet made it an improved experience. I was intrigued by Paul 2's observations from Epsom on the optimum gap between races. He was in favour of a higher tempo affair, perhaps more similar to the 15 minute turnaround from greyhound racing, but I didn't think that would allow enough time to do everything that surrounds a race.

If we stuck at a gap of around half an hour, eight races made the occasion as large an investment of your time as, say, a round of golf, which to me was always one of the game's failings. If you don't happen to have an eighty-day pass out, four or five hours following a hobby seems like quite a luxury for the average family man. Even with that pass out, on a personal level I couldn't hack it and left before the end to continue my journey up to Newcastle. The affliction known as Racecourse Fatigue Syndrome had really set in, and I headed to bed early in the new Hilton near the station, recognising that I was running on almost as empty as my car on the way back from Market Rasen. I really needed a good night's sleep.

I know this is going to sound daft, but I was expecting the fire alarm. It came at 2:12am, loud and shrill and immediate, like a child screaming in the night. Even so, I made a right bollocks of it.

Where is the lights switch? Why don't they automatically turn all the lights on? Where are my shoes? Lights, good. Coat, good. Still, where are my shoes? Leave everything, Neil, forget your sodding shoes. Ah, shoes! Key? Key. Open the door. Fumble with the catch-.....Christ come on Neil! Open the fucking door!

Corridor. No heat or smoke. Or fire. Dishevelled middle-aged men. One is going the wrong way, towards the lifts. This way, mate. I've studied the evacuation plan. Was expecting it, you see. Please, please let the stairwell be fine. It is, phew. Nobody is panicking, but everyone is taking it seriously. 4th floor, decent pace, 3rd, 2nd, 1st, out.

We were the first out of that exit, about four of us in the lead bunch, soon followed by dribs and drabs of others. There was the smell of smoke, then someone spotted it, billowing from the centre somewhere, over the low slung eastern end of the building.

Fire engines wailed. We went round to the front. A single hose trailed in through an archway to where a skip was smouldering. People congregated on the corner in various states of undress. Everyone was quiet except for a pissed guy who was shouting to his mate who had just

316

emerged. He was making a joke of it, but even in his state I could still hear the fear in his voice. Pubgoers had sluiced onto the street to witness the fractured blue light of the fire engine spilling onto the buildings all around.

It was all done quite quickly and we went back inside. Not many chose the lift. People were quiet on the way back up. Adrenaline still coursed through my body and I knew that sleep would be elusive. I wanted to call The Wife, who I hadn't seen for almost four days because of this stupid charade, and tell her that I loved her, but it was the middle of the night. It would have to wait, along with the return to sleep. As the minutes and hours ticked by the adrenaline was replaced with the empty ache of homesickness. I knew then that I would never do anything like this again in my life.

# 50) Newcastle

## Day 68 – Tuesday 19 May

I caught a few broken shards of sleep as it began to get light. I knew it was just a small fire in a skip next to the hotel, and not a big fire in the hotel itself, but for some reason it affected me. Outside my door was a photocopied message from the manager apologising for the early-hour shenanigans – it was a nice touch, even if its main intention was to ward off complaints at check-out. The breakfast was poor, but at least I could drink unlimited coffee, and I needed to because I had a big morning ahead of me.

Clive had set me up with one of his ex-colleagues now working in Newcastle (in a purely professional sense, you understand) and I arrived bang on time to be interviewed by BBC Radio. I'd interviewed quite a few people myself before and during my journey, but this was the first time that I would be answering the questions. I'd never quite settled on how to pitch my quest, but had actively baulked at it becoming a media circus because I felt it would somehow lose the purity of the project. However, this was to be one small, grudging nod to marketing.

I sat in the ante-room listening to the live feed, not sure that the caffeine was working. Just when I needed to be at my most sparkling and positive about my ludicrous adventure, I was feeling the most tired and homesick I'd been so far. I was able to hide behind the black and white, manufactured words of a blog, but I feared that the immediacy of live radio would not be so forgiving. I was ushered into the studio and suddenly I was sat next to the very cheery and encouraging Anna. A song was finishing so we had a minute before going on air.

"Pleased to meet you Neil, thanks for coming in! We'll just have a chat about why you're doing this, you crazy person, and I of course will get as many horse puns in as I can!"

I felt like I'd just sat down in an exam and been told I was following the wrong syllabus. I had been revising all morning about everything from the worst hog roast to the best performance by a three-year-old gelding after returning from an absence of more than 200 days, and suddenly realised I should have been swotting up on racing puns. But there was no time to rectify that – the song had finished and we were live. I wondered whether any noise would come out of my mouth.

"Are you in a *stable* relationship?" quipped Anna, and I managed to mumble something about my very understanding family. Then she went in for the kill, "So why are you doing this?"

"Yeah, I'd hoped that somewhere along the way I'd have found the answer to that, but I'm now fifty racecourses in, I've got two weeks left, and I'm still not sure why!" I admitted.

I could see Anna wasn't going to be fobbed off by that, though, and thought that for her, the listeners, and most importantly myself, for the first time I needed to attempt to put in words why I was performing this weird, wonderful, painful pantomime.

"I've been a racing fan for 25 years and I've always had this ridiculous idea and never been able to do it because of the day job, but that finished in September. I was a teacher for 17 years, and loved it for so many of those years, but stopped loving it. I had the opportunity of doing something different, and thought lets go for it, before I ended up in my rocking chair at the age of 85 regretting never doing it."

There, perhaps it really was as simple as that. In life opportunities to do something you really want are few and far between, especially when you're 43. There had always

319

been reasons not to do it, in particular my job, but at that point in my life those reasons had become less persuasive. Who knew where or what I would be doing the following March, but I would be unlikely to be in that unique position again. Anna had assumed the role of psychiatrist, asking an open question and then just letting me talk, not on a private couch but to thousands of strangers listening on BBC Radio Newcastle through the anonymity of the airwaves.

"Well good luck at the races this afternoon," said Anna as she wrapped up, leading to her finale, "it's not far from here so you should find it *neigh* bother!"

She'd really *got the bit between her teeth* now with the puns, but I didn't think to say that. I wasn't sure I was really cut out for radio. Or speaking, really, after a broken night's sleep following hot on the heels of a three-day jolly with Simon, but at least I was *entering the final furlong now*. Sorry, I'll stop. My 15 minutes of fame was over in a flash and I was escorted from the premises, wondering if I'd made any sense whatsoever. I phoned Jason who said not to worry as the Geordie listeners wouldn't have understood a word I was saying anyway. Good point.

I caught a taxi to the course, during which the cabbie explained his performance-related pay idea for his struggling football team with the words "only pay them if they bloody win!" I was amazed by the entrance as we pulled up. Newcastle racecourse seemed like a grand hotel from the outside, and they were happy to keep my luggage behind reception so I didn't have to trail it around like some vagrant, as at Redcar. They were possibly the most spacious facilities I had encountered so far, and again I thought back to my beloved Cheltenham and how claustrophobic that felt on Day 1 of my quest – admittedly they had 70,000 on Gold Cup Day, and I doubted Newcastle had 1% of that total for a rain-smeared Tuesday fixture, but perhaps that should tell Ian Renton something. I had arrived very early, and wallowed around in virtually empty halls getting the lie of the land. The beer was good and the food was pretty good. I drifted upstairs to a cocktail bar with a laid-back vibe, which afforded tremendous views from its own terrace. Big round tables with white tablecloths, as well as heaters to tackle the chill, encouraged people to sit and talk to each other, and because they were not competing for either a drink or their personal space, racegoers stopped fighting and started fraternising.

I believe this is the one most important challenge that horse racing has to tackle – how does it attract one million new customers a year without it seeming even more oppressive on the busy days? You can tinker all you like with prize money and horse populations, field sizes and fixtures lists, but punters won't come back if they feel harried, bullied or exploited.

The ARC-owned Newcastle was also attempting to tinker with those other aspects themselves, by planning a floodlit all-weather track. However, those plans were halted (for the 2015 fixture allocation at any rate) by the BHA refusing to give an exemption to the previously little-known rule F26.1 which stated that there must be a certain number of longer races on each card. With only the straight mile at Newcastle set to be floodlit, this would limit their ability to stage evening racing, and therefore made the £12 million investment unviable. ARC managing director Tony Kelly thought a compromise could be found if they started some twilight fixtures 15 or 30 minutes early and ran the longer races at the start of the card in daylight hours, but trainers had questioned the logic in ripping up what was generally considered a decent turf track, and preferred Catterick as a venue for the first northern all-weather surface.

The paddock was in front of the stands just by the winning post, and I thought of Market Rasen (which I nominated as my favourite course when put on the spot by Anna earlier) that had exactly the same configuration. This was a compromise – if you put the paddock there you couldn't fit in 1,000 more vertical drinkers by the course, but I felt it was the little things that added up to making a big difference. It was still raining as I surveyed the scene, and without the luxury of being able to watch them parade and return to the winners' enclosure from the shelter of the stand, racegoers would have missed an important part of proceedings.

However, if Paul 2 was surprised at the demographic at Epsom, he would have been aghast at the average age at Newcastle. Okay, it was a wet Tuesday afternoon, but it was quite possible that the horses outnumbered the punters, and there was definitely a higher proportion of greys in the audience than out on the course. I counted seven people dotted around the enormous food hall, and none of them was making a sound. It was disturbingly reminiscent of a restroom at an old-people's home. Somehow, despite the muted atmosphere, I really enjoyed the place and would love to come back to the city and the racecourse in the future, but my good betting run had come to an end with a winner-less day. That was alright, though, because I was soon to be flying home to my family, and that feeling really was priceless.

# 51) Goodwood

## Day 70 – Thursday 21 May

I'd come to mango late in life, but now I'd discovered it I was grasping every opportunity. I suppose it wasn't the worst thing to become addicted to on an eighty-day gambling and drinking spree, and for a man who was physically unable to drive past a corner shop when the Kit Kat Chunky was released onto an unsuspecting public many years ago, it was something of a breakthrough, although more expensive. I thought back to the start of the journey when the red motorway signs of Burger King and KFC haunted my progress, and how quickly that transformed on my internal dashboard to the green freshness of M&S and Waitrose. I was therefore excited, when I stopped at a garage on the way down to Goodwood in order to refuel in both senses, to discover fruit mango chews and loaded up with several packs. All that glittered was not gold, though, and indeed all that was described as mango was not mango-tasting. The unappealing little critters looked a little like rabbit droppings, and tasted about the same, although admittedly I was guessing on that latter point.

As the old adage goes, you only get one chance to make a first impression, and at Goodwood it was not a Good-one. The drive through the villages of Surrey and Sussex was pretty enough, but as soon as I got within sight of the racecourse the problems started. Signs for parking were not very large or clear. I made three aborted attempts to pull into a car park and eventually found my way to Car Park 9, eschewing the £5 charge for Car Park 8 that got you fractionally closer. I disliked the idea of driving past all the other car parks and pulling up on a scrubby piece of land about three miles from the grandstand, but perhaps that was just my dodgy knee? The shenanigans didn't stop by the time I'd reached the entrance, either. A gormless teenager asked me which enclosure I wanted, before looking me up and down and saying "oh, you can't get in the Richmond, I'll do you a Gordon." She then stabbed aimlessly at a laptop whilst saying "the system is really slow". I smiled politely and refrained from saying that the system was broken - I had cash, she had tickets and change, so why did the transaction need to take three minutes?

Finally I understood why I was so taken with Market Rasen. Everyone parked in the same spot (including Tom Scudamore) and despite there being different enclosures they melded seamlessly together. In fact if you were blindfolded and put in the cheapest at Market Rasen you would probably think it was Premier, such was the standard of the facilities at all three. I was intrigued why Anna at BBC Radio Newcastle had mentioned how posh Cheltenham appeared. I'd been there so many times and never once had that occurred to me. Despite me recently appreciating its failings, it remained a great leveller. It doesn't matter where you come from, where you went to school, or who your father knows – you go to Cheltenham and you stand legion to witness the greatness that the sport has to offer (if you can drag yourself away from the hospitality, that is).

Eventually I was in, and not often do people or institutions with such poor first impressions manage to turn it around so well on a second viewing. If I had to choose one word to form a litmus test for my appreciation of a racecourse over the previous 69 days it would be 'space', and Goodwood had that in abundance. Perhaps that was why us plebs had to park so bloody far away? The Richmond Enclosure, that I was only allowed to gawp at from afar, was reminiscent of Parisian café culture as stylish things soaked up the sun and bottles of champagne at small tables. For the un-double-barrelled in the Gordon Enclosure there were bandstands of beer outside as well as acres of options in the underground caverns. Furlongs of bars stood eager to serve, and although the food outlets were expensive (sausage rolls were available for £1 per inch, I kid you not – there's an obvious joke there but I'll let you make up your own), there was an astonishing array. It didn't stop there. Outside, beautifully manicured lawns beckoned racegoers out the front to find the benches dotted around, and there was a free, seated stand that commanded stunning views over the action. Families lounged on picnic blankets and there was more than one school party wondering around. Top marks to the management of the racecourse and the schools involved – this really did seem a cheap and effective way to secure the future of the sport. The track itself suffered slightly from the surprisingly common problem that a lot of the action was happening at least half a mile away, but somehow it got away with it.

In the fourth race I missed a bet. I was waiting for 3/1 on Resonant, the favourite, but I couldn't find it. I did my usual trick of asking a few bookies for my price, but they stood firm. I prowled the betting ring, pondering 11/4, but I knew I must stick to my principles – I truly believe in the concept of value betting. Resonant won like a good thing. As Ivan would say, a winner is a winner. The whole episode reminded me of my first visit to the Galway Festival, several years before the extraordinary four-day jolly with Clive and Simon. Jason and I decided we were going to have a large one on the Galway Plate and both individually studied the form for an intense five minutes. Eventually, we looked up at each other and simultaneously said "Moscow Express".

The remarkable chestnut gelding competed no less than 81 times in a career spanning eight seasons, and even ran in one of Best Mate's Gold Cups, but of course shall be best remembered for his victory in the 1999 Galway Plate.

Sadly, for reasons it is still hard to fathom, he won without the burden of any of our cash following him. He was quoted at 10/1 in the paper and when we got to the betting ring we were shocked to see only 4/1, and decided our cash would go elsewhere. I could try and argue that even back then we were exponents of value betting, but in reality I think he was still value at 4/1 and the only reason we defected was because of our artificially enhanced expectations via the SP forecast section of the racecard. It was almost like an inversion of a sale reduction – once we had seen the glitzy (and entirely hypothetical) 10/1 we were never going to be impressed with the more realistic odds. So Moscow Express seeped into our memories, and our language, as the one that got away. It became a phrase similar to Catch 22 in that it transferred from a niche arena into general use, coming to mean a missed opportunity. In some ways, dear old Moscow Express may even have been partly responsible for my ludicrous journey, for on that fine July afternoon in 1999 I decided that I should never pass up golden opportunities like that again. If in doubt, do it.

But of course some still slipped through the net, and Resonant at Goodwood became the latest in a long line of Moscow Expresses. The racecourse had unexpectedly won me over against the odds, but the one thing that was lacking, from my perspective anyway, was excitement.

On the drive back down the lanes I was shouting at bicycles to get out the way, red lights to turn green, and fellow motorists to stop being such morons. My route home took me past the college that I taught at for ten years, along roads that I had travelled thousands of times, and I thought back to my colleagues telling me a year before that I would miss teaching and would be back in the classroom before long. Not yet, dear friends.

But one thing did occur to me, my mind wondering whilst the driving part of my brain completed the autopilot journey I knew so well. It took me over ten years to start getting bored of teaching, and it had taken me less than ten weeks to start getting bored of horse racing. The authorities charged with evolving our sport need not worry too much at that shock revelation, as the people that they are trying to attract are unlikely to go racing five times a week, but it was a shock revelation to me. Of all the issues I had faced over the last two and a half months, and they had been many and varied, I never even considered that boredom would be one of them.

# 52) Musselburgh

## Day 71 – Friday 22 May

Eric drove me to Heathrow and again got fretful at the traffic situation, but it was not to prove a repeat of my journey to York via Kings Cross. This time, I had minutes rather than seconds to spare before boarding. On the flight to Edinburgh I sat next to Angus. He spotted that I was re-reading Four-iron in the Soul and we got chatting about golf. He had played all the big courses in Scotland, and I was slightly jealous. I liked his story about his caddie on The Old Course at St Andrews telling him to aim for the rough because of the devilish bunkers in the fairway where unsuspecting rounds had sunk without trace. Sometimes the road less travelled by can be more rewarding.

Angus said he didn't like betting on the horses because he didn't like losing. I know this sounds odd, but I really hadn't thought about it in those stark terms before. The sport that I had followed ardently for 25 years did indeed involve an awful lot of losing. It was certainly not as gratifying as, say, supporting Barcelona or Novak Djokovic who won most of the time. To extend the line of thought further, if Paul 2 was right that sports are fighting for attention not just between themselves but against the shopping malls on a Saturday afternoon, then it is an unfair contest because every time you go shopping you return with a prize and that warm fuzzy feeling inside. But to me, and I know this is going to sound even odder, I need the losers. Without the savage lows how can you fully appreciate the glorious highs? To return to golf, perhaps that is why I thought the 1995 Ryder Cup was the most fantastic thing in the universe (other than The Wife and kids, of course), until the 2010 and 2012 versions came along anyway. We had taken a beating from the Americans for years, but at Oak Hill we came from behind on the final day to claim a stunning victory, made all the sweeter by the previous savage defeats.

Angus didn't accept my view that owning investments and having a pension was the same as gambling, although he did wonder if his fund manager misappropriated some of the cash towards Ladbrokes. Not many people agree with me on this one, but there are many investors on this planet who know to their cost that stock and housing markets are a long way from a dead cert, yet for some reason we don't call this gambling despite it being a far more prevalent issue. Somehow owning a home seems a safer investment than the 20/1 outsider in the selling hurdle at Wincanton? Try telling that to the hundreds of thousands of people in the UK alone who lost everything in the property slumps of 2008 and 1990. Somehow investing in a pension seems more prudent than a Yankee on Saturday's televised races? Try telling that to the shareholders in the crash of 1987.

Let me make this clear: I'm happy to own (part of) a house and a small pension, but I don't see this as more or less morally superior than betting on a horse. I hope that they turn out to be good bets, and indeed they hold a greater significance than my horse wagers because of their relative scale, but they are still gambles. Perhaps you think your investments are longer-term than a two-minute horse race - after the property market slump you (hopefully) still have a home, and after the stock market crash you still have most of your pension, whereas after a losing bet it is all gone. That is true, but I don't gamble hundreds of thousands of pounds on the horses.

As we descended into Edinburgh, Angus pointed out the sights of the city, including Musselburgh racecourse directly beneath us, and it really did give me a new perspective on the sport. Like golf courses, they seem like such a luxury in terms of use of space in a built up area. Unlike their counterparts, though, racecourses are usually only employed for a fraction of the year, making their folly even more glaringly inefficient. Somehow, though, from above it seemed weirdly natural, squeezed onto the links land between conurbation and sea, nestled next to the ubiquitous golf course. He also picked out Arthur's Seat, which brought memories flooding back of a Scottish holiday with The Wife. As we came into land I closed my eyes and pictured her on top of the rocky peak, with Edinburgh laid out in the background. She had her eyes closed, her blonde hair wisping in the breeze, and her cheeks glowing rosy red after the walk up the hill.

At the airport I had to walk halfway to Edinburgh before picking up my hire car, but eventually I folded myself into my Economy option, which seemed to be a new creation called a Vauxhall Tiny. It did the job, though, and I scooted through the rush hour traffic to my hotel. The Roxburghe was a proper establishment and the last minute deal I found made it ludicrously good value. It needed to be, though, because the taxi to the races costs an arm and a leg. Then a brusque man at the turnstile asked me for £25 to enter. I asked him if I got a winner as well for that price, but he simply barked "eh?"

Musselburgh was busy and loud, even raucous in places, but somehow avoided crossing the line into 'rowdy' that Thirsk seemed to transcend so markedly. Angus had told me to look out for his brother Alistair, who was 6 foot 3 and would most likely be dressed as a Scottish dandy in pink tartan trousers. I could see the obligatory Stag in a horse and jockey outfit, the cast of Grease with a young man revelling in the role of Sandy, no less than seven Blues Brothers and some bruisers dressed in lounge suits left over from the 1980s (I wasn't sure if this last category was meant ironically or not, and didn't ask) but couldn't for the life of me see a tall dandy in pink tartan. It was like a Scottish version of Where's Wally set against the manic backdrop of a thronging racecourse crowd. Plenty were clearly present for the Boogie Night after racing, hosted by none other than Radio Forth, but I suspected that plenty weren't and I questioned the wisdom of effectively making all racegoers subsidise what only a minority would stay on for.

I discovered a stall selling Edinburgh Gin, and it really was a fantastic drink mixed with Fever Tree tonic and ice. The lady explained that their main competitors had grown too big now and had lost sight of what made them great, whereas Edinburgh Gin was made under Huxleys in the city and its 12 botanicals were all entirely natural. This of course was the mirror situation facing Cheltenham et al – success brings its own problems. Edinburgh Gin seemed more like Ludlow – local, authentic, independent, and producing a great product that was enjoyed by a diverse bunch.

I left after the fourth race and without a winner for the third meeting in a row, raising slight concerns that it might not all be plain sailing after my Rozene win. I was then treated to a crash course in Scottish, or at least the Edinburgh version of the language, by the cabbie on the way back. The main gist of it seemed to be that, if in doubt, just repeat "aye" and "ken" frequently, whether they fitted in the sentence or not. He liked having a bet on the horses, and won nine grand a few years back by all accounts, but liked the football more. He supported Man City and had recently seen them play Barcelona. He spent the whole game watching Messi, his movement off the ball and sublime skill on it.

"Aye ken, just couldna take my eyes off him, the runs, the passing, and incredible strength."

We had a big debate about the greatest of all time, where names like Pele and Best were suggested, but it was difficult comparing different eras, just like it was tough comparing racecourses. Back at the hotel, I was tempted by the Bar & Grill's set menu and they produced by far the best meal I'd had on my travels thus far. I opted for a delightful poached Scottish salmon salad to start, followed by an exquisite calves liver and bacon. They were nicely presented without being poncey, and the service was impeccable. The maitre d' kindly suggested two wines to accompany the dishes, which were superb, and £15 for two courses of that standard in central Edinburgh was simply astounding.

As I finished my meal the walls of the restaurant were bathed in a glorious sunset, the warm colours of heather reminding me of my new location for the day, and somehow signifying that the remaining seven days really did represent the dying embers of my dream. I forced myself to leave the hotel and headed down George Street to Tiger Lily, which Angus had recommended. I'd become adept at eating meals on my own but was still not skilled at solitary standing in trendy bars. They had Sam Adams on draught, which distracted me for a while, but really it was time to go. The first day of my biggest trip away of the entire tour had been pleasant enough, but I wouldn't be back to my family until the Wednesday evening, and that thought burned inside me as I walked back down George Street to the hotel.

# 53) Catterick

## Day 72 – Saturday 23 May

There were reasons to dislike Catterick before I even got there. Most obviously, it was a long way from Musselburgh. Less obviously, that day Eldest was rowing in the National Schools Championships in Nottingham. I tried for hours to find a combination of trains, planes, cars and taxis that would make it possible to see both my son race and some horses run at Catterick, but it was just not possible. So I mentally chalked up yet another one to the list of life moments I would never get back. In addition, Ivan had nominated the course as particularly unappealing (I think he used slightly different words), and it would be fair to say that expectation levels were low.

I had also forgotten, when I triumphantly proclaimed after Wincanton that the big driving was over, that I was actually hiring a car for the Scottish Swing. So that morning I had what turned out to be three and a half hours to get properly acquainted with my Vauxhall Tiny. I drove past some glorious views of the North Sea, but I was lacking cruise control and Tiny's accelerator pedal seemed to vibrate violently above 50mph. My mood was not enhanced by being unable to turn off the A1 because of unheralded roadworks. The detour meant that I missed the first race, and my Placepot plans would have to wait another day.

But what an unexpected treat! It started with easy parking just across the road and friendly staff at the gate who initially retained my ticket but then immediately returned it when I explained what I was doing, with the acknowledgement of "Fair play to you!" I entered next to the pretty paddock where there was a relaxed cafe and ragtime band strumming away. The adjacent paddock bar served a decent pint of Theakstons in, wait for it, a proper pint glass – the first of my entire journey! The facilities were neat and compact. It was busy but I could still get a bet on easily and found a lovely spot to watch the racing, past a dining marquee just beyond the finishing post. The racecourse commentator warned the crowd to keep up their fluids on this sunny Saturday, advice which some of the lads seemed to be taking a bit too literally, but it was still a decent enough atmosphere.

The odds at these smaller tracks quite often seem....at odds with the tipsters and betting forecast in the paper. I spotted a fine looking animal called Arcamante parading before the fourth race, but he was friendless in the tipsters table, most of whom selected the strong favourite Underwritten. However in the vibrant Catterick betting ring they were "flip-flopping", to use McCririck-speak. I managed to get 3/1 on Arcamante before he was backed into 2/1 favouritism and won well.

I headed to my hotel in Richmond just a few miles away. I'd heard good things about this pretty Yorkshire village and expected to pull up in a genteel square, but was instead presented with a funfair blaring out at five in the afternoon just yards from my abode. Unsurprisingly, I was not alerted to this at the time of booking. Over the din, I asked at reception for a room away from the noise and the cheery manager said "don't worry, you're down the side", by which she meant only marginally away from the noise, and steaming hot in the full glare of the sun.

This book is not intended to be a hotel review, but sometimes it's good to get things off your chest, so here goes. The Best Western Kings Head in Richmond is one of the worst hotels I've ever stayed in. In addition to the sweltering conditions akin to the black hole of Calcutta, there were wrinkled carpets and stains on the wall. Only a child could have got their knees under the desk, and the curtains refused to fully close against the oven-baked window. Most intriguing, though, was a small hole in the wall just by the bed. I wondered whether this was where the previous victim unfortunate enough to be incarcerated in Room 23 tried to tunnel-out in a Shawshank-esque bid for freedom? I asked at reception if there was an alternative room, but the shoddily-dressed chap peered at the computer before admitting the only other rooms were at the front, offering free fairground music piped directly into my brain until the early hours. The sauna it was, then.

I FaceTimed The Wife for the closing bits of Eurovision and we agreed that, yet again, the quality of the song had absolutely no bearing on the votes awarded. Graham did a good job, but I still missed Terry. We would normally watch it together and get pads of paper to write down our scores, out of ten, for both song and presentation (yes, I know that makes us sound a bit sad but we don't care). Not that night though – another facet of family life fallen by the wayside. I had been through a rollercoaster of emotions that day, but I was left with the darkest one at the end. It was one of shame and stupidity at the choice I had made ten weeks before, and the choices I continued to make every day in perpetuating the broken fairytale. The spectacular in Vienna drew to a close at the same time as the Richmond funfair quietened down, and eventually I drifted off into a hot and airless sleep.

# 54) Kelso

## Day 73 – Sunday 24 May

There were more shenanigans in the morning at the Kings Head, but I attempted to be stoical and look on the positive side of the many unsatisfactory situations. I didn't receive my wake up call, but that was okay because I'd lost half my bodyweight in sweat during the night and was up early anyway, seeking fluids like a desert nomad. The kettle didn't work, but that was okay because the cups were too dirty to drink from. And the showers was scalding hot, but that was also okay because once I'd burnt my shoulders I could soothe them on the only other available setting which was freezing cold. Downstairs in reception the youthful manager, Georgie, remained unerringly cheery as the ship sank around her. She was apologetic, reduced my bill, and dealt really rather well with my complaints. But even at half price it seemed a dreadful place to spend the night and I couldn't help but think she deserved a better hotel to start her career.

The A698 up to Jedburgh was spectacular as it swooped and cambered through gentle bends and tight hairpins. If it had formed a natural loop I was sure it would become our own version of the Nurburgring, but that didn't stop a variety of bikers from enjoying its unique charms on a Sunday morning. I decided to put Tiny through his paces, and discovered that he truly was a gutless piece of junk. On the uphill sections it was like someone had left the handbrake on, although my witty friends might suggest that I was the handbrake and the poor car was labouring under extenuating circumstances.

I switched on the radio and found BBC Newcastle. The presenter Sue had recorded a sound she had made and invited listeners to guess what it was. It was clearly a thick paper bag being rustled, but the good people of the North East came up with an astonishing variety of conspiracy theories, including dice being shaken in a Tupperware. As if this wasn't bizarre enough, Yazoo then came on – you don't hear them very often nowadays. The border crossing offered jaw-dropping views over the Scottish countryside. Somehow, I could sense the change in the landscape even without the big flags to mark it. I tried to keep momentum up for a punishing climb, just as Bryan Adams started telling me that everything he did was for me, but as he crooned to a close Tiny had virtually ground to a halt and I was holding up a cyclist. Then Sue revealed the answer that had kept us all on tenterhooks for the previous half hour – she was opening a packet of nail files. Tough one that, Sue.

I pulled up at the second Roxburghe Hotel in three days. It was a handsome thing, no doubt, with a roaring log fire in the impressive lobby, but it had a tough task ahead to better its Edinburgh namesake. I was shown through to the wonderful Library Bar for a spot of lunch before the races. I scanned through the extensive lunch menu and was suitably impressed. I hadn't realised when I hastily booked the hotel that I would be dining Chez Roux, and Albert of that dynasty in particular, although whether it was the great man himself or just his name that dressed the plates I wasn't sure. In order to expedite things before heading off to the track, I ordered a sandwich, but they seemed to be growing the wheat and catching the chicken, such is the French infatuation with doing things properly.

45 minutes, and a very fine sandwich, later I was on my way. The Satnav was in my luggage in the room, so I decided to test my skills, just for old times' sake, and found my own way to the course in double-quick fashion – yes, you've still got it Neil.

Kelso was "Britain's Friendliest Racecourse!" I was told by a big sign at the entrance to the car park, so imagined staff high-fiving me on the way through the gate and locals offering this newbie a wee dram in the bars. Neither happened, and although it was pleasant enough, perhaps there was something of an expectation gap. At Catterick yesterday I had very low expectations, and was pleasantly surprised, but plenty of people had told me how much I would enjoy Kelso and it left me slightly cold. Methinks the sign on the way in had protested too much, and have always thought that if you have to shout that something is brilliant, it probably isn't. There was a big crowd for Ladies Day, and as usual the ladies had made a fine effort, and as usual the gentlemen hadn't. It was a little tricky to move around. The cosy facilities produced a good atmosphere, and the people there clearly loved their racing, but trying to walk from A to B was like trying to cross central Paris at rush hour.

I thought back to when I was planning the schedule, trying to pick out the highlights of the racing calendar. Of course I went for the big meetings, the high-profile weekend fixtures, the feature days and festivals. Perhaps in hindsight I should have sought out the quieter days – it may not have been as glamorous, but it would probably have made for a more enjoyable journey. It was £25 to get into Members, but worth it I would suggest. I climbed some stairs to a small, tiered arrangement on the roof of the stand where I was rewarded with panoramic views over the course and town. They had a refreshingly casual attitude to health and safety, with a rickety old wooden structure and smoke billowing from a chimney over the assembled mountaineers.

It was another track where the on-course opinion held more sway than the accumulated off-course perceived wisdom. Just Awake should have been clear favourite for the second race according to the Racing Post, but was freely available at 4/1 and I couldn't resist; he was going ominously well before tipping up at the third last fence. The third race was delayed for more than 15 minutes as the groundsmen made running repairs to the track. They were putting down sand on the bends, presumably after reports of some loose turf. This was the right decision from a welfare perspective, but the wrong one for my Discoverie, who clearly went well on good ground but not sandy, and was pulled up. In the fourth I backed Neville Woods, who came a cropper on the walkway out to the course and was withdrawn before even reaching the start. It was not going well - three bets and none of them had even finished!

I retired to the hotel where I was kindly invited to dinner, in a still-paying-for-it kind of way. Why not? Back in the Library Bar I was treated to a Haggis bon-bon whilst selecting my supper. I got confused with all the veloutes and confits, and I know this sounds strange for me, but I wasn't that hungry and just fancied a salad. Monsieur Roux, though, clearly didn't approve of that sort of thing, as his menu was devoid of freshness and simplicity. I forced down a couple of plates of rich and unusual concoctions, but the food was nowhere near as beautifully balanced as the Edinburgh Roxburgh. In my humble opinion, gilding the lily is no substitute for simple classics cooked well, but perhaps my palate doesn't have enough Michelin stars to understand.

The food took an age to arrive as well - didn't they understand a man eating on his own wanted a quick steak and chips before going up to watch Match Of The Day? I amused myself in between courses by examining the racing paintings on the wall. Blink Bonny stared at me through the centuries with scared eyes bulging from her tiny head. Perhaps she too was alarmed by the veloute? The frame told me she won both the Oaks and the Derby in 1857, and I didn't even know that fillies ran in the Derby! It highlighted how far I had to go in horse racing, despite being just days from the end.

# 55) Cartmel

## Day 74 – Monday 25 May

I was treated to another spectacular drive on the way to the Lake District, and again Tiny struggled to cope. The A592 skirted around Ullswater and through the pretty villages of Glenridding and Patterdale before climbing the daunting Kirkstone Pass. There was plenty of second gear, even some first in places, but luckily Tiny wheezed his way up without having to resort to reversing up the steepest bits. I wasn't sure The Satnav was programmed correctly for a car with less horsepower than a horse. Then we started plunging down to Windermere and the road resembled something from a Top Gear special, with narrow passes and ravines to catch the unsuspecting. All of a sudden there were sheep in the road, and then signs warned that red squirrels may be crossing, and then (in an increasingly Pythonesque twist) signs said that blind people were roaming around as well. Jeremy Clarkson had never had to cope with this sort of thing.

I found the intriguingly named Burn How Garden Hotel, which seemed like it should be a question spoken by an arsonist on an insurance job. As I checked in I asked for a taxi to take me the twelve or so miles to Cartmel and the quote came back at £45! One way! It was busy there, apparently. No thanks, I'll drive. As it turned out, there was no traffic at all and I found an easy spot to park near the entrance to the Course enclosure. £45 my arse.

It was £13 to get into the middle, which seemed like a bargain to experience the unique offerings of this famous Bank Holiday shindig. We were held on the outside as the horses were already down at the start for the first race, but it was interesting watching them thunder around what was really one long home turn. It was clear that you needed a horse who liked going tight left-handed, and downhill, and uphill, and had speed to keep up but stamina for the gruelling finish. Tiny would not have fared well if they'd let cars have a go. That was not such an absurd idea, I discovered, because as soon as the horses were off the course it got reclaimed as a football pitch, cricket strip and lots else besides by the assorted humanity who had been temporarily constrained in the middle. I'd never been to Le Mans, but friends had told me it was one huge party with the occasional glimpse of some racing on the periphery, and I reckoned Cartmel must be fairly similar. Except for the bit about playing football on the track. The party had definitely already started, and there was a simply fantastic atmosphere.

If ever you need evidence of both how attached as a nation we have become to alcohol, but also how it can be used as a force for good to bring people together rather than tear them apart, then Cartmel races on a Bank Holiday Monday would be your data collection point. Plonk yourself anywhere at random and you will be less than five yards from a family enjoying a bottle of Pinot Grigio or working their way through a 12-pack of lager. That was the adults anyway, mostly. The fair blared out its existence like an attention-seeking child, but somehow it seemed to sit happily in its environment, whereas in a pretty Richmond square next to my bedroom window it seemed very wrong. There were all manner of stalls selling food from around the world, and you could buy gifts ranging from Panama hats to wooden ducks, the latter of which seemed surprisingly popular in this neck of the woods. There were two stands from local breweries and I can tell you that a red ale by Unsworths Yard called Lone Wolf is a thing of beauty.

Picnics and barbeques proliferated the Cumbrian turf, and each huddle was replete with folding chairs and cool boxes. Cartmel had resolved the issue of racegoers lacking personal space at busy meetings by letting them literally stake their claim to their own piece of land with windbreaks. It worked well in that everyone seemed relaxed and happy, but the one drawback was that it did create bottlenecks in key areas. The other problem, and this was of course by no means unique to Cartmel, was that it was yet again fiendishly difficult to buy a Racing Post. Without my daily comfort-blanket it just seemed like, well, gambling. But I was here to take part, so I made a random bet in the second race and went to watch it from a weird little mound of rock and grass on the final bend, where they met the rising ground before the finish. They appeared from behind a barn, dashed past almost within touching distance, and in the blink of an eye had disappeared around the crown of the bend. Then a couple of minutes later it happened again, but the horses were in a different order and more strung out. It was like watching a film that consisted of two still photos and I was expected to fill in the gaps as best I could.

At this point I saw Bill Bryson. At least, I was pretty sure it was him - a smallish, ginger-bearded chap with glasses and a thin but warm smile. He was dressed in tweed and just hanging around, taking it all in. I had a sudden pang of worry that the Guvnor of travelogues was completing his own tour of British racecourses and would steal my thunder, but was also excited to share my experiences and chew the cud with the old master. I couldn't let this moment pass; I just needed a subtle opening line in order to confirm his identity.

"Excuse me, are you Bill Bryson?" I said, in a brilliantly subtle manner.

"No," he replied, slightly bemused, in broad Mancunian "but I do know a Bill Price."

"No, sorry, Bill Bryson" I affirmed.

"Oh, Bill Bryson, no. Who is he anyway?"

"An author." I said quizzically. Surely everyone had heard of him?

"American, travel writer, oh yeah. I'm sure he's older than me, and he's got a full beard, as well, Bill Bryson. Did he not marry a Yorkshire girl? And he has lived over here quite a while, in Norfolk I think."

All of a sudden this guy had gone from never having heard of Bill Bryson to reciting a full Wikipedia entry. I suspected it really was the great man, and he was just feigning ignorance and a Manchester accent to throw his adoring fans off the scent.

"I was actually close to meeting him once. I went travelling round the world," continued Bill, philosophically referring to himself in the third person, "and prior to that he was actually doing a talk in the centre of Manchester about travelling, and I just missed it. I'd love to meet him one day." Yes, deep Bill, I know what you mean. I'm searching for my real self, too.

As the conversation continued I discovered that he was probably not Bill, but Tony who had worked on the railway for 20 years, and was known as Errol to his mates, as in Flynn. If he really was Bill it was a very convincing cover story, but the whole thing was getting more confusing by the minute, as he really didn't look much like the old film star in my opinion. But Bill, sorry Errol, I mean Tony was still talking, now about the transitory nature of money and selling his house but leaving the appliances because he didn't like leaving gaps behind, although he was leaving his girlfriend behind. It was amicable though, apparently.

"We had a Not-Lying Day yesterday." He said out of nowhere, and I asked him to explain further. "So you have to study when you're lying, and talk about it the next day, cos a lot of the time you don't even realise that you're lying. You need 24 hours reflection to see it."

So he was telling me, in riddles, that he was lying and really was Bill, but wouldn't realise he was misleading me until the next day? I was utterly confused. What was going on? I also noticed that his tweed hat didn't match the tweed of his suit, and thought that might be another giveaway? He was an intriguing guy, but I wasn't entirely sure I bought into his honesty crusade, and I wasn't sure he did either when I asked him whether Not-Lying Day was a regular feature.

"It was just a trial. This could never happen again, it's a one-off," he admitted, before explaining, "I couldn't lie to Sue last night and, gosh, she did give me some stares."

Yes, I thought, being truthful to your girlfriend would soon put a stop to all that not-lying nonsense. Then Tony was telling me about his Irish family back in Donegal, and that there were no words in Gaelic for "yes" and "no", just a variety of shrugs and expressions. I really wasn't sure whether I could believe a word he was saying, and needed a foothold in an increasing fractured unreality, so I dragged it back to the safer shores of horse racing and what was going to win the next.

"Tullamore Dew" he said simply.

When I asked why, he explained that he liked his whisky. That would certainly account for his ruddy complexion, and the nonsense that had been spouted over the previous twenty minutes. I wasn't even sure that it was Lucozade in his orange bottle any more. We wished each other good luck and drifted apart in the sea of soused partygoers that was Cartmel races, but we'd been chatting so long that the race was off before I could study the form and get a bet on. Tullamore Dew won by eight lengths at 6/1, and that's not a word of a lie.

I got back to the hotel and decided I would take a walk by the lake. Even in the dying light, the vista was achingly pretty, and I sat down on a bench for a while. It felt like the first time in three months that I had actually stopped. It was getting chillier and darker by the minute but I didn't mind. Everything had been so busy that I really hadn't contemplated what I was doing, or what I was about to do. I already knew that I felt guilty, sheepish and tired, but those emotions had always been quickly pushed to the side in order to deal with the next thing on the to-do list. That evening on a cold, Cumbrian bench, I just let them sit with me and sink in, without pushing them away. Then I took a Chinese back to my room (a meal, that is), ate it, and went to sleep.

# 56) Hexham

## Day 75 – Tuesday 26 May

The drive away from Windermere was, if anything, even prettier than the drive towards it the day before. With the sun on my back, the richness of the colours unfolded before me and, despite being on a tight schedule as usual, I simply had to stop the car to drink in the moment and take some photos. The Lakes and their alluring beauty had forced me to slow down and become reflective. Had I changed? If someone asked me what I did for a living, what would I say. I wasn't sure, but suspected the answer would no longer be "a teacher". It was more than just a question of defining an occupation, though.

The A686 past Melmerby turned a little worrying as I was told we were entering the Pennines and would climb to 1,903 feet. I feared for Tiny's long-term health even if we did make the summit, but we did, and were rewarded with astonishing vistas that must have spanned 50 miles. Suddenly the tiredness and homesickness of the last few weeks melted away and I felt utterly privileged to be passing through terrain as stunningly beautiful as that. Everything caught up with me in an instant, and I realised how lucky I had been, and that I would never get another chance like that in my life. I had a wonderful family who had allowed me to purge myself of a mid-life crisis by touring this wonderful island, and was determined to seize the opportunities the last few days might bring.

After less than two hours behind the wheel, a relatively short drive recently, I pulled into the grounds of Langley Castle. Wow. This was a proper castle, handsome and chunky and imposing. I enthused to Ben behind the desk and he gave me a potted history of the place as he led me to my room. It was built around 1350 during the reign of Edward III, and the turbulent nature of those times meant that it was soon burnt to the ground. It remained untouched for 500 years until restoration began in the late 20th century, therefore retaining its medieval character. Ben mentioned that the nearby Hadrian's Wall was originally 15 foot tall until people started nicking the stone to make their own houses, but the castle had somehow remained largely intact and its walls were seven feet thick!

I was in the converted stable block, which Ben explained was better in some ways because I could look at the castle rather than out of it. The last overnight stay of my journey was a bit of an extravagance - going out in style, let's call it. I could have accommodated several families in my suite for one, and everything was beautifully done. As Ben asked about my adventure and listed his CV of working at and near racecourses over the years (and it was quite a list), a lady appeared carrying fresh coffee and homemade shortbread, just to tide me over. Everyone was genuinely friendly and I immediately made a mental note to bring the family back some day.

It was sunny and warm, and encouraged by my Lakeland reflections, I spent ten minutes wandering around the gardens, examining the majestic building from different angles and aspects. A peacock cried in the background, and there was the distant, reassuring hum of a lawnmower. I was just three racecourses away from finishing my mission, but I still wouldn't quite let myself believe it. The Ffos Las farce on Day 3 had scarred me and I refused to become complacent. There was always something unexpected that could arise, as the Gods of Probability had already proved. Devon Loch in 1956 mysteriously sprawled to the ground just yards from Grand National glory, after all.

I got a cab to the racecourse and as we arrived I sensed that I had misjudged the clothing requirements. As people scurried inside in coats and scarves I feared that my short-sleeved shirt from the balmy oasis of Langley Castle would not cut it up on a windswept Northumbrian hillside, and I was right. The sign outside proclaimed that this was 'Britain's Most Scenic Racecourse', which worried me after Kelso's protestations about being friendly. I envisaged a nuclear power station in the middle, painted in landscape greens and blues, but when I got inside I found that the sign was absolutely right. The view was stunning, and the atmosphere was relaxed and friendly; I liked the place a lot.

I started with a winner in the first race called Tickenwolf, but I'd become a bit of a sheep with my betting strategy and I didn't I like it. I'd become obsessed with how the on-course movements at the smaller tracks had a life of their own, and I was going to back a different horse until I saw the support behind Tickenwolf, taking 11/4 before he was backed into 7/4 favourite. It somehow felt as though I wasn't taking the lead in my decision-making but blindly following others who may, or may not, know better than me.

However, securing the best odds was one aspect I had been pleased with over the last two and a half months. If I was betting at home I wouldn't have snapped up the same prices, and getting 11/4 on 7/4 shots makes a difference in the long run, and indeed could just make all the difference to the balance sheet at the end. I hadn't updated the spreadsheet for a while, and was banking on some vague notion that Rozene would get me out of trouble. After the first, I backed some frustrating placed horses who were hampered by some poorly judged rides.

I had to get back to the hotel where the manager had persuaded me to sample the Table d'Hote menu. Like the room, it was towards the 'ouch' end of the price scale, but also brilliantly carried off. I started with a pre-dinner drink in the enormous drawing room and couldn't resist sitting in the elevated window seat to eat my complimentary nibbles. I felt like a king sitting on a giant throne, looking down on the splendour of his castle, and again wished that the family were there to enjoy the moment with me. Ben kindly took a photo of me to show them on my return, but it wasn't quite the same. The nibbles appeared to be popcorn and quavers with "a hint of umami". As these were explained to me, I knew before even opening the menu that the food would be another triumph of style over substance.

Then the canapés arrived (or were they amuse-bouches, I get confused with these matters?) on tiny pedestals - tasty. Then I was seated in the wonderful, oak-panelled restaurant and the bread and amuse-bouche (or was it a palate cleanser?) of a quail's egg with pea smear were fantastic. The manager had earlier tried to persuade me towards the slow-cooked (to the extent of five hours!) duck egg, but I was drawn to the mushrooms on toast. When my starter arrived it was heavy on the cepe parfait, which was cruelly under-seasoned, and very light on the toast. Apparently there was an artichoke persillade in there somewhere, (whatever that is) and the waitress then flamboyantly poured a pot of swirling mist over the bowl which accounted for the "mushroom aromas".

I simply had to have the venison, which I'd never tried before, because it came from Cartmel as I just had, and was complimented by a chocolate sauce. I'd had chocolate before, frequently, but never with a main course and I was intrigued to see how it worked. It didn't. They then produced what I was almost certain was the palate cleanser, which was chef's take on a gin and tonic, replete with foam and freeze dried cucumber stick. It wasn't bad, but part of me felt like staging a protest against the over-fancification of an earlier promising meal by ordering a gin and tonic instead.

Onto dessert, and I opted for the rhubarb, which came in a fashionably deconstructed state, making it look like half the ingredients had tried to escape from the plate in a last minute bid for freedom. There was a parmesan crumb, little slabs of ginger sponge and an unexpected blob of ice cream, none of which improved the dish. Give me my mother's rhubarb crumble any day. I couldn't help but think that in amongst the theatre of the presentation, the impeccable service, and the undoubted culinary skills on display, the art of taste has got lost somewhere along the way. Perhaps it was just that the meal suffered in comparison to the recent triumph at the Roxburghe in Edinburgh, or perhaps my taste buds were just tired from 75 days on the road, like the rest of me.

# 57) Hamilton

## Day 76 – Wednesday 27 May

I slept well in my palatial bed and awoke to the distant cry of a peacock on a sunny morning. I called The Wife to update her on my castle experience and ask how they were all doing. They were spending a few days of half term with Frew, Rob, Katy and Fraser at Celtic Manor, the swanky golf enclave just into Wales that hosted the 2010 Ryder Cup. I was to get just one day with everyone in the resort, soaking up the historic vibes of a sublime sporting occasion, before we were to head home in order for me to complete my stupid escapade. A busy itinerary had been planned for the Thursday including Laser Quest, gym and swimming pool, although I had fortunately already missed the high ropes. They sounded like they were having a great time, and I couldn't wait to join them.

Things were going swimmingly, however that goes, for me too. Truth be told, I was just beginning to get a little bit smug. When Tiny consented to start that morning and I set off in good time for my penultimate destination, one more stumbling block had been cleared and for the first time I began to believe it was really going to happen. Despite my haphazard approach to planning and my flagrant disregard for timekeeping, I had actually managed to plot my way around all the British racecourses in eighty days. Well, 78, if you're being picky. Despite it being a frenetic three months, and feeling increasingly run down, I had managed to avoid illness and injury whilst surviving on a diet of Full English breakfasts, mango and adrenaline. Sure, Tiny's objections to going above 50mph had aggravated the sciatica from my slipped disc, but it was nothing I couldn't deal with. And nothing I couldn't continue to deal with over the important months that were to follow. I even had time to circumvent what would surely be the final game of Racing Post Hide And Seek by slipping into Gretna Services as I entered Scotland for the last time. They didn't have one, but Tiny started again, and I had just enough fuel to get me to the airport via the races. After the Ffos Las abandonment, I had earlier checked the going at both Hamilton and Stratford and, unless something biblical happened, they would both be going ahead. Quite an achievement, Neil, congratulations. Add your name to the list of great latter-day explorers!

It was just after Gretna that the ominous, brooding dark clouds gathered, and shortly afterwards they started dispatching their wet cargo in unrelenting fashion. Then the A74(M) stopped about a mile short of Junction 14, and a long way short of Junction 6 for Hamilton. No worries, I thought, as we could only be about a mile from the exit and then The Trusty Satnav (to give it its new title, with my new-found positivity) could be creative if needs be (even though it was still saying "No traffic ahead").

So I turned off the engine and busied myself with the last trappings of my tour. What was left to plan? Did I have 3G to update the shop? Should I get back to the guy about the taxi on Friday? Have I read that interesting article on page 17 of Monday's Racing Post? Only then did it occur to me that the persistent difficulties I'd faced in obtaining my daily form guide and eternal comfort blanket could have actually contributed to the situation – if I hadn't stopped at Gretna would I have been ahead of the hold-up? I quickly brushed the thought aside, though. If it was a crash up ahead, if I hadn't stopped I might have been in it rather than behind it. Thinking that way can mess you up after a while. It was what it was, and I was optimistic it would soon clear. But I didn't have any signal to try and confirm what was going on, so I sat in splendid isolation in a crappy rental car parked on the outside lane of a sodden Scottish motorway.

I looked at the time. 20 minutes had passed, and probably the first race as well. Some people had climbed out of their cars in the pouring rain to see what was going on. The going at Hamilton would be turning softer, and I made a mental note that, if and when I found a Racing Post, I would search for horses who appreciated a bit of cut in the ground. I was always thinking I never had enough time, anyway, so I decided I must use the bonus window productively and started writing to-do lists for after I'd finished. Then police cars and ambulances wailed up the hard shoulder, and I realised for the first time that it could be a bad one.

Half an hour had gone and we literally hadn't moved an inch. I was beginning to get a little worried, but surely it was just the Gods of Probability having their last laugh "We've rolled a six! Excellent! Let's make all the traffic stop before his penultimate racecourse, just to wind him up a bit!" It was still raining, persistent stuff, and I calculated that I had definitely missed the first race, and the second could be in doubt if we didn't start moving soon. I briefly flicked on the radio and trawled through a few local stations to find some information, but landed on nothing of note, and I didn't want to risk running down Tiny's battery or using up precious fuel which might mean I'd have to stop before the airport drop off.

After 45 minutes had elapsed fire engines started going up and down the other carriageway. Only then did I realise that there had been absolutely no traffic coming the other way in all that time. Gradually my ears picked out the menacing throb of a helicopter, but the skies were pretty murky and I couldn't see where it was. My travel-weary brain finally grasped the scale of the unfolding situation – if it was a really bad one the motorway could be shut for hours.

For the first time a raw panic crouched in the pit of my stomach. Up until that point all I had heard, other than the occasional wail of a siren, was the secure drum of the rain on Tiny's cheap metal roof. It was a curiously comforting sound, like the patter on a conservatory when you're all cosy inside, but the muffled, alien bellow of the unseen helicopter lent an air of malice to proceedings.

Suddenly I was snapped from my apathy and my brain engaged top gear. Panicking wouldn't do any good, I told myself. I was a veteran of the Great Fire of Newcastle 2015, and these little things would not faze me. I just needed to focus and make some cool and rational decisions. Suppose we were stuck for three hours and I had the choice of making the last race and keeping the ludicrous dream alive, or catching the flight from Edinburgh back to my family. I knew what The Wife would have said, if I'd had any signal to call her. She'd have told me to do Hamilton and catch a later flight, perhaps even the next day. Wow, she had been brilliant.

The stunning conclusion I came to was that if the traffic didn't start moving soon it would have slipped from my grasp, the great dream that took twenty years to become reality, washed away under the wet tyres of thousands of stationary vehicles. The last three months of quiet goodbyes, strained phone calls and savage homesickness would have all been for nothing.

The hour mark arrived, and if we didn't get going soon the third race would also be gone. Then a new thought occurred (I'd plenty of time for thinking, after all) It was still pouring it down, and what would I do if they had to abandon Hamilton? What was the soil like there? Did it drain well? Would it all still count if I got there after they'd abandoned but paid two pissed Glaswegians to race over the last furlong? Would I then still have seen racing at all the British racecourses?

I had been away from home for six days, and I was desperate to be back with my family, the family I had chosen to desert in one of its formative moments. They seemed to be forgiving me, but I was not sure forgiveness would come so easily to myself. What had once seemed an eccentric frivolity was quickly becoming a monumental error of judgement. Guilt is a powerful emotion, but love is a stronger one. Hopefully we could get through it, everything that life would have to throw at us, if we could just keep loving each other?

Gradually, to the persistent drumming of rain on a cheap metal roof, I realised it was not all about my guilt. I would have to process that, and a small price to pay it would be for as absurd a mid-life crisis as mine. And it certainly wasn't about the racecourses or the horses, the friends or the gambling – I'd worked that out a long time ago. My epiphany came late in the journey, and quite possibly at the very end of it if the A74(M) didn't start flowing soon:- this was a story about love. Swathes of water spilled down a glooped windscreen. Hairs stood up on the back of my neck. It had taken me 56 racecourses and 76 days to realise that this was a story about love.

However, my stunning revelation didn't make the traffic flow, and I had been static for over 70 minutes. It wasn't funny any more. I'd missed the third race now, and forced myself to work out the times in order to keep my mind active, before I burst into tears and started thrashing Tiny with a branch like Basil Fawlty. If I missed the fourth race at 3:40, would I have time to watch the fifth race and get to my flight? The fifth race was at 4:15, get away by 4:25, no traffic in 34 miles to the airport 5:10, faffing with hire car and long walk to the terminal 5:30, through security 5:50, gate 6:00, flight 6:15. That was cutting it fine, even for my casual approach. There could be another Kings Cross moment coming up.

So the summary was:- if we didn't start moving in the next ten minutes I would have missed the fourth race, and if I watched the fifth race about eighteen things would need to go right for me to make the flight. If I watched the sixth I would not.....

Woah! Hold on! Yes! Yes! Yes! Finally, we were moving! And my elation immediately drained away as we passed the accident on the other carriageway. It looked like two lorries. They could be okay but it was hard to tell. All the traffic on that side had turned around and gone back to Junction 14. Perhaps we had been held so that the helicopter could land on our side? I chided myself for putting my insignificant challenge ahead of the people potentially injured in the crash. I knew then the answer to my earlier calculations - if there were any more hold ups I would go straight to the airport. There were more important things in life than tours of racecourses.

However, all was not over just yet, and I adopted the clinical exactness of a brain surgeon, constantly monitoring the situation for possible problems and alternatives. The rain was heavier than ever, and spray flew off the road making driving conditions atrocious, but I couldn't take it easy as I had a race to watch and was increasingly worried that Hamilton would be forced to abandon under the watery onslaught. I shouted "come on!" as cars dithered in front of me, knowing that even though I had got through the hold up, the traffic in Hamilton itself may still be bad and every second was priceless.

Luckily, there weren't any more hold ups, and I arrived at 3:17 with time to take a deep breath before the fourth race. The lady on the gate was surprised to see somebody emerge from the murk after missing the first three races, but was still happy to take the full entrance fee. Frankly, I was so happy I'd finally arrived that I didn't even ask for a reduction. As soon as I was in I saw horses in the paddock and knew that it wasn't abandoned yet. I was at the course about half an hour and it seemed really nice. As I counted down the minutes to what I hoped would be the start of the fourth race at 3:40, I surveyed umpteen picnic benches (unemployed) and at least seven bars (fully employed, despite the crowd being small) and I wished I could give it more time, but there wasn't any left.

Remarkably, the going was still being described as good – they were obviously used to a bit of rain in these parts. I had a random bet and breathed a huge sigh of relief as I watched the fourth race which was won by an 18/1 outsider. Then I sprinted back to the car and charged across to Edinburgh, hoping for an incident-free passage. This time there were no hold ups, the fuel just held out, and I knew as I passed through a busy security hall with minutes to spare that, by the skin of my teeth, my fragile escapade was still intact. I could see the finishing post and, more importantly, I would see my family that night.

# 58) Stratford

## Day 78 – Friday 29 May

I spent a lovely day and two nights at Celtic Manor. Being on holiday, however briefly, gave us all a slightly suspended sense of reality as the freshness of new surroundings and the distraction of good company kept thoughts of the weekend pushed to the background. However, by the second evening I again felt the uncomfortable pinch of both the finale to my venture and a transition to a new life. We left early on the Friday morning to get back home and turn around quickly for the last meeting.

I had half an hour spare before we were due to set off for Stratford and tried to catch up with the spreadsheet. The record-keeping of my betting account had been jettisoned as one of the expendable items in my final push for the finish. I still had vague notions that, barring a completely ill-disciplined blowout on the final evening, I would secure an overall profit, but I wasn't entirely sure. I just needed Clive to be ten minutes late to get up to date and have a clear picture of the position. He was almost always late, and it was a spare ten minutes that I had already factored into my time management strategy with his even more casual approach to timekeeping than mine. But Clive had guaranteed me that he would arrive from work in London with Paul before 3pm, and astonishingly he was right. He pulled up on the driveway at 2:57 and the spreadsheet would have to wait for another day.

Then the taxi arrived and we were all set. It looked like it would be mission accomplished unless the M40 was shocking. We picked Andrew up en route, who said that the M40 was shocking, but the cabbie maintained that his satnav was showing only minor delays. I had sourced a Mercedes Viano to take us to Stratford. I wanted a table in the back that we could all sit around to swap anecdotes and enjoy a game of poker, but it soon became clear that the driver's aggressive approach to his trade, along with the virtually frictionless and tray-sized table, would make this a challenge. However, I was up for a challenge, so we persevered under trying conditions.

If you've seen the sketch of Tommy Cooper trying to perform a ventriloquist act on the set of a lurching ship in the midst of a storm you'll have some idea of the difficulties we faced. Clive, who was feeling car sick after only a few minutes under the guidance of Ayrton Senna, assumed the role of lookout, shouting "Braking!" and "Roundabout!" at appropriate moments so that we could all adopt the brace position and attempt to hang on to everything, but even with his early warning system, poker chips and cards frequently slewed onto the floor. This seemed to put Clive off his game and I managed to pull off an audacious bluff, which I reminded him of frequently throughout the evening.

In between hands, talk weaved between the usual banter and obscure minutiae of life. We agreed that the old BBC computer classic Elite was a triumph - there was something desperately hopeful about seeing tiny, bright pixels in the vastness of black and not knowing what it would be. Paul explained that he couldn't afford a self-centring joystick, and that he had to concoct his own solution with rubber bands. I had no idea that my dear friend had experienced such a deprived upbringing. Andrew challenged me to list all the courses in chronological order. No problem, I said, and rattled off Cheltenham, Uttoxeter, Not Ffos Las, .... um .... Taunton, Exeter .... no, it was gone.

The inevitable traffic jam on the M40 that everyone had predicted other than Ayrton's satnav at least offered some respite from the high g-force lurching and rolling. It did, however, mean that yet again I missed the first race. It had somehow become a regular feature of my venture, but that night it was a real shame because I had missed my debut before racing on the racecourse tannoy, to promote the project and celebrate the finish of my tour.

Two pieces of news caught my eye in the Racing Post. Firstly, Richard had achieved the extraordinary feat of collecting his first £100,000 for his two eminently worthy causes. He had passed his first significant milestone just as I was reaching my last, and I hoped he would pass many more over the remaining ten months of his walk.

Secondly, it was reported that striking French workers had caused the abandonment of racing at Maisons-Laffitte the previous day by blockading the entrance to the paddock. I felt fortunate, in many ways, to live on this side of the Channel, but had to admit that I never even considered a strike as a potential threat to my project. Fortunately, the staff at Stratford seemed cheery enough, and although there were frequent blockages at the entrance to the paddock as the horses came and went, no organised blockade was apparent.

We met Jason and Simon at the course and our merry band swelled to six. Somehow we had all individually decided to back Weather Babe in the second race of just five runners, but despite our support the Pipe-trained mare was drifting out in the betting. I sent Jason off with my poker winnings from the taxi to secure another punt at the enhanced odds and he came back in high-fiving mood with a voucher at a tasty 6/1. At almost three and a half miles, it must have been the longest hurdle race I'd ever witnessed, which allowed us time to recover from the taxi and continue the banter. I expressed my disapproval with Paul and Andrew that they had not brought their racing caps, and Jason (who was looking rather dashing in his) said it must be difficult for horses to coordinate all four legs. Turning for home on what seemed like the fifth lap of the course, the Babe looked all over the winner, but faltered coming to the last and finished a tired second.

We headed for the carvery as Andrew and Simon were, strangely, cycling around the Isle of Wight the following day and needed to prepare by Roast-Beef-loading before their exertions began. Ivan joined us and we were then a magnificent seven, comrades in the continuing war against the bookies. We were to win the battle that evening, but the fight was ongoing, and it was one that I would soon take leave of absence from for a few months. The food was okay, but the better part was that we all sat around a big table and chatted. Stories from the last three months were wheeled out, and I knew that some would become the fable of future banter – the Kings Cross train journey, the Sandown winners' enclosure, and of course my trials and tribulations with Black Narcissus all got another airing for old times' sake. The support of my friends had been immense and I was sure that I would look back on the journey with such great fondness, but for the moment I was enormously happy that Stratford would be my last racecourse for a while.

Andrew likened my dogged determination in finishing the course to that of an endurance athlete. It was very kind of him to say so, but as I scoffed my roast beef I thought the similarities were tenuous at best. He suggested that my refusal to quit in the face of adversity was due, like the athlete, to the mental visualisation I had gained from the many years I had spent dreaming of the finish. He was clearly trying to pick me up after a gruelling three months, but I insisted that making good choices about family situations was not the same as quitting, and if I had chosen that route it would have been for all the right reasons. If a marathon runner stopped half way through a race all they would gain was an hour of their life, and a vague notion that they had performed poorly. If I had stopped I would have gained weeks, if not months, of my life back to spend with my family, support The Wife, watch rowing races and football matches, cook lasagne, attend birthday parties, prepare for the future, and just be there. Really, there is no substitute for just being there, which I wasn't for a majority of those three months. As I sat there with my positive, encouraging, funny, smiling, wonderful table of dear friends, I knew that my own internal jury was still out considering the verdict, and it could be some time before one was reached.

After failing to insure against a Twiston-Davies kick in the goolies in the previous race, when Speed Master beat our valiant Weather Babe, Ivan was smarting, as you would be, and insurance-backed in the third with a new trainer because he "didn't want to commit suicide if Nicholls won". However, after the third race, which wasn't won by Nicholls, it was clear that it was not a day for favourites. They had watered the course earlier in the week and it had been hosing it down most of the day, so the conditions on the course seemed almost as testing as in the taxi. Accordingly, I started backing big outsiders. Big outsiders did indeed win the remainder of the races, although not the ones I'd chosen.

Later in the evening there was an outbreak of winning in the gang, although I managed to avoid most of the contagion. Some of us caught on to Catch Tammy at 80/1 each way who soldiered on for third. Then the whole bunch, except me, backed Iguacu at 10/1 in the last under Ivan's assertion that Richard Johnson would not have come to Stratford for just one ride if it wasn't worth his while. I pointed out that I had gone to Hamilton for just one race only two days earlier and that didn't result in a winner, so I broke from the crowd for the last bet of my tour. With the spreadsheet incomplete, I went into the last race not quite knowing the situation, and was quite glad of that. I didn't want to be intimidated into a betting corner where the whole adventure ended with a whimper because I was trying to stay in the black. Sometimes, it appeared, ignorance really was bliss.

I don't need to tell you the result, but I should tell you that it was a roaringly tight finish and Paul, Jason, Andrew, Ivan, Clive and Simon were all dancing around the steps of the grandstand in joy, and I couldn't stop myself from joining in. The racecourse after a rousing and winning finale is a wonderful place to be, and I, of course, was celebrating a greater victory anyway – the successful completion of my challenge.

Tammy had selected Simon to be her on-course representative that evening, and had earlier texted through her raft of selections, which Simon completely forgot about until it was too late. His face as he read them out, and we confirmed that, of course, most of them had won, was priceless. His voice was a barely audible whisper as he reached the end of the list and realised the extent of his lapse. Unsurprisingly, Tammy had also caught on to Catch Tammy, with a generous £8 each way.

Suddenly it was all over. I hugged goodbye to Jason and Ivan, and the rest of us trooped back to Ayrton in the Viano. I had expected it to be a hugely emotional moment for me, but if anything I felt slightly numb. I had just completed my amazing odyssey, something I had dreamt of for more than 20 years, planned for months, and stuck with, for better or worse, throughout an increasingly confusing, punishing and absurd 78 days, but somehow it just hadn't all sunk in yet. I thought back to Chesterfield John looking lost in the Taunton taxi, and recognised that I too would have to soon face the imponderable question of "what next?"

I had climbed my Mount Everest and the view from the top was shrouded in cloud. The adrenaline had waned now my goal was reached, and in the immediate aftermath of an extraordinary challenge it became a matter of getting down the mountain as quickly as possible before my oxygen ran out and frostbite set in.

I wondered when, if at all, the magnitude of my achievement, the extent of my sacrifice, and the emotion of the moment would catch up with me. The answer was obvious: when I got home.

## Beverley

A mutant daisy gets the better of me

## Fakenham

Alright Benny leads from pillar to post

## Oaksey House

Equicizers in the state-of-the-art gym

## Walking The Courses

Richard after his lap of Wincanton

## York

One of the finest racecourses in the world?

## Thirsk

Barry's collection
of truncheons

## Goodwood

Quite close to
being glorious

## Newcastle

The slightly
alarming turnout
and demographic
at a lovely course

## Reflections

The stunning beauty of Lake Ullswater refreshes the soul

## Going Out In Style

The majestic Langley Castle, the final overnight stay of my tour

## Mission Accomplished

The usual suspects at Stratford

# Part 3

*Stewards Enquiry*

# State Of The Nation

I am happy to report that horse racing is alive and well, indeed flourishing throughout the many corners of our land. For all the various, well-documented issues that it faces at this key point in its evolution, I think it is time to celebrate the rich variety and amazing spectacle on offer around our racecourses.

No other sport has the ability to bring together such a diverse bunch of followers. I have been welcomed by senior stakeholders and chatted with complete strangers in friendly, open and humorous atmospheres across the portfolio. The only requirement for entry to this most social of clubs is a shared passion for, or at least a passing interest in, horse racing. I have attended the glittering festivals and seen some amazing moments of the highest drama, but have found the relaxed warmth of the less glamorous venues to be the real heartbeat of our sport. Some of them are quirky, some even slightly eccentric, (and Cartmel is completely bonkers!) but I see this as a unique selling point of our sport, rather than something that needs standardising or streamlining.

British racing needs to find a way to grow and secure its future without losing the essence of what makes it great. Of course we need to attract new people to the sport through the mass appeal of feature days and added extras, but we must also cherish the Market Rasens and Ludlows, the Hexhams and Beverleys, that provide such a valuable service in bringing communities together. Without the many rungs to its ladder our sport would not stand as tall against the modern backdrop of increasing competition for disposable income and available time.

Sure, there are issues to address. It is hard to think of many public arenas where the customer is treated so poorly in terms of the availability of good quality and easily accessible food and drink. Today's consumer no longer thinks of this as something that occurs outside of their leisure activity, it is part and parcel of it, and yet racing seems largely happy to let its punters jostle for extended periods to get an expensive but mediocre product. If Twickenham can serve 80,000 fans food and drink in the compressed mayhem of a twenty-minute half-time interval, why do most racecourses fail to deliver so effectively to a fraction of that attendance in six such opportunities throughout an afternoon?

In addition, how does a sport that is trying to attract an interested and invested fan of the future deal with the fact that most of the action occurs way beyond the view of a majority of customers? Putting up a large TV may help, but raises the question as to why you wouldn't watch it on your large TV at home?

However, here is possibly the biggest concern:- how does horse racing ensure the experience is just as enjoyable at the large meetings as the small? How can one piece of land accommodate 5,000 customers on some months and 50,000 at others, yet still send everyone home happy? It is a problem most other sports never have to address - Twickenham and Stamford Bridge have the same number of seats for every match, and they are usually full. More than that, though, the customer has a piece of territory for the duration of the event (their seat!), rather than constantly trying to find and retain personal space. It is hard to think of another sport where the fans are more constantly on the move, and yet horse racing doesn't seem to have fully reconciled the fluidity of its crowds with the set piece nature of the action. Golf galleries, for example, are often on the move as well, but if somebody nips to the loo they can pick up the action on another hole or with another group fairly quickly. If you are at a racecourse and have to queue for 20 minutes you are probably going to miss a race.

This is why, irrespective of the food and drink, or whether I could see what was happening on the far side of the course, I cherished the smaller meetings. What I may have lost in atmosphere and the quality of the horses was more than made up for in the ease with which I could enjoy my day. The one astonishing exception to this rule was Aintree, which was a revelation in how a big, high-profile venue can put on a spectacular show that will have all walks of life going home happy. My beloved Cheltenham needs to take note and try to replicate that feeling from the Grand National which was at once exhilarating, thriving and joyously riotous, but also somehow comfortable and personable. I never thought I'd say this, but the 'home' of National Hunt racing has a lot of catching up to do, at least in terms of the feel of its big meetings for the common punter on the ground.

# The Final Reckoning

When non-gamblers asked me about my adventure the first question was usually "What on earth are you doing that for?" When gamblers asked, it was almost invariably "Are you ahead?" The truth is that for several months afterwards I didn't actually know. Despite the lovely Rozene putting me tidily ahead when she won at Ripon with less than two weeks to go, the last ten days of the tour were not kind and only produced a handful of winners.

I had a conversation with the cabbie on the way to Hexham races on the same subject, and he asked a very astute question:

"If you knew the position going into the last day, would it affect your betting?"

Luckily I was never in that position, and I punted at Stratford like any other day, but I would like to think that it would not have affected my decision-making. The eighty-day window artificially framed my betting, but in reality it is a continuum (that makes it sound like I'm a compulsive gambler, but if The Wife is still reading this far, I'd like to make it clear that I have rarely bet since). If I'd spotted an outstanding opportunity at Stratford I hope I would have backed it accordingly, irrespective of the possible effect on finishing the tour in profit or loss.

Again I come back to this elusive concept of 'value' - the mathematician within me simply refuses to ignore the logic. If I consistently bet on horses available at, say, 16/1 that in reality have a 10/1 chance of winning, I must make money in the long run. The renowned Racing Post tipster Tom Segal, operating under the title of Pricewise, has made a very successful career out of this beautifully simple idea. To clarify, the idea is simple, but in practice identifying the 'real' odds of a horse winning is fiendishly difficult.

The other problem is that even if you manage to get 16/1 on what should really be a 10/1 chance, it's still only a 10/1 chance and will lose 91% of the time. Tom Segal, for all his undoubted skill and immense knowledge, can have long losing runs, but at the end of the season invariably shows a decent profit. That I attempted to match and even beat the great man, who has made his working life one long search for value, should tell you that I fall into the 'eternal optimist' category of punters.

So, when I finally caught up with the spreadsheet I was pleased to find that, astonishingly, I had actually turned a profit over my 78 days – a small victory in the ongoing war against the bookies, however tiny that profit was compared to the turnover of cash, race after race, day after day. Rest assured, I'm certainly not retiring just yet. As I don't bet in large sums, a return on investment of just 1.3% was really neither here nor there, even if it was tax-free. The interesting analysis for me was whether there are 'sweet-spots' where the punting is more profitable.

That multi-variable analysis could go on for much longer than the original project, but in particular I was intrigued by the question of whether you should ever back at odds-on. Scottish Robert would be screaming "No, no, no!" at this point, and you certainly wouldn't find esteemed tipsters such as Pricewise selecting horses anywhere near this range. My spreadsheet, however, showed that five of the seven horses I backed at odds of less than Evens won, returning a profit of 25%. My statistical background warns that this is a very small sample size on which to make sweeping conclusions, but it does suggest that it's not necessarily the complete mugs game that most think it to be. I stand by my explanation to Robert in a crowded bar at Ayr – if someone offered me 1/2 on rolling 1 to 5 on an unbiased dice, that is a bet I would willingly take all day long.

At the other end of the scale, my examination of horses priced at 10/1 or more showed just six returns despite making over 100 bets in this range, representing about a third of my overall selections! Until now I had literally no idea that such a large proportion of my bets were on these outsiders, and can only deduce that there is an innate skew in the smaller-stakes punter towards bigger odds – having a fiver on the 2/1 shot is unlikely to pay for the next round, let alone make a significant difference to the monthly finances. Naturally, given the odds, some of those six returns (such as Wayward Prince, again at Ayr) were large, but still not enough to prevent a 4% loss on investment in this category. You may not be surprised at this, thinking that betting up in these dizzy heights is similar to buying a lottery ticket, but actually an awful lot of Tom Segal's tips are in this range. Perhaps (okay, admit it Neil, almost definitely) I'm just not as good as Pricewise, and I certainly don't have the flair of Jason in pulling off 66/1 coups in four-horse races.

I'm not stupid enough to think that backing horses is the easy way to quick money. My time spent travelling around the racecourses of Britain has again demonstrated that fortunes can swing on the narrowest of margins. If I hadn't lost out in my first six photo finishes I might have done a whole lot better, but if Rozene hadn't held on I would have done a whole lot worse. I like playing games, and cash is an easy way of keeping score. Fortunately throughout my 25 years of backing horses the negatives have been small enough to cope with and the positives have brought me great happiness. I still get a buzz out of finding a winner, even though it's unlikely that it will be enough to substantially change the course of my life. Equally, I still get annoyed with myself when I make a silly bet or choose incorrectly, even though I can afford to do so.

So overall I've done okay. The really bad bets were few, and I must admit that I'm rather chuffed that I can call myself a winner. I can always question the wisdom of completing such a preposterous undertaking, but at least I cannot castigate myself for squandering my family's inheritance. Not yet, anyway.....

# Reflections

As I write, more than five months have passed since Stratford, and as the dust has slowly settled on my grand tour I have been able to gain perspective on the thing, in the same way that you can only really gauge the scale and absurdity of an enormous folly if you stop living in it and go far enough beyond the walls to view it from a distance.

The truth is, I think I was a pretty crap husband, father, son and friend those eighty days. People close to me got fragments of my former self, not just in terms of the long chunks of time spent away from home, but even during the brief, distracted moments I spent in their presence. I was incredibly fortunate that most of these people still remembered me on my return, and some of them even seemed to have forgiven my aberration. A few even celebrated my absence and have enquired when I might be going away again, but I shan't name names.

It was an enormous undertaking for my amazing wife and she dealt with it all remarkably well. Not just the cooking of the chicken nuggets and the writing of two critically-acclaimed guest blogs, but the way our life together was compressed into gaps between me finishing the latest chunk of writing and sodding off again to get more material. She was enormously positive throughout the whole escapade, and picked me up several times when I really felt like I didn't want to do it any more. If this book stands testament to anybody's efforts it is hers, not mine.

She would say I was stressed during the trip. I don't think it was stress, not like trying to teach and control, push and cajole a classroom full of youngsters. I must admit I was in a flap sometimes as I tried to get out the door for a train, and often loudly cursed the various bits of technology that frequently and deliberately let me down just when I needed them not to, but I think that was purely a lack of time, rather than proper stress.

When I was a teacher everything was pigeonholed into neat segments and if the timetable said the lesson finished at 10:30 that's when we finished (for all our sakes). I have always taken solace in the definitive and the absolute truth of mathematics, yet my eighty days was crammed full of the opposite – motorways that didn't work, writing that expanded to fit the space available and often beyond, and a variety of unusual feelings that were slightly alien to someone as emotionally intelligent as a stone.

I loved the discipline of writing every day, but severely underestimated the toll it would take. I suppose I should have realised that transitioning from the exact world of mathematics to the expansive and occasionally chaotic world of travelling and writing would test me like never before. Perhaps it was overly-ambitious of me, a man with no journalistic training, little writing pedigree, and frankly only the feeblest grasp of the English language, to write up to 2,000 words a day for three months. Add to that the travel, frequently in excess of four hours, and sometimes as much as eight hours driving a day, not to mention the time spent at the races (which was, after all, the point of the project!) and the snatching of brief moments with my family. It was simply a very, very busy period of my life.

I thought when I set out this would be a love story. Indeed it has been, but perhaps not in the way I expected. I thought this would be a memoir about my continuing infatuation with a sport I have known for longer than my wife and children, and most of my friends. Horse racing does indeed have a lot of things going for it and, bar a few courses and meetings, I'd recommend it to anyone, especially those seeking a backdrop for a mid-life crisis. Despite a certain element of racecourse fatigue setting in towards the end, it usually remained a fun way to spend an afternoon, and I can think of very few things in life that I could do to such an extent over a three-month stretch and

374

not get bored of to some degree. On the whole, I have loved the horses and the courses, the people and the places. It has been a truly fantastic voyage, but I have only been racing once since I finished the tour, and of course that was to Cheltenham for its first, and my favourite, meeting of the season. It was a day trip that affirmed that I was still in love with this beautiful and mysterious sport, but I was also very glad it was only a day trip!

I wondered if I would be attracted to the romantic notion of being a writer. In the months leading up to my venture when people asked me what I did for a living I would simply say "I'm a teacher". Having not yet transitioned to a new life, I was still clinging to the remnants of the old one. It wasn't that I was without a purpose, given the unique circumstances of my family this past year, but it was hard to label that purpose easily. Now I would say I am a writer. I may not say that out loud, and if somebody asks I might mumble "pursuing other interests" or some such euphemism for a mid-life crisis, but if they really press the point, I feel I have just about earned the elbow-patches to call myself a writer. I have written after all, and now I've gone and compounded that mistake by publishing as well, and you've gone and amplified the error by reading it. So, if that doesn't make me a writer then I don't know what does. I may have so far escaped the international fame and glorious riches that have plagued JK Rowling and the like, but it is surely only a matter of time.

I thought I might fall for the quixotic allure of travelling and the mesmeric rhythm of going racing every day, but life on the road isn't all it's cracked up to be, however attractive it seems in novels or films. In airport restaurants I would stare at the menu, craving something but not knowing quite what. In motorway service stations I would be presented with an abundance of shiny wrappers, and feel overwhelmed. Of course, it wasn't until I finished and had time to reflect that I realised it was not the fault of the restaurant or the shop – I was searching for things that could not be found on menus or shelves.

So I enjoyed the racing and the writing, if not the travel, but none of them are at the heart of this particular love story. Instead, it is much simpler than that, and a story that is replayed a million times a day in corners all around the globe, some of which at least have never even heard of horse racing. In the end the toughest foes on my travels were not the bookmakers or the blinking cursors on empty pages, but the melancholy and loneliness that signified my desperate longing to be with my wife and boys at one of life's defining moments for a family unit. This book is really a love story dedicated to those three remarkable people who I've discovered I really can't live without. I know that resisting the urge to chuck it all in didn't make me a stronger person, but that time away from them did at least allow me the perspective to fully comprehend their amazing qualities.

Against the odds, I completed my challenge. The mathematician can tick the box because the numbers don't lie. 58 racecourses in 78 days. Mission accomplished. The rest, though - the hours of anguish, the fear of failure, the savage homesickness and the constant guilt were all immeasurable. Later on, the depths of my soul that I faced, that we all faced together, in a summer that was darker than any of our previous seasons on this planet, and the extraordinary bravery shown by my wife and two boys throughout it all - they cannot be expressed in numbers. But my revelation from a drenched and static Scottish motorway turned out to be true – we can get through anything if we just keep loving each other.

I spent three months of my life following my dream, and that was enough. I am so, so glad that I have done it, but I am equally happy to have now stopped doing it. I saw some beautiful parts of Britain, stayed in some wonderful places, and began to scrape the surface of the incredibly diverse people and cultures that surround our similarly

376

varied racecourses. Many people have asked which racecourse was my favourite, and you can flick forward a few pages for that, but only a few have asked the bigger question about my odyssey:-

If I could spend more time in just one place that I had briefly passed through, a part of the country where I was really taken with the people and the surroundings, where would that be? Easy – home.

# Epilogue

On 13 August 2015, less than three months after I'd finished, the BHA published the fixture list for 2016.

"We are pleased to be able to publish the fixture list earlier than in recent years to allow our customers to plan accordingly" Nick Rust, chief executive of the BHA announced at its unveiling, although it is unclear whether he was referring to Around The Races In Eighty Days pilgrims in particular.

Despite widespread concerns voiced over many years about small field sizes, uncompetitive racing and falling populations of both horses and owners, the number of fixtures has grown since 2012 and there shall be 1482 opportunities to go racing next year. With the recent conversion of Newcastle, the number of all-weather fixtures has also grown which will no doubt reopen the debate on the role of this Marmite offering in the future of our sport.

But these are industry-wide issues, and the publication of this list has always been a very personal moment in my year. I relished sitting down and working through the many iterations of my ludicrous dream, an annual process that was (until recently) an entirely hypothetical exercise. Twenty years ago, the eighty-day period was always bookended by Gold Cup Day and the Derby, a link that has been lost over the years due to the vagaries of where Easter falls in the calendar, as well of the expansion of the Festival to four days.

I couldn't help but peek once again this year, and smiled ruefully after discovering the reinstatement of the eleven-week interval between the pinnacles of the jumps and flat seasons. The holy grail of an eighty-day gap remains unattainable, however, and seems set to continue unless Cheltenham decide to go back to a three day Festival, or Epsom moves the Derby to the Sunday, both of which would surely be happily quoted at 100/1 by any bookmaker.

This then immediately raised a deeper question as to whether I felt the urge to use the lessons learned from my first iteration (such as don't try to go to Ffos Las in March) to perfect the tour, starting perhaps with the Thursday of the Cheltenham Festival (which would at least avoid the oppressive vibe of the Friday) and culminating in the Derby. The simple answer to that was no.

My odyssey was indeed far from perfect. In fact, it was littered with imperfections - long trips and bad hotels, nasty food and unlucky losers (bets, that is, not my friends), missed opportunities and experience gained. The biggest adrenaline rushes came not from tight finishes to races, but from almost-missed trains and 2am fire alarms. I never caught up with Tracksuit Dave and Scottish Robert, or spoke to Tommo and Nick Luck, and my epiphany was really a dawning realisation that I was doing it for no other reason than the absence of reasons not to at that peculiar time of my life. Stephen Fry once said "never regret the things you've done, only the things you haven't", and whilst I'm not entirely sure I agree in every scenario, those sentiments do seem to aptly summarise this situation. It was my journey and one that I would not change even if I had the luxury of going back in time. A ten-hour round trip to Carlisle was an absurdity, for example, but then again so was the whole project. It shall stand as its own epitaph, with the rough corners unrounded and the flaws shining brightly in the granite worktop of reality.

My journey is done, and its shortcomings only add character to the rich tapestry of its timeline. I must move on and let younger and fresher dreamers fill the void with their search for their own individual brand of perfection. If you feel as though my tour was a little too sedate, why not try watching racing at all the different tracks within a racecourse (eg Old and New at Cheltenham, July and Rowley Mile at Newmarket, or indeed jumps v flat v all-weather layouts at the many dual-code racecourses). That should keep you occupied in the fixture list spreadsheet for a few hours.

Perhaps see if you can do them all alphabetically, or attend each meeting in a pantomime horse outfit. A friend once said to me "If in doubt, do it!", and dear old Moscow Express confirmed that the gnawing pain of missed opportunities can far outweigh the easy gain of sticking to what you know. Your journey may not be perfect either, but it shall be yours rather than mine, and it shall tell its own story.

# Appendix 1 - The Neils

In my very own version of the Oscars, I shall now unveil the eagerly awaited highs (and lows) of my tour. There are no gold statuettes for the winners, although those whose achievements are recognised here should feel free to type up and print off their own certificate if that would make them feel better. I offer more than merely shiny and expensive prizes – my selections shall receive worldwide acclaim, as well as that warm fuzzy feeling inside when you know you've done a great job.

Of course, my views are entirely subjective and determined by the vagaries of the weather, the people, and how many winners I'd backed. I had only a handful of hours to form my impressions, and a snapshot can never paint the full picture, but that was all I had. Note that I have ignored all 'previous course form', which is why my beloved Cheltenham is noticeably absent from the credits.

The eagle-eyed amongst you will notice that some of the awards have very little to do with horses, but as I'm sure you will have realised by now, my adventure has been more than simply going racing. It has been an odyssey of people and places, pubs and hotels, and of course food which has been recognised by no less than three awards. I am opening the envelope…..

## Hotel/B&B

1st – Langley Castle (Kelso):- A simply stunning setting for an unforgettable stay, and one of the warmest welcomes of my tour. The food may have been a little too clever for its own good, but everything else was faultless and despite it being 400 miles from home, I shall take my family there one day.

2nd – The Old Deanery (Ripon):- Literally a stone's throw from an exquisite cathedral which could be surveyed from our spacious room, and a relaxed bar with comfy sofas crying out for an afternoon drifting to its own rhythm.

3rd – Premier Inn, Castleford (Pontefract):- Perhaps a shock choice, but when I walked in everyone smiled at me and that goes a long way. It's a Premier Inn on a trading estate, and that it still makes its way onto the roll of honour should tell you all that you need to know.

Worst – Best Western Kings Head, Richmond (Catterick):- One of the worst hotels I've ever stayed in, let alone over the three months of my tour. My room was a tiny sauna of shame – stains on the ceiling, a hole in the wall, a dysfunctional shower and desk, and a faulty kettle with grubby cups. Oh, and don't forget the added bonus of a fair that literally screamed fun at my window until late.

## Pub/Bar

1st – The Strand (Cheltenham):- The one shining light on a disappointing Gold Cup day, but what a glorious way to end the Festival and begin my journey. The patchwork quilt of racing folk blended seamlessly to the sounds of a local band. It was riotously good fun, and Paul and I found ourselves unable to avoid the dancefloor in the heady atmosphere.

2nd – Ship & Mitre, Liverpool (Haydock):- Ivan marched me through the streets to this gem that he had unearthed. An unassuming exterior leads into a humming and friendly interior, with the biggest range of beer I have ever encountered (with the possible exception of the Cambridge Blue). It's the sort of place you could go to every day of the year and not get bored.

3rd – The Imperial (Exeter):- Yes, it's a Wetherspoons, but it serves decent beer at very decent prices, and the cavernous layout (including a stunning orangery) gives ample opportunity to find a niche and sample the extraordinary range.

Worst –The Royal (Thirsk):- This may well be the best pub in Thirsk, judged by the maniacal screams emanating from the other offerings on the main square, but was certainly the worst hostelry of my eighty days. It's the sort of place where you suddenly discover a penchant for bolting lager before remembering you're late for an imaginary appointment.

Breakfast

1st – Burn How Garden Hotel (Cartmel):- Nothing particularly fancy at this strangely named establishment, but efficient and friendly service and a fine fruit selection to start. Everything in my Full English was perfectly cooked and delicious.

2nd – Best Western Queen Hotel (Chester):- Sometimes, it's the little things that distinguish what is a fairly standard meal. Complimentary Bucks Fizz and a girl with a guitar certainly did that, but also a wonderful range of pastries and some proper fried potatoes, rather than those weird triangular hash brown things.

3rd – Homemade Cafe (Nottingham):- They served good coffee, a fine Full English, and a tempting range of homemade cakes. The cafe is part of the pavilion that looks out over the playing fields, and with a range of board games and a great mix tape on the speakers, Jason and I would have stayed all morning if the schedule had allowed.

Worst – Bills (York):- Pleasant surroundings and painfully friendly staff front of house, but they seemed to have forgotten to employ a chef, and when it finally arrived it was clear that a clown had waved some anaemic bacon near a lukewarm pan.

## Lunch/Evening Meal

1st – The Roxburgh Bar & Grill (Edinburgh):- This was one of the best meals I've ever had, let alone during my nationwide odyssey. Local ingredients beautifully balanced and impeccably served. The set menu at £15 for two courses was simply astonishing value. The maitre d' helped me choose two glasses of wine that complimented the food superbly.

2nd – Premier Inn, Castleford (Pontefract):- I was glad I opted for the hotel meal package rather than wandering across the road to one of the many fast food outlets. Tasty food, decent servings, and outstanding value. And a happy hour at the bar before sitting down always helps.

3rd – Pitcher & Piano (York):- I finally worked out how to get a good lunch when going racing – eat nowhere near the racecourse! A sunny terrace by the river proved an oasis of calm just yards from the throng of the city centre. A decent club sandwich and well-kept beer – you can't ask for much more than that.

Worst – Prezzo (Ripon):- Awful wine that was changed grudgingly, agonisingly slow service, ordinary food, and a special acoustic reminiscent of a soft play centre on a Sunday morning. Enough said.

## Racecourse Food

1st - The Carvery (Newton Abbot):- Local meats expertly roasted, a wide range of accompaniments, and speedy service despite the high volume of footfall just before the first race. The head chef (who was carving and overseeing the whole operation in an efficient but friendly manner) deserves a huge pat on the back for pulling off the improbable and proving that racecourse food can, and should, be a whole lot more than the usual dross on offer.

2nd – The Chinese Van (Plumpton):- What an unexpected treat! The noodles looked great but I was drawn to the sweet and sour chicken with rice which was superb. Properly cooked fresh to order - remarkable.

3rd – The Noodle Bar (Lingfield):- At the end of racing, what better way to send the weary traveller on his way than with a huge box of steaming chicken noodles than even two grown men failed to dismantle (and boy, Simon can eat). I would advocate adding chips for the perfect combining-carbs hit.

Worst – Roast Beef bap (Sandown):- This was the easiest decision of them all, despite Sedgefield's pathetic attempt at going Around The World In A Jacket Potato. My roast beef bap was stringy and tasteless to the point of being inedible (and this was a second choice after I had ordered the pork and was told that it wouldn't be ready for another ten minutes, after my money was taken!)

## Racecourse Atmosphere

1st – Aintree:- A day at the Grand National delivers on so many levels, but the whole shindig is driven by the feel good factor of the great race itself. It was frantically busy and roaringly drunken, but there was no hint of trouble. Somehow, everyone was having such a great time that racegoers surfed through the afternoon on a wave of affability.

2nd – Wincanton:- The most sought after commodity of my tour was space, and Wincanton has this in spades. Somehow, this enhanced the atmosphere rather than dissipating it. People talked to each other, and a stag party in frocks for Ladies Day were embraced (not literally) as part of the spectacle and interviewed in the paddock.

3rd – Cartmel:- It was all a bit bonkers, but it somehow epitomised the endearing charm of our sport. If ever you needed an advert for how homogenising our sport would make it poorer, this is it. But get your Racing Post before you go.

Worst – Uttoxeter:- Day 2 of my adventure was a low point, as overcrowded as Cheltenham but without the excitement of the racing to distract you, and with a slightly nasty undercurrent weaving through the melee. There really was nothing nice at all about this place; the best bit was leaving.

## Racecourse Facilities

1st – York:- A stunning four-tiered grandstand with fantastic views and a variety of cleverly arranged eating and drinking options, and we were not even in the premier enclosure. This is probably the blueprint for future racecourse design (should it ever be required!)

2nd – Market Rasen:- All three enclosures sat harmoniously next to each other with great views out over the action from the spacious stands. I know this sounds silly, but facing north means you can see everything a lot more clearly! The amenities were generous and sparkling, and there was a little shed that sold coconut mushrooms.

3rd – Newcastle:- It was desperately sad that this fine establishment was so underwhelmed by support on the wet Tuesday of my visit. The entrance seems to suggest country club more than racecourse, and upstairs the cocktail bar overlooking the parade ring and finishing post is a thing of beauty.

Worst – Plumpton:- People were having a good time, but the facilities could at best be described as rudimentary, and at worst woeful. It's basically two sheds hidden in the Sussex countryside, and even with the fantastic Chinese van, you cannot escape the feeling that punters deserve more.

## Racecourse Overall

1st – Market Rasen:- This Lincolnshire outpost just shaded it as the best all rounder, and I was smitten with this unheralded provincial track. The course is compact and pretty, with the paddock sited in front of the finishing straight, promoting the feeling of being totally immersed in the action. If I had a teleport machine, this is where I'd take a horse racing newbie to explain my passion for the sport.

2nd – Wincanton:- Perhaps walking the course with Richard before racing made me feel an affinity with the place, but there was a huge amount to recommend – an excellent variety of food and drink options, friendly and efficient staff, and a relaxed vibe throughout.

3rd – Beverley:- There was nothing particularly special about this independent track (hence it not appearing in any other category), but everything was done very well and it managed to be greater than the sum of its parts. It was tangible on my visit how experienced and friendly staff made a huge impact to proceedings.

Worst – Huntingdon:- The problems started early with farcical arrangements for parking and entering the course, and the experience got worse once inside. Flickering TVs symbolised the tiredness that emanated from the facilities, and employing youngsters at the food and drink outlets was a false economy.

# Appendix 2 - ATRIED in Numbers

0    Penalty points accumulated whilst driving (perhaps the longest-priced winner of the tour, other than the next entry?)

0    Pounds (lbs) gained (medical science is still puzzled by this, and it may well form the basis of the next Horizon investigation into the new superfood that is the hog roast)

0.3   Seconds left before the doors closed as I boarded the 10:30 from Kings Cross to York (thanks again to Simon for his impersonation of an ageing Thunderbirds puppet when boarding the train to delay the guard)

1    Abandoned meeting in my eighty-day window, and I managed to find it on Day 3 (Ffos Las)

1    Meeting I didn't bet at (Chester)

2    Meetings with only a single bet (the rearranged Ffos Las, and Hamilton)

4    Complimentary entrance tickets (many thanks to Warwick, Newbury, Aintree and Towcester)

5    £ for the most expensive beer (quite disgraceful really)

7    Flights (four of them return day trips to Ayr and Perth)

7    Odds-on bets (five of them won to give a profit of 25%, demonstrating that even odds-on shots can be value bets in the correct circumstances)

| | |
|---:|---|
| 8 | Photo finishes involving my selections (the first 6 of them lost!) |
| 14.8 | Average odds of my selections (although this mean average was skewed by some extreme outsiders – if you're really into this sort of thing the median was 6/1 and the mode was 5/1) |
| 15 | Longest sequence of losing bets, right at the start (thanks must go to Perspicace and the Pipe/Scudamore combo for breaking that demoralising sequence) |
| 16 | Winner-less meetings |
| 17 | Train journeys, most of them pleasant and punctual |
| 18 | Hotels and B&Bs |
| 19 | Full English/Welsh/Scottish breakfasts (if you include the strange tray of reheated gloop that British Airways presented me with on the way to Ayr) |
| 26 | Winning meetings |
| 26 | Flat meetings |
| 31 | Losing meetings |
| 31 | Jumps meetings (no connection in the last four entries!) |
| 36 | Fewest runners at a meeting (Fakenham) |
| 58.65 | The rather insignificant £ betting profit at the end of 78 days, a return on investment of just 1.3% (excluding significant expenses!), but at least it was a profit, and it was tax-free! |
| 72 | Winners |

| | |
|---|---|
| 140 | Most runners at a meeting (Cheltenham on Gold Cup day – no wonder it was difficult to find a winner!) |
| 307 | Bets |
| 448 | Smallest racecourse attendance (at the eerily quiet Wolverhampton, and some of those could have been Holiday Inn customers who had gone through the wrong door) |
| 6,889 | Miles driven (excluding taxis, lifts, trains and planes) |
| 68,957 | Largest racecourse attendance of my eighty days (at Cheltenham, and it felt like it, although Aintree had only slightly less and it felt a lot more spacious |